D1745139

WITHDRAWN
FROM
UNIVERSITIES
AT
MEDWAY
LIBRARY

MW
TP090144.22
BOKSSPSSR

3026497

Luck Egalitarianism

EQUALITY, RESPONSIBILITY, AND JUSTICE

Carl Knight

UNIVERSITIES AT MEDWAY LIBRARY

EDINBURGH UNIVERSITY PRESS

2 3 JUL 2010

© Carl Knight, 2009

Edinburgh University Press Ltd
22 George Square, Edinburgh

www.euppublishing.com

Typeset in Sabon
by Servis Filmsetting Ltd, Stockport, Cheshire, and
printed and bound in Great Britain by
CPI Antony Rowe, Chippenham and Eastbourne

A CIP record for this book is available from the British Library

ISBN 978 0 7486 3869 7 (hardback)

The right of Carl Knight
to be identified as author of this work
has been asserted in accordance with
the Copyright, Designs and Patents Act 1988.

Contents

Acknowledgements

Hillel Steiner provided insightful commentary on an early draft of the entire book, and Jonathan Quong and Stephen de Wijze also supplied valuable comments on several chapters. Dick Arneson went through with me the final two-thirds of the book in some detail, enabling me to make several major improvements. I am grateful also for the input of Alan Hamlin, Matt Matravers, Catriona McKinnon, Peter Vallentyne, and participants at events at the University of St Andrews, the University of Wales, Newport, the University of Manchester, University College Dublin, and the University of Glasgow.

I was fortunate enough to be an Arts and Humanities Research Council Doctoral Award holder for the three years spent working on the book at the University of Manchester. A small proportion of the material presented here originated while I was at the University of York where I was funded by a York Alumni Fund Postgraduate Studentship. A Global Exchange Programme Award from the Worldwide University Network and the University of Manchester facilitated my spell as a Visiting Scholar at the University of California, San Diego in May and June 2006. I am happy to be able to acknowledge these sources of generous support.

Some of the work presented here has been published elsewhere. Chapter 2 includes material from 'Egalitarian Justice and Valuational Judgment', *Journal of Moral Philosophy*, in press, © 2009 Koninklijke Brill NV, Leiden, by permission of Brill. Chapter 3 is based on 'Describing Equality', *Law and Philosophy*, in press, by permission of Springer, © 2009. Chapter 4 includes a large amount of material from 'In Defence of Luck Egalitarianism', *Res Publica*, 11, 1 (2005), 55–73, © 2005 Springer, by permission of Springer. The bulk of Chapter 5 is derived from 'The Metaphysical Case for Luck Egalitarianism', *Social Theory and Practice*, 32, 2 (April 2006), 173–89, by permission of *Social Theory and Practice*, © 2006. I appreciate the assistance of the editors and referees for these journals, and especially that of Eddie Clark, Neil Curtis, Nicola Ramsey, and anonymous reviewers for Edinburgh University Press.

ACKNOWLEDGEMENTS

Many friends at the University of Manchester and the University of Glasgow have provided encouragement during the preparation of the book – too many, alas, to mention by name, but they have my thanks. My greatest debt by far is owed to my family, particularly my brother Roger, my father David, and my mother Cora.

In memory of my mother

Introduction

Equality, Responsibility, and Justice

In a celebrated article of 1989, G. A. Cohen declared that '[Ronald] Dworkin has, in effect, performed for egalitarianism the considerable service of incorporating within it the most powerful idea in the arsenal of the anti-egalitarian right: the idea of choice and responsibility.'[1] The general view inspired by Dworkin's accomplishment has become known as 'responsibility-sensitive egalitarianism', 'equality of fortune', or more commonly, 'luck egalitarianism'.[2] While it is widely accepted that luck egalitarianism seeks to combine the traditionally radical idea of distributive equality with the traditionally conservative concern for holding people responsible for their actions, there is much disagreement about (1) the specific nature of its objective, (2) the most appropriate way of realizing the objective, and (3) the desirability, from various perspectives, of the objective and its particular realizations. In this work I hope to shed some light on all three of these issues.

(1) receives the briefest treatment. The version of the luck-egalitarian objective that I will focus on is the view that variations in the levels of advantage held by different persons are justified if, and only if, those persons are responsible for those levels.[3] This is, it seems to me, the purest form of luck egalitarianism. One might say that there is a presumption in favour of equality, because inequalities have to be justified. And the only available grounds for justification are grounds of responsibility. It is hard to see how it would be possible to give equality or responsibility sensitivity a more prominent role in an account of distributive justice without compromising one or the other. Indeed, it is argued that neither equality nor responsibility sensitivity could be given a more prominent role in such an account at all. The arguments of this book are also most relevant to the understanding of less demanding definitions of luck egalitarianism, because they appeal to similar ideas.[4]

(2) is the subject of a much lengthier discussion. The luck egalitarian objective is typically said to recommend that disadvantages that arise from congenital disability, poor native endowment of talent,

1

and birth into unfavourable social or economic circumstance give rise to entitlements for compensation, for they do not derive from responsible acts, whereas those that arise from choices to make more or less effort, or to pursue some goals rather than others, do not, for they reflect differential responsibility. While this is, in the end, roughly right, the journey from the objective to a distributive theory, let alone public policy, is rather less straightforward than might be imagined. It is necessary to devise some theory that describes the correct (or most correct) measure of advantage and disadvantage, and successfully explains how these might be varied as individual responsibility varies. Part 1 appraises the two principal candidates for this role.

Chapter 1 examines and extends Dworkin's 'equality of resources'. Dworkin suggests that one might measure equality and advantage by use of the envy test, inequality and disadvantage being present wherever any individual favours another's bundle of resources rather than their own. It is argued that this captures some important parts of (dis) advantage, and that a responsibility-corrected form of the test is possible. This fails as an account of egalitarianism, however, as it cannot recognize inequalities in the circumstances of the hypothetical choice that is central to the envy test. Dworkin's favoured approach to distribution, which relies on hypothetical insurance markets, does not even get this far, because its notion of equalizing gives aggregative considerations a key role.

Chapter 2 considers 'equal opportunity for welfare', as advocated by Richard Arneson and John Roemer. The discussion begins by identifying the variety or varieties of bad luck that appear to be compensable. It is maintained that compensation for 'bad price luck' – typically, unluckiness in the expense of one's tastes – is appropriate, and that Cohen's broader view of which kinds of luck are compensable is unacceptable, for the luck egalitarian at least. The bad-price-luck argument is then defended against a few objections raised by Dworkin. As its success is largely dependent on the availability of a robust conception of welfare, an attempt is made to set out such a conception. This 'present-mood' account of welfare focuses on affective states – on how it feels from the inside – and appears to overcome many of the problems faced by better-known accounts. Cohen's attempt to reintroduce a resourcist element to egalitarian justice is resisted at the close of the chapter.

Part 2 begins the extensive analysis of (3) – the question of the desirability of luck egalitarianism. It is particularly concerned with equal opportunity for welfare's credentials *as an account of equality,* but equality of resources and certain non-luck egalitarian theories are also assessed on this basis.

Chapter 3 notes that, because every major theory of distributive justice can be construed as egalitarian in some senses (for instance, in giving each individual the same rights), we need more discriminating conditions for a theory or principle to qualify as substantively egalitarian. Three such conditions are set out. In short, the theory or principle has genuinely to treat like cases alike, treat all fully and equally, and pursue equality in a dimension that is of value to egalitarians. While libertarian, utilitarian, and priority for the worst off views can meet one or two of these conditions, they cannot meet all three of them as various forms of outcome egalitarianism (the view that individual levels of advantage should be made as equal as possible) can. Luck egalitarianism can tick the first two boxes, and there is a decent prima facie case for it ticking the third.

Chapter 4 begins by outlining a luck-egalitarian approach to public policy which is sensitive to various problems concerning information gathering. A wide range of arguments for the non-egalitarian character of luck egalitarianism presented by writers such as Elizabeth Anderson, Marc Fleurbaey, and Jonathan Wolff is then handled. The claims that luck egalitarianism insults persons, injures the irresponsible worse off, or injures the non-negligent appear to be significantly overstated. The negligent needy might, in principle, be abandoned by luck egalitarianism but this is unlikely in practice. A more pressing practical problem might be the mistreatment of dependent care-takers but this can easily be rectified by small theoretical additions. Luck egalitarianism's prescriptions appear to be particularly attractive to the egalitarian when compared to those of 'democratic equality', the alternative theory put forward by Anderson.

Confirmation of luck egalitarianism's ability to satisfy the third condition for substantive egalitarianism comes in Chapter 4. In Part 3, the broadest sense of (3) – luck egalitarianism's attractiveness *as an account of justice* – is considered.

Chapter 5 explores the role of responsibility in luck egalitarianism. Some writers – Susan Hurley being the most prominent – aver that the marriage of equality and responsibility is an unhappy one. It is here contended that, quite to the contrary, full responsibilitarianism implies luck egalitarianism, provided there have been responsible acts. Other critics, such as Samuel Scheffler, suggest that luck egalitarianism's use of responsibility renders it implausible for metaphysically based reasons. In reply, it is urged that luck egalitarianism is actually unusually sensitive to our metaphysical uncertainty. Other theories, such as outcome egalitarianism, appear to make just the untenable assumptions that luck egalitarianism is alleged to make. Furthermore, luck egalitarianism's metaphysical sensitivity can be readily accommodated at the level of application.

The sixth and final chapter puts the spotlight on those considerations of distributive justice which are neither egalitarian nor responsibilitarian. It is argued that, while luck egalitarianism can be adjusted in a minor way to ensure that basic needs are met, it cannot respond satisfactorily to other matters concerning absolute (non-comparative) levels of advantage. In this connection, four main forms of inefficiency are identified, and suggestions made about their likely effects. Even when combined with other principles of justice, luck egalitarianism leads that combination towards one or another form of injustice. A stronger account of distributive justice, however, may include certain significant elements of responsibilitarianism and luck egalitarianism.

Before the argument gets under way properly, some comments on the method and scope of this book are no doubt in order. I endorse the Rawlsian approach to moral epistemology known as the *method of reflective equilibrium*. We take our considered moral judgements – those judgements made under idealized circumstances and without errors – as the starting point. We then attempt to match these judgements to moral principles through a process of philosophical reflection and reconciliation, until the judgements and principles lie in equilibrium.[5] My favoured construal of the method is *wide*, in that it admits the consideration of background theories in support of, or in opposition to, the moral judgements. It is also *radical,* meaning that initial considered judgements may be revised, and new principles introduced, during the reflective process. Finally, the outcome of the method is to be understood as *fallible*: we do not claim that the resultant principles are true, but just that they are justified.[6] To be sure, there is nothing particularly startling about all this. Thomas Scanlon's remark that the method of reflective equilibrium 'prescribes, so to speak, a level playing field of intuitive justification on which principles and judgements of all levels of generality must compete for our allegiance'[7] is particularly applicable to my construal of that method. But, in the inevitable absence of knock-down arguments relying solely on morally neutral facts, I think this is the best we can do. The specific arguments of this work are not explicitly cast using the terminology of the Rawlsian method, because this would distract from the arguments themselves, but I hope my intent of working in 'a level playing field of intuitive justification' is nevertheless apparent.

A couple of further deep assumptions of method should be mentioned. The book, like the bulk of the work that it engages with, has an individualist outlook, taking the person as the basic concern of justice, and (though it makes few claims beyond those concerning justice) as the basic concern of social and philosophical enquiry. This does not, of course, mean that it is indifferent to the moral or other significance of groups of persons, but just that it treats any such significance as ultimately deriving from the significance of individuals. It is also assumed that the rightness of distributive bodies' actions is to be judged by their consequences. I do not think that this last point shapes the conclusions in any decisive way, because the kind of consequences under consideration are very broad including, for example, the extent to which rights are acknowledged, but some of the arguments for the conclusions may strike some as having a specifically consequentialist bent.

As may be clear, this work is concerned with distributive justice in a quite familiar sense of the term. It assumes, without argument, that distributive justice is concerned with assigning benefits and burdens to human beings, and thus is concerned with non-human animals and the natural environment only for their instrumental value. Intergenerational justice is also not treated in anything approaching systematic fashion although there are several remarks relating to this issue. Likewise, criminal justice is mentioned occasionally but only to draw attention to possible contrasts between luck egalitarianism and retributive accounts of punishment.

I will say slightly more about what I take to be the most practically significant constraint of scope. This is the book's concern with justice as something that applies to the society within a nation state. The work offers no sustained discussion of how justice applies between different nations or cultures within a state[8] or, more particularly, of how justice applies beyond the boundaries of the nation state. Now the significance of this should be obvious right away. Strongly redistributive theories of justice, such as the luck-egalitarian theories discussed in this book, have radically different implications where they are applied to different groups of people.

For simplicity, let us begin by considering two different versions of outcome egalitarianism. On the *domestic* model assumed in this book, outcome egalitarianism will be concerned with making a particular country's worse off better off and its better off worse off, relative to their starting positions.[9] In practice, this would probably involve more extreme versions of existing redistributive policies (for example, highly progressive income taxes), and such policies would be identified as being left wing in quite a familiar sense.

The specific practical implications of the alternative *cosmopolitan* model of outcome egalitarianism are harder to pin down, but their broad shape can be suggested. In the present case, the outcome egalitarian is interested in making the global worse off better off and the global better off worse off. Now the precise definition of these groups will depend on the kind of outcome egalitarianism under consideration, and we will not discuss its particular forms until Chapter 3. But it seems clear enough that the poor of developed countries, who generally earn five digit pound or dollar salaries and/or have a wide variety of needs met through social services, are better off than the majority of persons in developing countries, who generally earn three digit salaries, and often lack access to health care, food, and clean drinking water. So the switch from a domestic view to a cosmopolitan view is likely to have the effect of not only ceasing the transfer of resources to the poor of developed countries, but also starting a transfer of resources away from these people to the global poor. If such policies are left wing, they are certainly not so in a traditional way.

How are these practical implications altered by a shift from simple outcome egalitarianism to luck egalitarianism? One of this book's conclusions, often denied by other writers, is that domestic luck egalitarianism has strongly egalitarian policy implications. Might it be, then, that luck egalitarianism has a surprisingly traditional left-wing policy in the domestic and in the cosmopolitan cases, broadly concurring with outcome egalitarianism in the former instance but repudiating its more unconventional trans-domestic conclusions? I think not. If anything, bringing responsibility into the picture carries the cosmopolitan judgement even further away from the domestic judgement.

Poor people in poor countries present the most spectacular case of disadvantage combined with absence of responsibility for that disadvantage.[10] While it is, I argue, often the case that poor people in rich countries are not responsible for the disadvantage they have relative to their fellow citizens, the imbalance between level of advantage and level of responsibility is on the whole far less extreme than it is for the global poor. The poor of rich countries usually had the opportunity to be rich, in the weak sense that, had they performed to the absolute maximum of their capabilities at school and in their working lives, they would most likely have succeeded. The presence of such limited opportunity is obviously, for a luck egalitarian, nothing like sufficient grounds for justifying the full scale of existing inequalities, because it is unreasonable to expect any persons to operate at 100 per cent all the time: the poor should be judged only on the same terms as the rich, and the rich have typically not got where they have through sheer hard work. The point is rather that the global poor often lack even this limited opportunity – there is no course of action for them which would reliably have made them (by global standards) rich. Even to have achieved the level of advantage of the poor in rich countries would have required extraordinary efforts, if even that were possible. The global poor are then not only poor compared to the poor of rich countries, but they are also even more obviously not responsible for their disadvantaged position. Responsibility considerations actually reinforce the cosmopolitan case for large-scale redistribution to the global poor, even to the extent of moving assets away from the poor of rich countries.

The apparent extremity of the cosmopolitan view is one possible motivation for a third *communitarian* position. Here our favoured principles are to hold not between persons across the globe, but rather between certain communities, such as states, nations, or subnational social entities. The best known communitarian view is Rawls's 'law of peoples' although the distributive implications of his view are, in stark contrast to his position on the domestic case, fairly weak.[11] Usually, as in the case of Rawls, communitarianism involves demanding domestic principles of justice and less demanding trans-domestic principles, this asymmetry being grounded in some account of how certain rights and responsibilities arise only within communities (in my broad sense). There does not seem to be a great deal of appeal to the idea of applying outcome egalitarianism or luck egalitarianism between communities, so that states are equal in their total or average levels of advantage (corrected for responsibility in the latter case). If one accepts that strong redistributive rights and responsibilities hold trans-domestically, it seems strange then to apply them only between states, rather than, as the cosmopolitan would have it, between people. So the most likely use of communitarianism by outcome egalitarians or luck egalitarians is as part of an attempt to limit the scope of their egalitarian principles. They can say: 'egalitarianism applies only domestically, because the conditions for full distributive justice do not hold trans-domestically, but we are not indifferent to global justice as we have these other principles, which are grounded in conditions which do hold trans-domestically'.

The foregoing should give some indication of the kind of positions on global justice that luck egalitarians may assume. Although, as I say, this work assumes the domestic model, its arguments would be largely compatible with the communitarian model, because that model is concerned only to apply luck egalitarianism at the domestic level. The discussion should also suggest the practical importance of the choice of a trans-domestic position. Depending on the position taken, luck egalitarianism may take a fairly conventional left-wing view (perhaps focusing on the expansion of existing welfare states), a very radical view (perhaps introducing something equivalent to the welfare state on a global basis), or – should a communitarian stance be taken – something between the two (perhaps involving a mechanism for substantial humanitarian intervention but no permanent redistributive functions).

Given the real world significance described above, it might be asked why I have not felt the need to engage with these issues more systematically. My answer is twofold. First, the literature on luck egalitarianism generally assumes the domestic model, and it would be quite impossible to engage with much of it without sharing that assumption. If one tried to write a book about luck egalitarianism that assumed cosmopolitanism, that argued for it, or that tried to stay neutral on the issue, it would be a very different book, and one inevitably on global distributive justice instead of luck egalitarianism, for most of the key issues would be global, and many of the central topics in recent egalitarian debates would be precluded. Second, with global justice, as with the other matters of method and scope mentioned earlier, I claim only to offer a rough idea of the conceptual backdrop of the central arguments that come later, rather than a fully worked-out view of these various matters, each of which is philosophically complex in its own right. I hope (and believe) that this is no great impediment to the value of what follows.

Notes

1 Cohen 1989, 933; see Dworkin 1981.
2 The last two phrases were coined in Anderson 1999a. Although Dworkin has certainly been a strong influence on luck egalitarians, he states that his 'equality of resources' is not itself luck egalitarian; see Chapter 1.

3 This is equivalent to what I describe as 'equity' in 6.3 (that is, Chapter 6, section 3).
4 See, in particular, the Conclusion.
5 Rawls 1999a, sec. 9, 1975; Daniels 1996.
6 See Knight 2006b.
7 Scanlon 2003, 151.
8 But see the comments on cultural accommodation in 4.2, and also Knight 2004.
9 Of course, it is possible that the best outcome egalitarian response to some particular circumstance is to do nothing, just to make the worse off better off, or just to make the better off worst off. I discuss the phenomenon of 'levelling down' in Chapter 6 but, for the moment, it suffices to say that in most countries a mixture of policies would best achieve outcome egalitarian objectives.
10 See Knight 2008.
11 Rawls 1999b; cf. Rawls 1999a.

Part 1

Luck Egalitarianisms

Equality of Resources

---

1. Introductory Remarks

I will start my discussion by looking at the first significant theory that has been identified as luck egalitarian – Ronald Dworkin's 'equality of resources'.[1] From an egalitarian perspective, this theory marks an advance on the renowned work of John Rawls in a number of areas.[2] Two of these areas are especially noteworthy here.[3] First, Dworkin insists as a matter of justice that individuals' choices influence the size of their holdings, whereas Rawls proposes that all inequalities in social goods, however they were arrived at, are open to redistribution if that is to the benefit of the worst off. This is the most obvious reason why it is appropriate to say that Dworkin, not Rawls, presented the first significant luck-egalitarian theory.[4] Second, Dworkin proposes mechanisms for setting the value of goods and the fairness of their distribution not only for social but also for natural goods; he consequently avoids Rawls's 'primary goods fetishism', whereby natural inequalities are overlooked.[5] In my view this second move also leads Dworkin's theory to be more faithfully luck egalitarian although this is for the more contentious reason that it overcomes shortfalls in Rawls's account of distributive equality itself – shortfalls that would be present even in a Rawlsian account that did accommodate considerations of choice and responsibility.[6]

My analysis of equality of resources as a luck-egalitarian theory is presented in three stages. The first stage, which takes up the first half of the chapter, aims to show that envy-test equality is well equipped to overcome many of the criticisms that have been raised against Dworkinian equality of resources by welfarist critics. The objective of the second stage, which comes in sections 6 and 7, is to establish that, impressive as they are, Dworkin's distributive mechanisms do not, from a luck-egalitarian perspective, go far enough in redressing inequalities in natural endowments. In fact, Dworkin's favoured insurance markets fail to realize the luck-egalitarian ideal set out by Dworkin's account of responsibility, which is better captured by the envy test that he refuses to apply consistently. The final stage, which is started and completed in the final section of this chapter, seeks to demonstrate that envy-test equality fails to recognize one important source of inequality.

2. Envy-Test Equality

Dworkin draws a distinction between *choice* and *circumstance*. People's choices, he says, are linked to their personality which is made up principally of their ambition (broadly understood) and character:

> Someone's ambitions include all his tastes, preferences, and convictions as well as his overall plan of life: his ambitions furnish his reasons or motives for making one choice rather than another. Someone's character consists of those traits of personality that do not supply him with motives but that nevertheless affect his pursuit of his ambitions: these include his application, energy, industry, doggedness, and ability to work now for distant rewards, each of which might be, for anyone, a positive or negative quality.[7]

Circumstances, by contrast, consist of an individual's personal and impersonal resources. Personal resources are an individual's physical and mental capabilities, including the market value of their talents. Impersonal resources are socially transferable goods, such as an individual's wealth and property and her legal opportunities to make use of that wealth and property.[8]

Dworkin proposes the *envy test* as the measure of a fair distribution of resources. This states that '[n]o division of resources is an equal division of resources if, once the division is complete, any [individual] would prefer someone else's bundle of resources to his own bundle'.[9] In other words, a fair distribution is *envy free*.[10]

For the moment let us set aside the relationship between the envy test and Dworkin's firm distributive proposals. Consider the following account of distributive equality, *envy-test equality*, which states that to be just a distribution must be equal, and to be equal a distribution must be envy free. On this account the test is to be applied to resources all told – that is, jointly to personal and impersonal resources, as well as to all subcategories of personal and impersonal resources. There is no need for, say, personal resources to be equal (that is, to result in envy freeness) provided that impersonal resources are unequal in just such a way as to offset any inequality (that is, to render the distribution envy free). Nor is there any need for money (a subcategory of impersonal resources) to be equally distributed.

Although envy-test equality denies that equality need be secured in every aspect or dimension of equality,[11] many cases remain in which the envy test recommends redistribution. Anyone who, prior to transfer, prefers someone else's bundle of resources to their own, is viewed as disadvantaged and, considerations of responsibility aside,[12] as such entitled to compensation up to that level at which envy freeness is secured. Conversely, an individual who, prior to transfer, prefers no one else's bundle of resources to their own, is viewed as non-disadvantaged. Such an individual is liable to expropriation down to that level at which the envy of other individuals is removed.

The simplest case of redistribution is that where the only variations that have an impact on the envy test are income and wealth. If A's income is £10,000 and B's and C's incomes are £20,000 apiece, and they all have relevantly identical physical constitutions and preferences, it is clear enough that, assuming a general desire for income, A will envy B's and C's resources. A transfer of income from B and C to A is the obvious solution here. Variations in talent do little to complicate the situation because talent is just one cause (and often not the most significant cause) of income and wealth inequalities.

The situation becomes significantly knottier where there are variations in physical constitutions and preferences. Suppose that we have equalized the income of A, B, and C. But B was born paraplegic, and this is a permanent condition.[13] C was born with expensive tastes that, on reflection, she feels she 'could do without'. In this section I will consider cases of the first type, leaving cases like that of C until the next section.

Suppose that B strongly wishes that she was not paraplegic.[14] B qualifies for special compensation – that is, resources beyond what an able-bodied person who is otherwise identical would receive – as she prefers A's bundle of resources. For the envy test to be satisfied, B would have to favour her set of resources to the set of resources enjoyed by everybody else, or be indifferent to the choice. This will usually mean transferring impersonal resources to her to make up for her personal resource shortfall.

Is this way of dealing with disabilities *acceptable to the disabled*? Peter Handley claims that Dworkin's view of disabilities as giving rise to 'special needs' and compensation leaves 'wider structural and attitudinal factors that relate to disability unquestioned'.[15] Regardless, however of whether Dworkin would be prepared to provide compensation in the form of the removal of social barriers – to my knowledge he nowhere says that he would or would not – the envy test is perfectly capable of providing such compensation. The envy test embodies a first-person understanding of equality, being based on each individual's appraisal of their situation vis-à-vis everyone else's.[16] Consequently compensation will be made only in the form and to the extent to which it improves the individual's life *as she judges it*. Hence, the envy test is very far removed from the much-bemoaned medical approach to disability where that is understood as the tendency to regard impaired persons as suffering from 'personal deficits' that require medical treatment, regardless of whether that treatment furthers the patients' ambitions, and without any consideration of ways of alleviating socially imposed disadvantages. Rather, it provides a rationale for addressing Handley's 'wide attitudinal and structural factors', and assigns any associated costs to persons such as A.[17] This appears to show that equality of resources (so far conceived) does not neglect B.

3. No Accounting for Taste?

We turn now to cases like that of C, who has a taste for skiing. A large part of Dworkin's original motivation for formulating equality of resources was the weaknesses he perceived in equality of welfare, the main alternative egalitarian theory. Foremost among these is equality of welfare's implication 'that those with champagne tastes, who need more income simply to achieve the same level of welfare as those with less expensive tastes, should have more income on that account'; Dworkin asserts that 'this seems counter-intuitive'.[18] Critics such as G. A. Cohen, Richard Arneson and John Roemer have argued, however, that it is only counter-intuitive to compensate for expensive tastes where their holders can fairly be held responsible for cultivating them.[19] The apparent intuitive force of Dworkin's criticism dissipates where those with expensive tastes are not responsible for possessing them. Cohen puts the case thus:

> For Dworkin, it is not choice but preference which excuses what would otherwise be an unjustly unequal distribution. He proposes compensation for power deficiencies, but not for expensive tastes, whereas I believe that we should compensate for disadvantage beyond a person's control, as such, and that we should not, accordingly, draw a line between unfortunate resource endowment and unfortunate utility function. A person with *wantonly* expensive tastes has no claim on us, but neither does a person whose powers are feeble because he recklessly failed to develop them.[20]

Roemer adds that Dworkin's theory seems to presume 'an apparently peculiar conception of responsibility, for that term usually denotes an aspect of a person's situation associated with actions over which she has had control, and one may not be responsible for one's preferences under this construal'.[21] In fact, tastes seem to be in the same boat as resources; whether disadvantages are fair or unfair depends upon whether they were arrived at due to choice or to unchosen circumstance. It seems inconsistent to compensate for unfortunate resource endowments but not for unfortunate tastes because both can be matters of unchosen circumstances.[22] Cohen consequently urges that '[t]he right cut is between responsibility and bad luck, not between preferences and resources'.[23]

The broad claim to be considered is that resource egalitarianism is insensitive to morally relevant disadvantages brought about by certain conjunctions of taste and responsibility. I start my discussion by examining John Rawls's reasons for offering no compensation for any kind of taste. Were these reasons sound, envy-test equality would have an answer to the objection at hand, although its treatment of taste would be flawed for other reasons.

Rawls notes that 'as moral persons citizens have some part in forming and cultivating their final ends and preferences'.[24] He goes on to criticize arguments like those of his and Dworkin's critics:

> [The critic] must argue . . . that it is unreasonable, if not unjust, to hold such persons [that is, those with expensive tastes] responsible for their preferences and to require them to make out as best they can. But to argue this seems to presuppose that citizens' preferences are beyond their control as propensities or cravings which simply happen.[25]

The starting point of Rawls's argument seems uncontroversial. It is probably true that cases where preferences are formed *entirely* independently of the individual's conscious choices do not exist. The critics' point retains force, however, so long as *some part* of preference formation is independent of the individual's choices, for they can maintain that it is this part that requires compensation. The procedure might be similar to that used in Tort Law. On the available evidence an individual's expensive taste might be said to be, say, 60 per cent attributable to his choices and 40 per cent attributable to his circumstances, in which case he would meet 60 per cent of the expense.[26] Thus Rawls's conclusion is far too strong. Arneson, Cohen and Roemer claim only that citizens' preferences and tastes are beyond their control insofar as they happen to be beyond their control in each case, not that they are necessarily fully beyond their control.[27]

Rawls nevertheless pushes towards the strong conclusion by appealing to what he says are common-sense notions of responsibility. He writes that it is a 'normal part of being human to cope with the preferences our upbringing leaves us with' and that taking responsibility for our ends 'whether or not they have arisen from our actual choices . . . is something we must learn to deal with'.[28]

Two objections can be raised to such an approach. In the first place its conclusions, if consistently applied, seem deeply at odds with egalitarianism. Arneson writes that the idea that individuals are to be held fully responsible for their tastes and preferences, however they are formed, 'undermines any concern for distributive equality': 'The poor, handicapped and untalented individual could simply choose a conception of the good life that is fully satisfiable despite these adverse circumstances.' [29] Perhaps some would be happy to accept this conclusion but, nevertheless, specify that goods should be distributed in egalitarian fashion in full knowledge that that distribution will not help the disadvantaged equally to pursue their conceptions of the good life. But such a distribution then seems seriously undermotivated from either a Rawlsian or a Dworkinian perspective.

If Rawls's argument was sound, then this first objection to it could be brushed aside easily enough. We would simply have to forget about equality, at least in any distributive sense. But Rawls's argument is not sound. It is quite possible that it is simultaneously the case both that people have learned to bear the costs of their unchosen expensive tastes, and that justice says they should not have to because they cannot be blamed for holding them. An appeal to the claim that the disadvantaged do or should cope with that disadvantage begs the question in favour of the normative principles embodied in existing, possibly unjust, social institutions. As Roemer notes in a different context, '[p]references are often adjusted to what the person falsely deems to be necessity, and society does her no favour by accepting the consequences that follow from exercising them'.[30] Rawls's move is a strange one for him given that he evidently does not think it a strong case against redistribution of income and wealth that poor people may have learned to live with deprivation. Stripped of its appeal to common sense, his position amounts to an undefended assertion that people *should* take responsibility for *all* their tastes, even though some of these are completely beyond their control. This is not a compelling case.

4. Dworkinian Advantage

Unlike Rawls, Dworkin allows that certain tastes do, indeed, require compensation. Dworkin explains his position as follows:

> The distinction required by equality of resources is the distinction between those beliefs and attitudes that define what a successful life would be like, which the ideal assigns to the person, and those features of body or mind or personality that provide means or impediments to that success, which the ideal assigns to the person's circumstances.[31]

I will refer to these life-defining beliefs and attitudes as *ambitions*; the personal features which are 'means or impediments' to the idea of a successful life that ambitions set are *resources*. On the Dworkinian account, an individual's *advantage* is some part of her (chosen or unchosen) resources that is continuous with her ambitions by furthering their fulfilment. A *disadvantage* is some part of an individual's resources that hinders the fulfilment of her ambitions and therefore fails the continuity test.[32] As the Dworkin quote suggests, certain tastes may be disadvantageous in this sense. Dworkin calls these 'cravings' and says that they may demand compensation in the same manner as disabilities. In other words, for a taste to be a compensation-entitling disadvantage, its holder must *disidentify* with it or *disprefer* it (I will use these terms interchangeably). Suppose a man finds that his tap water tastes unbearably sour and therefore has the expensive taste for bottled water. Dworkin says that he 'would prefer not to have that disability: his condition is a handicap, and equality of resources would regard it as such'.[33] For Dworkin, compensation for cravings should be set by a hypothetical insurance market, as we shall see below. Envy-test equality simply enters them as (disadvantageous) resources in the envy test. Thus, the man with an expensive taste for bottled water would compare his resources, unwanted expensive taste and all, with those of others, and would find himself entitled to compensation up to the level at which he no longer envies the resources of otherwise similarly positioned tap-water drinkers.

The flip side of the Dworkinian account of advantage's treatment of tastes is that those tastes that are continuous with the individual's ambitions do not require compensation, however expensive they may be. There is no basis for a claim for compensation for preferred expensive tastes because, from the first-person perspective of the envy test, they are not a disadvantage. They merely make the promotion of the bearer's welfare expensive, and Dworkinians are interested in ambitions, not welfare.

What, then, of the claim that resource egalitarianism is insensitive to morally relevant disadvantages brought about by certain conjunctions of taste and responsibility? This claim can be supported by arguments of two types. The first type of argument maintains that envy-test equality overlooks disadvantages arising from taste variations on account of its *inadequate conception of advantage*. The second type maintains that it does so on account of its *neglect of responsibility*.

I turn first to consider three inadequate-conception-of-advantage arguments presented by Cohen.[34] The first of these has only superficial appeal. Cohen asks us to imagine the case of an individual with an expensive taste that can be eradicated by therapy:

> If he agrees to the therapy, then, so I believe, the ideal of equality says he should get it, regardless of whether he says farewell to his taste with unmixed relief or, instead, with a regret which reflects some degree of identification. This suggests that identification and disidentification matter for egalitarian justice only if and insofar as they indicate presence and absence of choice.[35]

Contrary to Cohen's claim, whether the craver is unreservedly happy about losing his taste or has mixed feelings about it is irrelevant to the resource egalitarian. The continuity test asks a simple Yes/No question: 'All things considered, does this individual favour having this taste?' There is no question of therapy being withdrawn if the answer is, 'No, all things considered I do not want this taste, but that said, part of me would feel sad if I lose it.' In this case, equality of resources is concerned only with the first clause of this answer and ignores any reservations.[36] This is quite appropriate, for a taste that is judged by its bearer to be on the whole a disadvantage is still, though it may have small benefits, on the whole a disadvantage and should be treated as such.

The second argument has more, though not much more, going for it. It attempts to show, by way of example, that envy-test equality fails to acknowledge the disadvantage of expensive tastes. Consider two people with different pastimes. Paul loves photography, which is expensive, while Fred loves fishing, which is not. Paul cannot enjoy or value any less expensive pastime (such as fishing). Moreover, he cannot afford to pursue his pastime while Fred can his; Paul consequently has a less enjoyable and (from his perspective) less meaningful life than his fisherman peer. The egalitarian, it may be granted, should recognize that Paul is in a position of comparative disadvantage. But

Cohen claims that the 'envy test for equality of resources is satisfied: Paul can afford to go fishing as readily as Fred can'.[37] Thus envy-test equality apparently fails to capture an important part of what matters for egalitarians.

Cohen's conclusion that the envy test is satisfied without compensation for Paul rests on the mistake of thinking that the envy test is to be applied objectively. He asks 'Does Paul objectively have the same resources as Fred?' or 'Does Paul have the resources to *do* what Fred can?' [38] Cohen's criticism is inapplicable to envy-test equality, however, as it uses a subjective measure of resources. Indeed, the relevant measure is subjective not merely in the sense of being concerned with individuals' tastes and interests; it is outright first person, and is as a result sensitive to variations in tastes and in ambitions.[39] We do not merely ask if Paul's resources allow him to do what Fred can but, rather, if Paul would trade resources *and* tastes in pastime with Fred. If he would trade, he is entitled to compensation, for he cannot get as much value as Fred can out of the same activity. Far from undermining envy-test equality's egalitarian credentials, the case of Paul and Fred actually reinforces them, showing how it, unlike objective theories, recognizes Paul's disadvantage.

Cohen has recently expanded on the second argument by reference to one of Dworkin's examples. Suppose that someone has a taste for bottled water and finds tap water repulsive. As this person disidentifies with this taste, Dworkin holds that he is due compensation.[40] Cohen claims that this amounts to an abandonment of his opposition to compensation for expensive brute taste, for the compensation 'can only be [issued] because bottled water is expensive, so that what he regrets is that he has an expensive taste, and it is to precisely *that* object of regret that equality (here misnamed 'of resources') is responding'.[41] For such compensation to be more than merely dressed up as resource based, Cohen asserts that it must be forthcoming on grounds other than the holder's wants: 'But we get the stated mere guise when "resources" of physical constitution are treated as handicapping a person's "ability to lead the life he wishes to lead", and *that* means, *ex hypothesi,* in the relevant context, nothing more than that he wishes to lead a life without the deleterious welfare effects of that constitution.' [42] If the resource egalitarian cannot recommend compensation in these apparently compelling cases without falling back into welfarism then, so one might ask, why work within her framework at all?

As before, the argument rests upon the illegitimate assumption that Dworkin's resources are objective. This is especially evident in Cohen's belief that Dworkin's justification for compensation for expensive tastes must be 'the fact that the source of the illfare in question is a person's physical constitution' or, more specifically, 'the constitution that makes them want' expensive foods.[43] The assumption appears to be that it is only such things as income, wealth, legal rights, and physical capability (including talent) that can be equalized by resource egalitarians. Any reference to preference and taste under the guise of 'physical constitution' amounts to a retreat into welfarism, for these particular kinds of physical constitution result only in a welfare deficit, not a resource deficit.

Yet at the core of equality of resources are mechanisms that require subjective input. My favoured version of equality of resources takes the envy test as the most important mechanism in this kind of case. Here the aim is to compensate fully for bad brute luck – for instance, by ensuring that, among those who have exercised equivalent responsibility, the envy test is satisfied. There is space between envy-test equality and equality of (opportunity for) welfare simply because the situation where, as regards taste, the envy test is satisfied – that is, everyone identifies with their own taste – is not necessarily the same scenario as that where equality of welfare holds. People may well identify with a taste that is detrimental to their own welfare. They may not subscribe to the 'correct' account of welfare, or they may have second-order preferences (perhaps other-regarding ones) that endorse their taste even though they acknowledge that it does not further their own welfare. Provided that people can conceivably pursue things other than their own welfare, 'unofficial' (envy-test) resource egalitarianism and welfare egalitarianism remain apart in theory. Provided that people sometimes actually pursue things other than their own welfare, the two accounts remain apart in practice. Similar points can be made about the 'official' version of equality of resources, which will be discussed later.[44]

Both versions of equality of resources refer to (dis)identification, be it as grounds for insurance or an impediment to envy freeness, and neither requires that this (dis)identification be *completely independent* of welfare considerations. But, in both cases, the rationale for compensation is non-welfarist. All that matters is the disidentification itself, and whether that has arisen from reasons of welfare or from reasons of anything else is neither here nor there.[45] For this reason, there is no need to dress the cause of welfare in objectivist language ('physical constitution' and so on). Someone may reply that any theory that allows so much subjective input is misnamed 'equality of resources'. This may be so. But whatever one might want to call this theory, it can compensate in such cases without being welfarist in any of the usual senses.

The third argument is not explicitly concerned with tastes but is nevertheless relevant here. Cohen maintains that equality of resources is unable to compensate for *pain*. He starts by noting that the egalitarian will grant treatment to a man who suffers from a condition that triggers pain in his arms when they move but that does not decrease his ability to use them. The argument concludes that equality of resources does not do everything an egalitarian theory should for 'providing the medicine cannot be represented as compensating for a resource incapacity'.[46]

This argument relies on the same misrepresentation of the resource-egalitarian position as the previous one. It stands or falls on the claim that '[a] would-be resource egalitarian who said, "Compensation is in order here because the man lacks the resource of being able to avoid pain," would be invoking the idea of equal opportunity for welfare, even if he would be using resourcist language to describe it'.[47] This claim may well be true of objective accounts of resources but it is manifestly false when applied to the Dworkinian account. If an individual with this condition would prefer to have arms he could move without pain – as (nearly?) everybody would – he would envy everybody without that condition, and would therefore, according to envy-test equality, be entitled to treatment. As such a condition would (presumably) be discontinuous with his ambitions, he would also be entitled to some – in my view insufficient, but nevertheless significant – level of compensation under Dworkin's hypothetical insurance-market scheme.[48] A (hedonistic) welfare egalitarian would also recommend treatment but on the very different grounds that the individual suffered a welfare deficit; the attitude of the individual towards his condition would be irrelevant. Cohen's argument again serves only to highlight a major advantage envy-test equality has over objective theories, namely its sensitivity to morally relevant interpersonal variations.

5. Responsibility

So far, envy-test equality's conception of advantage seems tenable. But what of its supposed neglect of responsibility? Here the claim is that equality of resources fails to realize the luck-egalitarian objective of making individuals' resources responsibility sensitive.[49] Cohen suggests that one's degree of responsibility for one's taste, rather than one's degree of identification with it, is the appropriate basis on which to assess claims for compensation:

> [A] craver prefers not to have his unfortunate preference yet, by hypothesis, persists in having it. That rather suggests that he cannot help having it, and that in turn raises the suspicion that it is its unchosen and uncontrolled, rather than its dispreferred, character that renders compensation for it appropriate. Would not Dworkin's attitude to the music craver be less solicitous if he learned that he had been warned not to cultivate his particular musical interest by a sapient teacher who knew it would cause frustration?[50]

This passage can be interpreted as raising two distinct claims against envy-test equality. The first and weaker one is just that it fails to make compensation for a taste conditional on it being unchosen and uncontrolled. Here Cohen is on to something. Suppose that Fiona and Gina have the same dispreferred expensive tastes for pre-phylloxera clarets and plovers' eggs.[51] Unlike Fiona, however, Gina deliberately cultivated her tastes, or somehow brought them about through negligence. Perhaps the combined effect of Fiona's native endowment and upbringing is such that she holds her expensive tastes after numerous attempts to adapt to less expensive fare, while Gina's endowment and upbringing left her with averagely expensive tastes that she chose to override in adulthood by consuming only the finest food and drink. There is, many believe, a morally relevant difference between Fiona and Gina that requires us to compensate the former but not the latter.[52] Otherwise Fiona will be disadvantaged for circumstances over which (we stipulate) she has no control and Gina will not be held responsible for the consequences of her choices.

Arneson has proposed a rival account of egalitarian justice, *equal opportunity for welfare*, which handles compensation for tastes in just the responsibility-sensitive way recommended by Cohen.[53] We will examine this and closely related views in the next chapter but, for the moment, it is sufficient to consider Arneson's statement of the key extended sense of equal opportunity for welfare:

> We may say that in an extended sense people share equal opportunity for welfare just in case there is some time at which their opportunities [for welfare] are equal and if any inequalities in their opportunities at later times are due to their voluntary choice or differentially negligent behaviour for which they are rightly deemed responsible.[54]

Equal opportunity for welfare is sensitive to the difference between Fiona and Gina. Fiona's tastes are things that she is not responsible for and that undermine her welfare prospects; as such, they are prime candidates for compensation on an equal-opportunity-for-welfare scheme. Gina's tastes, by contrast, have resulted from her choices; as such she must bear their costs. What, then, can be said of equality of resources?

It is debatable whether Dworkin himself recognizes the moral difference between Gina's situation and Fiona's. The discussion of responsibility that he offers suggests that he does. He notes that people take responsibility for their choices on several levels: we blame ourselves when we are free to choose but choose badly, '[w]e evaluate and criticize the ambitions out of which our choices are made', and 'we try to reform or overcome those character traits that have led us to make choices we would prefer not to have made'. Circumstances are a different kettle of fish. They result not from our own actions but from facts of the social and natural world over which we have no power – or rather, no power until we start making choices. Consequently, '[i]t makes no sense to take responsibility for these unless they are the upshot of [our] choices'. This assignment of responsibility, Dworkin says, is central to our personal ethics. Even if we are philosophically convinced that we have no free will, our commitment to distinguishing between choice and circumstance remains unchallenged, for '[w]e cannot plan or judge our lives except by distinguishing what we must take responsibility for, because we chose it, and what we cannot take responsibility for because it was beyond our control'.[55]

Next Dworkin describes a contrast between 'ethically sensitive' (or 'continuous') theories of justice and 'ethically insensitive' (or 'discontinuous') theories. The former view justice as continuous with personal ethics, making assignments of responsibility on the same grounds as everyday morality, which the latter do not. Dworkin makes it plain that equality of resources falls into the former category. Taking this commitment together with his account of responsibility in personal ethics, Dworkin's distributive-ideal theory 'aims to make people's impersonal resources sensitive to their choices but insensitive to their circumstances'.[56]

Dworkin believes that this objective lays moral weight on a distinction between two different types of luck. *Option luck* encompasses the consequences of gambles willingly taken in the full knowledge of their possible consequences. *Brute luck* encompasses the consequences of risks that were either unchosen, taken unwillingly, or taken without knowledge of their possible consequences.[57] The fallout of one's choices are set by option luck whereas one's circumstances are established by brute luck (except insofar as they are affected by one's choices). Hence, instances of bad brute luck give rise to legitimate claims for compensation whereas instances of bad option luck do not.

Dworkin's response to the case of Fiona and Gina is apparently confirmed in one of the new chapters of *Sovereign Virtue* where the explanation of how to identify those tastes that require compensation seems to make relevant whether the acquisition of a taste is bad luck.[58] Yet in 'What is Equality? Part Two' Dworkin does not say that a craving should be compensated only if it is unchosen.[59] The explanation for this is that Dworkin does not believe that any tastes are genuinely chosen because all tastes are themselves the result of uncultivated second-order tastes.[60] Gina may *look* more responsible for her tastes than Fiona is for hers but, in fact, she is not. Gina's attempts to develop her tastes did themselves result from certain other preferences she held and, even if she was responsible for holding those other preferences, there will, at some anterior point in the chain, be further preferences, for which she is not responsible, that guided all her behaviour. For this reason, Dworkin holds that it would be unreasonable to treat Fiona and Gina differently on the grounds of a difference that is only skin deep. Little surprise, then, that Dworkin has recently distanced himself from interpretations of his theory that cast it as luck egalitarian.[61]

The reasoning leading to Dworkin's position clearly has a strongly deterministic character. This raises questions concerning the relation between metaphysics and justice, some of which will be addressed in Chapter 5. Here it is enough to note that, shorn either of this account of the genesis of preferences, or of the particular moral conclusions, resource egalitarianism would still distribute in luck-egalitarian fashion: in the first case because there is a deep difference between Fiona and Gina; in the second case because, although that difference is relatively shallow, it is morally relevant.[62] Such a strategy sits more comfortably, at least linguistically, with Dworkin's intentions of making impersonal resource distribution choice sensitive but (unchosen) circumstance insensitive, option-luck sensitive but brute-luck insensitive, ambition sensitive but endowment insensitive.[63] Although these sensitivity–insensitivity pairs are not equivalent to one another, here they all point in the same direction. For, as the case has been described, Fiona's holding of her tastes is the result of brute luck, endowment, and (unchosen) circumstances, whereas Gina's holding of her tastes is the result of option luck, ambition, and choice.

In spite of Dworkin's stated position, I believe that the resource egalitarian should accept that only those disadvantages for which the holder is not *responsible* are unfair or unjust. The plausibility of resource egalitarianism *as a theory of luck egalitarianism* obviously depends on this move.[64] I will take 'disadvantages for which the holder is not responsible' as equivalent to unchosen or uncontrolled disadvantages, or disadvantages that arise from circumstance or brute luck; like Dworkin, Cohen, and Arneson, I will most commonly refer to choice. The resource-egalitarian theory that accommodates this position is *responsibility-sensitive envy-test equality*, which states that, to be just, a distribution must be either equal (= envy free) or unequal in ways that are wholly attributable to individual choice. This theory, like equal opportunity for welfare, is clearly a variety of luck egalitarianism. It also has obvious inspiration in major themes of Dworkin's work.

The possibility of responsibility-sensitive envy-test equality is denied by the second and stronger claim apparently present in the quote from Cohen given at the start of the section. Here, the objection is not merely that envy-test equality fails to be responsibility sensitive, but that the resource egalitarian's focus on identification is actually incompatible with such sensitivity. Thus, Cohen asserts that it follows from the idea that a taste should be compensated only if it is unchosen that it must be such a taste's 'unchosen and uncontrolled, *rather* than its dispreferred, character that renders compensation for it appropriate'. This may well follow if we treat choice and identification as rival *principles of distribution* – perhaps because we think that this must be the proposed role of identification, as we assume (with most welfarists and resource objectivists) that it does not have anything to do with advantage. From there is easy enough to get to the view that the 'principles' of choice and identification cannot be simultaneously affirmed, for they differ in their prescriptions in many cases.[65] But this reasoning is possible only where the role of identification in equality of resources is misunderstood. As I have emphasized, identification plays a key role in the constitution of advantage itself on the Dworkinian account. Once we understand this, there is little difficulty in maintaining that dispreferred tastes, as disadvantages, are compensation entitling where, according to our favoured distributive principle, they are unfair – according to the luck-egalitarian principle, which is I believe attributable to Dworkin, where they are unchosen.

According to responsibility-sensitive envy-test equality, then, it is a craving's unchosen character, *together* with its dispreferred character, that justify compensation.[66] Hence, although equal opportunity for welfare and responsibility-sensitive envy-test equality treat Fiona and Gina in the same way, they compensate Fiona for different reasons: the former focuses on the fact that her taste is unchosen and expensive while the latter focuses on the fact that her taste is unchosen and dispreferred.[67] Moreover, equal opportunity for welfare and responsibility-sensitive envy-test equality would diverge in their treatment of Fiona in just the same way as equality of welfare and envy-test equality would were she to identify with her tastes. The difference in both cases is evidently a matter of advantage. Contrary to the stronger claim I have hesitantly attributed to Cohen, responsibility raises no more difficulty for the resourcist than it does for the welfarist.

6. Hypothetical Insurance Markets

Dworkin's favoured distributive mechanism for equality of resources, *the hypothetical insurance market*, is importantly different from the mechanism I have described above. I will now make the case that Dworkin's favoured mechanism is inconsistent with his account of advantage and responsibility, for it offers insufficient compensation to certain disadvantaged persons to account fully for their bad brute luck. I could make this claim even if I wholeheartedly accepted Dworkin's treatment of taste because the cases in question concern matters of physical constitution which Dworkin accepts may be chosen or unchosen.

Dworkin proposes to set compensation for each disability at the level the average member of society would have bought insurance against that handicap from behind a veil of ignorance. The veil is thin enough for the frequency of the disability's occurrence in the population to be known but thick enough for each individual to be ignorant of their chance of acquiring the disability. The premiums would be paid for through earnings contributions from those who were not disabled.[68] So, if there was a 1 in 1,000 chance of acquiring a disability, the average person might decide to buy coverage such that, if they acquired this disability, they would receive, say, £20,000 per year; this would require insurance contributions of (on average just over) £20 per year from those 999 who did not acquire the disability.[69]

The strategy for coping with illnesses and accidents that Dworkin endorses follows the same path. He proposes to base levels of medical coverage in the United States on 'what kind of medical care and

insurance it would be prudent for most Americans to buy for themselves' from a position in which there is relative equality of wealth and
a veil of ignorance that prevents everybody from knowing anything
about the likelihood of each individual requiring treatment.[70] In
practice, the insurance payouts would be paid by the welfare system
and the (hypothetical) insurance contributions levied as income tax.[71]
Furthermore, Dworkin suggests a similar approach for dealing with
variations in income-producing talent, asking at what level people
would buy insurance against not achieving a certain income level; the
premiums would be paid from income achieved above this level.[72] For
instance, if there was a 1 in 3 chance of earning less than £10,000 per
annum, and the average person chose to buy coverage at this level,
this would require insurance contributions of (on average) £5,000
from those two-thirds above that level.

These insurance mechanisms may be impressive in design and
appealing in their conclusions. But the question before us is whether
they realize Dworkin's stated objective, 'that an equal share of
resources should be devoted to the lives of each person',[73] where
resources are defined to include both personal and impersonal
resources, as we have seen Dworkin defines them.[74] Jan Narveson
notes that, once the mechanisms are in place, inequalities will in
all likelihood persist: 'In what clear sense is Jones – who is highly
talented, quite unhandicapped, and earns a very good income which
is still, after taxes, very far in advance of that of Smith, who is quite
untalented, usually unemployed, and enjoys only the insurance-
support-level income – possessed of *equal resources* with Smith?' [75]
The presence of inequalities alone, however, is not enough to judge
against Dworkin. The theory of responsibility sketched earlier makes
both the talented and the untalented responsible for the upshot of
their choices so, if Jones has made more profitable choices than
Smith, Smith can have no legitimate complaint from the point of
view of equality if he ends up with fewer resources than Jones as a
result.

A successful case against Dworkin's conception of equality of
resources needs to show not only that its proposed institutions result
in inequalities of resources, but also that those inequalities are the
result of brute luck or circumstance. Suppose that there are two
people and that the insurance mechanism for disabilities is instituted.
Angela is disabled while Beth is not, so Angela is compensated at the
level settled on by everyone in society before the distribution of disabilities was known, while Beth contributes to that compensation.

After redistribution, Angela has her disability plus an equal share of impersonal resources plus her compensation, while Beth has no disability plus an equal share of impersonal resources minus compensation tax. John Roemer urges that it is 'not obvious . . . that resources have been appropriately equalized between these two. After all, they have identical preferences and took identical actions. Is the *difference* in their final states not a matter of brute luck, is it not a difference which is morally arbitrary?' [76] On the envy test, for there to be no morally relevant difference in the resources possessed by Angela and Beth, Angela must view the compensation as adequate fully to compensate her for her disability. Thus, the envy test will not be satisfied and bad brute luck will remain where no insurance is available that is both at an acceptable price to parties who are uncertain whether or not they are disabled, and that offers full compensation.[77]

I would have thought it obvious that the level at which the average person would have bought insurance against a given handicap is lower than the level required for a handicapped person to enjoy equal resources, taking the handicap into account. Philippe van Parijs implies, however, that Dworkin's agents would indeed insure at a level that provides full compensation. He argues that they would be inclined to *maximize minimum utility* (maximin) rather than to maximize expected utility (which he takes to be the strategy underpinning the assumption that less than full compensation would be assured).[78]

It may be noted preliminarily that Dworkin himself does not think his agents would insure at such a high level, believing that his hypothetical insurance markets would take a similar shape to actual insurance markets once these are corrected for inequalities.[79] In any case, quite independently of Dworkin's stance, Van Parijs's argument is unconvincing. The basic problem with maximin as a decision rule is that '[i]t is extremely irrational to make your behaviour wholly dependent on some highly unlikely unfavourable contingencies *regardless of how little probability you are willing to assign to them*'.[80] Van Parijs's case hinges upon the one-off weightiness of the insurance-level problem: 'Maximin makes a lot of sense when what is at issue is not one of the many decisions which you take in the course of your life, but the one big decision which determines how much will be put at your disposal to conduct the whole of your life.' [81] This is merely an unsupported assertion. Certainly, the fact that the choice before Dworkin's agents is decisive for their entire life chances is reason for them to take particular care in making their decision.

But it is by itself no reason to choose one decision rule rather than another.

The issue swings decisively away from maximin when we consider the effects of using it for this life-chance-defining decision. The cost to the non-disabled of insuring at the level required for equality of resources would, as the 'expensive resource transfer' of Chapter 6 suggests, be severe. Van Parijs's proposal implies that people would sooner leave themselves materially deprived in (say) 99 out of 100 outcomes than run the 1 in 100 risk of being disabled with less than full compensation, where that compensation may both run into the most outlandish extravagance *and* offer the beneficiary the most trifling gain in well-being. It *may* be true that some people are this risk averse. But to say that the *average person* is this risk averse – which implies that *every person* is this risk averse (for no one can be more so) – is absurd in the extreme.

As maximin does not seem a plausible strategy for the average person, Dworkin's insurance mechanisms will not offer full compensation to the disabled. The same is true for the underemployed and unhealthy, for the obvious reason that the levels at which the average person would have bought underemployment and health insurance are far below the level required fully to compensate the underemployed and the unhealthy. The average person is (by definition) not disadvantaged, so it will be rational for them to set the level of compensation for many disadvantages much lower than that required for envy freeness. As a consequence, inequalities of resources may result from variations in brute luck and circumstance, as some are born disabled or untalented or develop illnesses while others do not.[82] These results, as Eric Rakowski remarks, 'seem to offend the fundamental principle, affirmed by Dworkin, that people ought to start life with an equal bundle of resources and that equality should be maintained over time except insofar as somebody works less hard or accepts more desirable work or has poorer option luck or finds less generous friends'.[83] The insurance mechanisms upset this principle by balancing the worst-off individuals' use of resources with the uses they could have been put to by other people. Someone's brute bad luck of being disabled, untalented, or ill is not in any way alleviated by the argument that the average person behind a veil of ignorance would have preferred to risk having more resources and leaving themselves relatively unprotected against that bad luck. Many people are left with a disadvantage for which they are in no way responsible; hence resources are not equalized.

7. Three Dworkinian Responses

Of course, Dworkin is well aware that his insurance mechanisms fail to satisfy equality of resources as set by the envy test.[84] Consider three defences of this inconsistency. First, Dworkin explains in a recent paper that 'equality of resources means that people should be equally situated with respect to risk rather than that they should be equally situated after the uncertainties of risk have been resolved'.[85] The envy test should be applied *ex ante* to the distribution of disabilities, talents, and illnesses so that people are assured not an equal bundle of resources after their emergence but a hypothetical equal opportunity to insure against them.[86] That is, 'the appropriate [that is, synchronic, *ex ante*] version' of the envy test 'requires not . . . that people be fully compensated for any bad luck after it has occurred, but rather that people be made equal, so far as this is possible, in their opportunity to insure or provide against bad luck before it has occurred, or, if that is not possible, that people be awarded the compensation it is likely they would have insured to have if they had had that opportunity'.[87]

Positioning people equally only with respect to risk is, on Dworkin's account of responsibility, fair enough where running the risk is a matter of choice and option luck. But where the risk is a matter of circumstance and brute luck, with the opportunity to insure being hypothetical, this strategy leaves the distribution partially sensitive to circumstance and brute luck. Suppose that Christina is born with a dispreferred disability and Diana is not. This inequality in personal resources is not fully corrected by hypothetical insurance-market compensation, and this cannot be justified *in egalitarian terms* – let alone luck-egalitarian terms – by saying that, had Christina had the opportunity to insure before the cards were dealt, she would have settled on this level of compensation. If Christina would have made that choice, she would have done so because she was prepared to trade an egalitarian distribution for one which, on the balance of probabilities, offered her better prospects. Dworkin's move to the *ex ante* allows hypothetical individuals to trade circumstance insensitivity for a share of the spoils of circumstance sensitivity but this is to contradict the core ideas of egalitarianism.

Second, Dworkin believes that any attempt to satisfy better the envy test with regard to natural talents has undesirable consequences. Regarding underemployment insurance, for example, he argues that high levels of compensation for the untalented may drastically restrict the occupational freedoms of the talented:

> If the level of coverage is high then this will enslave the insured, not simply because the premium is high, but because it is extremely unlikely that his talents will much surpass the level he has chosen, which means that he must indeed work at full stretch, and that he will not have much choice about what kind of work to do.[88]

If this result counts against high levels of compensation, it may have serious implications for equality of resources as I earlier described it. It may equally undermine certain otherwise attractive combinations of equality of resources and non-egalitarian considerations. For instance, utility is usually promoted by the more talented working longer hours as they produce more per hour, in which case the alleged injustice would be endorsed by both elements of a resource-egalitarian–utilitarian tie-up.

Dworkin's argument against this 'slavery of the talented' relies upon the envy test, insisting 'that people should not be penalized for talent'.[89] He claims that, where there are high levels of compensation for the untalented, the talented will envy the amount of leisure time or freedom to work less productively that is enjoyed by the untalented. Van Parijs puts the argument like this: 'one must . . . require that no one be forced to have less *leisure* in consequence of *more* native talent'.[90] But to focus the envy test on one type of resource – leisure time – in this fashion is perverse. When the talented's resources as a whole, including leisure time, are considered, they are not disadvantaged relative to the untalented – if they were, the compensation would go the other way. They may be enslaved by their insurance payments but only in the same sense that the untalented are enslaved by their lack of talent.[91] Egalitarianism accepts the former type of 'enslavement' as necessary where such measures bring the untalented from a position of disadvantage to one of equality. The talented are not entitled to preferential treatment.[92]

Finally, there is the possibility that, while the hypothetical insurance markets fail to equalize resources, they are the best we can hope to do in the difficult conditions of the real world. Will Kymlicka puts the case like this:

> If we cannot fully equalize real-world circumstances, then what else can we do to live up to our convictions about the arbitrariness of one's place in the distribution of natural and social circumstances? Dworkin does not say that his scheme fully compensates for undeserved inequalities, just that it is the best we can do to live up to our convictions of justice.[93]

I hope to have shown that we can do *more* to redress these inequalities than Dworkin supposes. It is certainly the case, as Kymlicka says, however, that we cannot fully equalize circumstances, for some persons' shares can never be raised to the level of other persons no matter how many resources we devote to them. Dworkin himself offers the existence of such persons as grounds for limiting compensation to that set by the hypothetical insurance markets, as the alternative 'provides no upper bound to initial compensation, but must leave this to a political compromise likely to be less generous'.[94] But while it is true that a policy of full compensation would never gain majority assent, that is hardly a relevant consideration when we are concerned with devising a philosophically sound conception of luck equality. Moreover, the danger of compensation being set too low by political compromise may be increased rather than decreased by compromise in the conception of equality itself. The outcome of negotiations will often be less egalitarian where egalitarians can only table a conception of equality that is already watered down by the aggregative considerations of the insurance markets.

David Johnston offers an alternative argument for a similar conclusion:

> If no amount of compensation can bring the overall value of a person's means index up to an adequate or near-adequate level, then compensation is inappropriate. If we want political and social arrangements to serve our generalizable interest in having the means necessary to be effective agents, then it makes no sense to compensate people for shortfalls in those means in ways that still leave them unable to pursue projects or try to realize the values they conceive.[95]

Johnston's argument is tainted by the assumption, also shared by Rawls, that our sole generalizable interest is to reach an 'adequate' level at which we are 'effective agents'. This has particularly inegalitarian consequences given Johnston's observation that 'adequacy or normality usually has a reasonably firm basis in the organization of that society's practical affairs'.[96] This seems to put anyone who cannot be raised to adequacy, as that is defined by social convention, beyond the pale. Many people with disabilities may be raised to this level by the kinds of measures suggested by the social approach to disability. But, nevertheless, Johnston has at the drop of a hat removed perhaps the majority of the mentally disabled, and many of the more severely physically disabled, from the ambit of justice.

In fact, it is people such as these, the most disadvantaged, for whom the egalitarian has the greatest concern. The obvious thing for the resource egalitarian to do here is to try to make the distribution of resources as close to equality as possible.[97] Provided more resources can actually improve the worst off's position vis-à-vis everybody else's, it is neither here nor there that there is no possibility that even more resources could bring them to a state of equality or adequacy (as socially conceived).[98] In terms of the envy test, we keep increasing the worst-off person's resources until they would no longer prefer to have more resources.

The most that Dworkin's hypothetical insurance scheme can be said to achieve is sensitivity to some circumstances, or equality of impersonal resources plus limited compensation for personal resource inequality. As it stops short of giving the disabled, the unhealthy, and the underemployed as many resources all told as the able bodied, the healthy, and the fully employed, it cannot be said to realize equality in the currency of resources.

8. Disadvantage without Envy

We have found Dworkin's 'official' version of equality of resources to be unsatisfactory as an interpretation of luck egalitarianism. So far, we have found that responsibility-sensitive envy-test equality fares far better. There is, however, a final objection to be considered. Consider the following illustration of the problem, which Cohen attributes to a private communication from Justine Burley:

> [W]hen it comes to reproductive capacities for example, the greater financial burdens imposed on women by virtue of their unique biological endowments probably will not be compensated on Dworkin's view. A woman's complaint is only deemed legitimate if there is penis envy, as it were . . . To demand that a woman *want to be a man* to support compensation is simply ridiculous.[99]

Cohen believes that this is an instance of the envy test being 'relevantly false because I can think myself better off with my preferences ill-satisfied than I would be with your preferences well-satisfied'.[100] But if this is the cause of the trouble, how is it any different from other, less problematic examples? In the Fred and Paul example mentioned earlier, Paul's compensation is conditional on his willingness to exchange both resources (where Fred's are greater) and tastes in pastime. (It is also conditional on Paul's taste being unchosen, but I will leave that aside.) In other words, Paul must be willing to have his taste in photography removed and replaced with a taste in fishing.

There are several ways in which the dilemma facing Paul is dissimilar to that facing the woman in the Burley example (whom I will call Justine). For instance, the former concerns a taste while the latter concerns physical attributes. This does not itself strike me as morally weighty: if Paul is utterly devoted to photography, and the physical attributes in question are much less important than those connected to gender (for instance, a permanent but minor change in hair colour is on offer), I think we have more sympathy for Paul's predicament than Justine's. It does, however, suggest the possibility that the relevant thing is whether the person in question could imagine themselves changed in the proposed way – that is, whether they would really be the same person at all. It is safe enough to suggest that Justine would no longer really be Justine were her gender changed. Paul's case is far trickier, as his taste can be defined as stronger or weaker, but it seems likely that he would still be Paul without it. This might appear to explain our different intuitive responses to the cases of Justine and Paul, particularly where the latter's taste is weak. One might imagine, then, that responsibility-sensitive envy-test equality's problems might be overcome simply by restricting the kinds of things of which the parties' bundles may be made up. Some personal resources – certainly gender, and maybe others – are ring-fenced on the grounds that their admission may distort the distribution set by the envy test.

I do not believe that this solution works. Consider Henry, who not only has a more financially and welfare-expensive taste in pastime than Fred, but also has more than averagely expensive tastes and preferences about everything else – food, drink, music, cinema, architecture, horticulture, politics, philosophy, and anything else one might choose to name – and this through no fault of his own. (Perhaps Henry had an unusual upbringing, or fled political persecution in a distant land and finds that he can satisfy his tastes in his new home only by importing goods at great cost.) Here, the only way that Henry can live reasonably free from frustration and despair, as Fred does, is if he would, hypothetically, be willing to exchange tastes and resources with Fred. But, if he actually did this, it seems clear that Henry would not really be Henry; in fact, he would be far closer to being Fred. This shows that the envy test may make compensation conditional on someone willing that they were utterly other than they are even where some personal resources are excluded. But it is just as unreasonable to hold someone responsible for their state, however miserable, just because they choose to decline a personality transplant, as it is to deny compensation when they refuse to swap their gender. In both cases unchosen inequalities will go unchecked, for an individual is clearly disadvantaged relative to another if the first can achieve a reasonable level of satisfaction or enjoyment only by willing to have something happen to them that few would agree to and that none can be expected to agree to, while the second receives equivalent benefits unconditionally.

This last point suggests another: that the root problem is not really to do with the special importance of individual identity at all. For while the conditions attached to Justine's and Henry's compensation are particularly harsh, and their injustice therefore obvious, there is a similar injustice even in the case of Paul, and even if his taste is weak. For Paul can have a taste in pastime that he can satisfy only by willing that his taste in pastime was other than it is. But Fred need do nothing of the sort, either hypothetically or actually, to satisfy his pastime. It is not enough to say, 'well, clearly Paul cares more about his particular pastime than he does about his own welfare or about having a taste than can be fully satisfied. That is his choice.' This does not address the fact that Paul and Fred did not face equivalent options: whether Fred cares more for his pastimes than for his welfare or taste satisfaction does not matter because he can have his cake and eat it, while Paul must choose one or the other. But both parties would sooner have increased welfare and endorse their actual pastime. Since this is not allowed for, those with more expensive tastes are disadvantaged. The mere presence of (hypothetical) choice does not make someone's situation *relevantly* chosen, for assessments of responsibility are always relative to circumstances. The circumstances created by the envy test are not ones of equality, as the account of advantage it provides overlooks a certain source of advantage and disadvantage.[101]

Can this inequality be corrected by responsibility sensitivity? There is no reason to think so. If someone comes to envy others' holdings through no fault of their own (they are injured after being struck by lightning, say), responsibility-sensitive envy-test equality suggests that they are entitled to compensation. But the problem was precisely that persons with expensive tastes (whether they are for photography or for being a woman!) can be disadvantaged without envying. An unchosen expensive taste is non-compensable according to responsibility-sensitive envy-test equality, simply because it is not recognized as a disadvantage.[102]

9. Concluding Remarks

No version of equality of resources is a wholly adequate account of equality. Inequalities will patently remain after the distribution mandated by hypothetical insurance markets, because it would be irrational for people choosing from behind a veil of ignorance to insure at high enough levels for the *ex post* distribution to be equally favourable to all by any faintly plausible measure. While the envy test can ensure that people's situations are equalized in many significant respects, we have now seen that it fails to account for some inequalities in the circumstances of the hypothetical choice the test presents. Although the envy test can be combined with responsibility sensitivity, there is nothing about responsibility sensitivity that corrects the envy test's refusal to accept that expensive tastes can be disadvantaging even in the absence of envy. For this reason, responsibility-sensitive envy-test equality ultimately fails as an account of luck egalitarianism.

Notes

1 The first important statement of this theory is Dworkin 1981. This paper is reprinted together with some notable new chapters in Dworkin 2000.
2 Rawls 1999a; 1996.
3 Other areas of advance include Dworkin's avoidance of the excessively rigid 'lexical' ordering of Rawls's principles; his refusal to make the primary focus of justice an arbitrarily defined worst-off class as Rawls does; and the irrelevance for Dworkin's project of Rawls's problem of indexing primary goods (see Arneson 1992, 223–4).
4 See Scheffler 2003a.
5 Sen 1980.
6 Rawls sees his arguments in the two areas as connected; see section 3 below.
7 Dworkin 2000, 322.
8 Dworkin 2000, 322–3.
9 Dworkin 1981, p. 285. Hobbes may have had something similar in mind when he wrote that 'there is not ordinarily a greater signe of the equall distribution of any thing, than that every man is contented with his share' (Hobbes 1996, I, XI).
10 A full account of equality of resources would state that to be equal a distribution must be *fairly* envy free. A fair envy-free division is that set by an auction in which each individual has an equal role in the construction of bundles and equal buying power; see Dworkin 1981, 285–7 and note 102 below. I do not discuss the kind of unfairness that

the auction is designed to combat, but I take it as read that equality of resources requires fair envy freeness.

11 I discuss Anderson 1999a's alternative to this stance in section 4.7. See also McKerlie 2001.

12 In the first part of this chapter it is assumed that whatever criteria of (non)-responsibility there may be for transfer have been satisfied. Responsibility will be considered later in this chapter.

13 Were B's injuries treatable, much of the following discussion would, *mutatis mutandis*, apply if the treatment could not fully restore B's condition or if the treatment was extremely expensive. If B could make a full recovery at modest expense then, assuming that she dispreferred that injury, the envy test would recommend that she receive the treatment, as well as compensation for the injury.

14 The disabled persons in my examples would, except where stated, prefer to be able-bodied. This is not because I assume that such persons in the real world have such preferences, but rather because this combination of impairment and preference is for the moment the interesting one as it gives rise to compensation. On the envy test an impairment that is not dispreferred presents no case for compensation.

15 Handley 2003, 111.

16 Clayton 2000, 175.

17 Regarding these costs, see Chapter 6.

18 Dworkin 1981, 228.

19 Arneson 1989, 83–4.

20 Cohen 1989, 922, footnotes suppressed, original emphasis.

21 Roemer 1996, 263.

22 Cohen 1989, 932–3.

23 Cohen 1989, 922.

24 Rawls 1982, 168.

25 Rawls 1982, 168–9.

26 The remainder would be met either by whoever was responsible for the individual's circumstances – for example, a parent who has nurtured the expensive taste – or by society if no one can be fairly held responsible – if, for example, the taste was congenital; see Steiner 1997.

27 Arneson 1989, 79; Cohen 1989, 913–14.

28 Rawls 1996, 185 n.15, 185.

29 Arneson 1992, 218–19.

30 Roemer 1998, 19; see also Elster 1982.

31 Dworkin 1981, 303; see also Dworkin 2000, 322–3.

32 Andrew Williams writes that the basic idea of the continuity test is 'that a political community should regard certain conditions as disadvantaging some of its members only if those members' own views about what it is to live well also imply that those conditions disadvantage them' (Williams 2002, 387). See Dworkin 1981, 302–4.

33 Dworkin 2000, 291.

34 Cohen also refers to responsibility in these arguments. But he does so only in order to make it clear that the (allegedly) overlooked disadvantages are unfair. The fundamental question at this point is whether the disadvantages are actually overlooked by envy-test equality.

35 Cohen 1989, 927. The final sentence of the quote is suggestive of the stronger claim against equality of resources that I consider in section 5.

36 Of course, in some real-world cases the second clause may become relevant as an indicator. For example, if there was only one course of treatment available and two cravers the resource egalitarian might give the treatment to the craver who made less qualification on the usually reasonable assumption that that reflected her stronger disidentification.

37 Cohen 1989, 923.

38 Cf. Cohen 1989, 917–18, 935.

39 Thomas Scanlon describes a subjective criterion of well-being as one according to which 'the level of well-being enjoyed by a person in given material circumstances or the importance for that person of a given benefit or sacrifice is to be estimated by evaluating those material circumstances or that benefit or that sacrifice *solely from the point of view of that person's tastes and interests*' (Scanlon 1975, 656, emphasis added). On my understanding both equality of welfare and envy-test equality provide criteria that are subjective in this sense, but they interpret the italicized portion differently: equality of welfare takes the point of view of persons' interests to be embodied in welfare, while envy-test equality takes persons' interests to be embodied in their point of view (cf. Arneson 1990).

40 Dworkin 2000, 288, 291.

41 Cohen 2004, 9.

42 Cohen 2004, 10.

43 Cohen 2004, 10.

44 According to Dworkin's favoured version of equality of resources the most important mechanism for the present discussion is the handicap insurance market. Here compensation is assigned in those cases and only those cases where individuals disprefer a taste and choose to insure against having it, the level of insurance being decided by personal risk aversion and, significantly, welfare considerations; see Dworkin 1981; Dworkin 2004, 348–9. Despite the reference to welfare, this account is neither equality of welfare nor equal opportunity for welfare (see section 5 below). The most obvious of its differences from the former is that it makes distributions partially sensitive to choice. Unlike the latter it does not aim to make welfare fully sensitive to responsibility, for some instances of very bad brute luck will go

without full compensation simply because insuring to that level would have been a very bad gamble.

45 Dworkin 2004, 350.

46 Cohen 1989, 919.

47 Cohen 1989, 919. Equal opportunity for welfare is described in the next section.

48 Dworkin 2000, 297.

49 Strictly speaking the objective described in the text is only luck egalitarian if we understand luck thinly with regard to responsibility – i.e. as 'just the absence or negation of whatever it is that makes for responsibility' (Hurley 2002, 80). Note that both the claim against envy-test equality and my response to it presume that either (metaphysical) libertarianism or compatibilism is true; for relevant discussion see Chapter 5.

50 Cohen 1989, 927.

51 These classic examples of expensive tastes were introduced in Arrow 1973, 254.

52 Larry Temkin writes that 'egalitarians are not committed to the view that deserved inequalities . . . are as bad as undeserved ones . . . Rather, what is objectionable is some being worse off than others *through no fault of their own*' (Temkin 1993, 17, original emphasis; see also Cohen 1989, 920, 939–40; Nagel 1991, 71).

53 Arneson 1989. Arneson now rejects this theory in favour of 'responsibility-catering prioritarianism'. Cohen's favoured theory is 'equal access to advantage', although his favoured interpretation of this has changed. Whatever the relative merits of the three theories, I refer to equal opportunity for welfare as it is the more obvious rival to responsibility sensitive equality in the regards relevant to this chapter as, unlike the other theories, it is both egalitarian (not prioritarian) and subjectivist (not a hybrid of subjectivism and objectivism). For a discussion of responsibility sensitive prioritarianism, see Chapter 6.

54 Arneson 1989, 86.

55 Dworkin 2000, 323.

56 Dworkin 2000, 323.

57 Dworkin 1981, 293.

58 Dworkin 2000, 291.

59 Dworkin 1981, esp. 303.

60 See Dworkin 2000, ch. 7; Dworkin 2004, 346–7, 391 n.22.

61 Dworkin 2003, esp. 191. Cf. Scheffler 2003b, 200.

62 Even if we accept Dworkin's preference genealogy and conclusions we may still, in principle at least, be luck egalitarians; see Chapter 5, note 48.

63 Dworkin 2000, 323; Dworkin 1981, 293–5, 311.

64 This assertion is much narrower and weaker than Timothy Hinton's

(2002) claim that Dworkin's qualified luck egalitarianism is untenable, and that egalitarians therefore need to take a firm stance one way or the other on brute luck and choice.

65 Perhaps this is not Cohen's line of thought. But I cannot see how else one gets to the stronger objection. Or if, alternatively, the strong objection is not attributable to Cohen, I do not see why he does not accept, or even consider, a resource-egalitarian response to the weaker objection that is parallel to the welfare egalitarian's response to Dworkin's expensive tastes objection, given that he endorses the latter response.

66 Surprisingly enough Cohen himself arrives at this position, or something very much like it, when he proposes to 'compensate for disadvantages which are not traceable to the subject's choice *and* which the subject would choose not to suffer from' (Cohen 1989, 937, original emphasis). This proposal arises as a response to an example of Scanlon's; no mention is made of the second clause's obvious similarity to Dworkin's position on cravings rejected earlier in the same paper.

67 The extent of this divergence, and others I mention later, depends on which conception of welfare is in use. See Chapter 2.

68 Dworkin 1981, 297–8.

69 To some extent the hypothetical insurance market does seem to presuppose the medical approach to disability, in that compensation is set by the average person rather than by the disabled person herself.

70 Dworkin 2000, 313.

71 Dworkin 2000, 312–13.

72 Dworkin 2000, 315–17.

73 Dworkin 2000, 305.

74 Dworkin 2000, 300–4.

75 Narveson 1983, 18, original emphasis.

76 Roemer 1996, 250, original emphasis.

77 Otsuka 2002, 44–6, 50–1.

78 Van Parijs 1995, 85.

79 Dworkin 1981, 299.

80 Harsanyi 1975, 595, original emphasis. Harsanyi's comment was directed at Rawls, who also employed maximin (Rawls 1999a; see also Hare 1973; Barry 1973, ch. 9).

81 Van Parijs 1995, 85.

82 See McLeod 1998, chs 4 and 5; Otsuka 2002; 2004; Cohen Christofidis 2004, 285.

83 Rakowski 1991, 99.

84 Dworkin 1981, 329; 2000, 340–1; 2002, 121.

85 Dworkin 2002, 121.

86 Dworkin 2002, 123–4.

87 Dworkin 2003, 191. On Dworkin's current terminology, responsibility

sensitive envy-test equality takes the diachronic version of the envy test to be the appropriate one; see Otsuka 2004, 157 n.17.

88 Dworkin 1981, 322.

89 Dworkin 1981, 312. Cf. Kymlicka 1990, 80.

90 Van Parijs 1995, 65, original emphasis.

91 Miriam Cohen Christofidis points out that '[w]hat Dworkin calls "slavery" . . . should actually be called restricted choice' (Cohen Christofidis 2004, 271).

92 Cohen Christofidis 2004, 267, 283 n.14.

93 Kymlicka 1990, 81.

94 Dworkin 1981, 300.

95 Johnston 1994, 166.

96 Johnston 1994, 146.

97 Rakowski 1991, 101.

98 In considering equality of success Dworkin takes this proposition as unproblematical, holding that 'equality of success . . . recommends distribution and transfer of resources until no further transfer can decrease the extent to which people differ in . . . success' (Dworkin 1981, 191).

99 Cohen 2004, 25, original emphasis.

100 Cohen 2004, 25.

101 Dworkin's favoured variant of equality of resources is not subject to this objection as it does not distribute on the basis of the envy test. He claims that the Burley counterexample is inapplicable because a 'just society' would provide the appropriate compensation; see Dworkin 2004, 350. This compensation would presumably be set by a hypothetical insurance market, and would therefore be limited in the way that all compensation is on such schemes.

102 Fair envy freeness (see note 10, above) does nothing to address this problem. If supply and demand are such that an individual has to use up many of his tokens in the auction to secure the materials required to practise photography, while fishing materials can be purchased with few tokens, Paul will in that regard be disadvantaged relative to Fred, since he has fewer tokens to spend on other things.

2

Equal Opportunity for Welfare

1. Introductory Remarks

Consider the following simplified scenario:

1. (a) Steve holds £10.
   (b) Harry holds £10.
2. (a) Steve's taste is such that he would obtain 1 unit of welfare (hereafter: unit) from consuming a hamburger.
   (b) Steve's taste is such that he would obtain 10 units from consuming a steak.
   (c) Harry's taste is such that he would obtain 10 units from consuming a hamburger.
   (d) Harry's taste is such that he would obtain 1 unit from consuming a steak.
   (e) No change in the tastes of Steve or Harry is now possible.
3. (a) A hamburger now costs £2.
   (b) A steak now costs £10.
4. Steve would now prefer to have Harry's taste.
   (a) Prior to t (= a point in the past) Steve's taste was that of Harry's.
   (b) Harry has not deliberately cultivated his taste, nor could he ever have eliminated it.
   (c) Steve deliberately cultivated his present taste at t.

Which of these facts is relevant to egalitarian distributive justice? A wealth egalitarian replies that 1 alone is relevant, and that the existing distribution is perfectly just. A welfare egalitarian begs to differ: on her account, 2 and 3 also come into play. She views the distribution as unjust, on the grounds that Steve is only able to secure 10 units with his funds, whereas Harry is able to secure 50 units with his. Steve has *expensive taste*, in the sense that he is only able to secure below-average welfare with average income. The welfare egalitarian views Steve's expensive taste as a disadvantage that entitles him to compensation.

44

In his highly influential article, 'What is Equality?', Ronald Dworkin criticized the welfare egalitarian's stance on 'champagne tastes' as counter-intuitive.[1] His favoured theory of equality of resources did not, however, agree with equality of wealth's stance that 1 is the only relevant fact. Dworkin suggested that 4 is also relevant for, on his scheme, those with *dispreferred tastes* (or 'cravings') are entitled to compensation.

Another position was proposed in response to Dworkin by G. A. Cohen, Richard Arneson, and John Roemer,[2] who urge that compensation for expensive tastes did not appear counter-intuitive where those tastes were unchosen;[3] on the contrary, such compensation was mandated by justice. On this account, which may be referred to as *equal opportunity for welfare*, 1, 2, 3, and 5 all appear to be relevant. For equal opportunity for welfare to hold at any given time, individuals must face what Arneson calls *'effectively* equivalent options' in terms of expected welfare, which Cohen prefers to signify with 'equal *access*' (as opposed to mere equal opportunity).[4] It is not enough that individuals have equivalent options; awareness of options, and the ability and character to choose among them, must also be taken into account. For persons to enjoy effectively equivalent options, one of three conditions must therefore hold:

> (1) the options are equivalent and the persons are on a par in their ability to 'negotiate' these options, or (2) the options are nonequivalent in such a way as to counterbalance exactly any inequalities in people's negotiating abilities, or (3) the options are equivalent and any inequalities in people's negotiating abilities are due to causes for which it is proper to hold the individuals themselves personally responsible.[5]

Equal opportunity for welfare, however, does not require that one of these conditions holds at any one time. Some people may, through responsible action, come to have better options as well as better negotiating abilities.[6] Equal opportunity for welfare *in the extended sense* requires either that options are effectively equivalent, or that they are non-equivalent as a result of differences in voluntary choices. Arneson comments that, '[w]hen persons enjoy equal opportunity for welfare in the extended sense, any actual inequality of welfare in the positions they reach is due to factors that lie within each individual's control', and concludes that this makes 'any such inequality . . . non-problematic from the standpoint of distributive equality'.[7] This establishes the centrality of 5 for equal opportunity for welfare's treatment of the steak and hamburger case: the presence or absence of deliberate cultivation of taste is pivotal, because an inequality resulting from an expensive taste may be consistent with equal opportunity for welfare in the most important extended sense (all following references to equal opportunity for welfare are to the extended sense).

Cohen has recently modified his account, suggesting that some tastes that are chosen are nevertheless compensable.[8] In the first part of this chapter (sections 2, 3, and 4) I identify the relevant varieties of luck, and argue that the position that Cohen now wants to occupy either makes distributive decisions on morally arbitrary grounds or comes close to collapsing into equality of welfare. In section 5 I move on to defend the general shape of equal opportunity for welfare's argument for compensation for bad price luck. Whether this argument is ultimately successful depends on the availability of a compelling account of welfare – something which Dworkin denies is possible. I proceed, in sections 6 to 9, to describe an unusual affective-state account of welfare that appears to overcome many of the problems facing more conventional accounts. In section 10 I combine this specific account of welfare with equal opportunity for welfare, confront an objection to a similar combination presented by Dworkin, and show how this combination can justify compensation for bad price luck. Section 11 considers Cohen's arguments for the position that advantage should in part be measured using objective resources.

2. Luck and Taste

In 'Expensive Taste Rides Again', Cohen states that he wishes to revise the following first sentence of the 'flagship statement' of his earlier essay 'On the Currency of Egalitarian Justice': 'I distinguish among expensive tastes according to whether or not their bearer can reasonably be held responsible for them.'[9] Cohen now says that this sentence (together with similar statements in 'Currency') is poorly formulated. A suitable reformulation would replace 'them' with 'the fact that her tastes are expensive'. He adds the following: 'It is, as I made it abundantly clear elsewhere in "Currency," precisely *that* fact for which the question of responsibility is crucial.'[10]

Without this clarification the first sentence of the flagship statement is at best ambiguous and at worst morally implausible. The original formulation may be read as suggesting that justice distinguishes between responsibility and lack of responsibility for *the existence of tastes that now happen to be expensive*. Persons are entitled

46

to compensation if they have what Dworkin calls *bad preference luck*, 'which is their bad luck in having the preferences that they do because these preferences are expensive'.[11] On this account, the bare fact that Steve chose to generate his taste (fact 5) disqualifies his claim for compensation. But suppose that Steve's taste was not expensive when he cultivated his taste, and that he could not have predicted that it would become so in the future. He has been unlucky, not in having the taste that he previously cultivated, but rather in that his taste has since become expensive. He has an unchosen disadvantage (a taste for an expensive food) which would be overlooked by one concerned only with bad preference luck. This possibility suggests that responsibility for holding the taste does not matter in the absence of responsibility of for its expensiveness.

For this reason Cohen now makes it clear that it is responsibility for the *expensiveness* of one's taste that matters.[12] People are entitled to compensation on this account where they have what Dworkin describes as *bad price luck,* 'which is bad luck in the high cost of the preferences they have'.[13] This would be a relevant set of facts on such an account:

6. (a) At *t* a steak cost £2.
   (b) At *t* a hamburger cost £2.
   (c) Steve could not reasonably have been expected to anticipate the rise in price of steaks from *t* to the present.

Cohen believes that it would be unfair to penalize Steve for the unforeseen economic changes that have replaced the favourable circumstances depicted in 6 with the unfavourable circumstances depicted in 3. No transfer would be due if Steve knew such changes were likely to occur but gambled that they would not, or hoped that they would, perhaps because he views expense as itself desirable.[14] But this is not the case here. As it is, Steve suffers from a welfare deficit for which he is not relevantly responsible; such deficits are compensable on Cohen's scheme, and the first element of the reformulation of his flagship statement reflects that.

The second sentence of Cohen's original flagship statement reads thus: 'There are those [tastes] which he [an individual] could not have helped forming and/or could not now unform, and then there are those for which, by contrast, he can be held responsible, because he could have forestalled them/and or because he could now unlearn them.'[15] Cohen believes that the failings of this second sentence are more substantial than those of the first. The problem is not merely that his position is poorly expressed; the position itself is at fault. While Cohen still believes that some chosen tastes are non-compensable, he now maintains that others do give rise to valid claims for compensation. The former category are *brute tastes*, 'which do not embody judgments of valuation'.[16] Cohen offers the example of 'my own liking for Diet Coke, which embodies no particular *approval* of it'.[17] *Judgemental tastes*, by contrast, '*are* informed by valuational judgment'. Cohen writes that 'I no longer think that the mere fact that people chose to develop and/or could now school themselves out of an expensive judgmental taste means that they should pick up the tab for it, and that is precisely because they *did* and *do* identify with it, and therefore cannot *reasonably* be expected to have not developed it or to rid themselves of it.'[18] The moral idea driving the distributive proposal is that some persons are disadvantaged by their identification with certain tastes that turn out to be expensive, because that identification leads them to develop those tastes. Cohen observes that this takes his position even further away from Dworkin's:

> So what Dworkin gives as a reason for withholding compensation – the subjects' approving identification with their expensive tastes – is something that I regard as a reason for offering it, since, where identification *is* present, it is, standardly, the agents' very bad luck that a preference with which they strongly identify happens to be expensive, and to expect them to forgo or to restrict satisfaction of that preference (because it is expensive) is, therefore, to ask them to accept an alienation from what is deep in them.[19]

Cohen's move should not exactly be to turn Dworkin on his head. One may recall that Dworkin is interested in the presence or absence of identification with taste *right now*: hence, on his account, fact 4 in the hamburger-and-steak case mentioned at the outset justifies compensation for Steve (given fact 1). Here Cohen, like Dworkin, focuses on present (dis)identification: unfair disadvantage arises 'where identification *is* present'. We have seen that elsewhere in the same paper, however, he focuses on the *history* of identification as well: persons who did identify or who do identify with a taste '. . . cannot *reasonably* be expected to have not developed it or to rid themselves of it'. In other words, present (dis)identification matters for establishing whether it is reasonable to expect an expensive taste to be unlearned, while past (dis)identification matters for the key issue of establishing whether it is reasonable to hold someone accountable for their choice to develop a taste.

So why should Cohen occupy the second of these positions? An answer becomes clear when we consider the case of someone who initially had no identification with an expensive taste, but nevertheless developed it, and subsequently came to identify with it. Cohen has no reason for thinking that it would be unreasonable to ask such a person to bear the costs of their tastes whether they can now be rid of them or not, for that cost has arisen directly from a choice that she was not predisposed to make. It is a history of identification that excuses an individual of the cost of their expensive taste; present identification tells us only that an individual who has been so excused cannot be expected to dispose of their taste.

3. Problems with Cohen's Revised Account

The discussion of the previous section indicates that the following would be an example of an additional relevant fact on Cohen's scheme:

7. Prior to and at t, Steve disidentified with the taste he then had and identified with the taste he now has.

This embodies my stipulation, given as an interpretation of Cohen, that the (dis)identification must not come after the possession of the taste – it must be what we might call 'pre(dis)identification'. According to Cohen, the presence of this fact diminishes Steve's liability for his present expensive taste. It shows that, even if Steve is responsible for the fact that the taste he holds is expensive, it would be unreasonable to make him bear its cost.[20]

The implications of this revised account are no simple matter. To see them one must first try to establish what exactly a *chosen expensive brute taste* might look like. This is because it is (with one important exception to be mentioned in due course) the only kind of expensive taste that Cohen now refuses to compensate, and as such it appears to be the only source of disagreement between Cohen and equality of welfare. I will maintain that, from what little Cohen says about chosen brute taste, it is not clear that such tastes can exist in a form that is differentiated from chosen judgemental taste by any morally significant characteristic. In the one case, Cohen's account amounts to no more or less than equality of welfare,[21] insofar as it is concerned with welfare;[22] in the other, it amounts to something with (even) less justification.

The feature that makes a taste brute in Cohen's sense is that it 'does not embody judgments of valuation'. For reasons that should be obvious from the earlier discussion, the kind of judgements of valuation that they do not embody are those that are *temporally prior* to the taste itself. Steve's taste for steak does not go from being judgemental to being brute simply because he stops identifying with it some time after he has acquired it, for Cohen's question of whether Steve could reasonably have been expected to turn down the opportunity to cultivate that taste, given the cost that would be imposed upon him, can obviously apply only before taste acquisition. The kind of taste we are looking for is one that is chosen *and* initially not supported by value judgements.

How might the origins of Cohen's own taste for Diet Coke meet both these criteria? Were Jerry (as I will call this character) brought up to have this taste or hypnotized into having it, it would fail to meet the first of the criteria.[23] This would also be the case if his first sip had him hooked, and that sip resulted from, say, a bar-keeping error or lack of alternative beverages. Contrariwise, if Jerry made a deliberate attempt to cultivate that taste, it would fail to meet the second of the criteria. That attempt must be based on some kind of value judgement, however sensible or fatuous it may be, for otherwise his behaviour is inexplicable.

There are further possibilities that may appear to salvage chosen brute taste. First, suppose that Jerry makes no deliberate attempt to cultivate a taste for Diet Coke and has no pre-identification with it, but that he tries it anyway. Perhaps he just wants to see what it tastes like. Or perhaps he has decided to live his life as a 'free spirit' which, right now, means trying some Diet Coke for no particular reason. Either way, Jerry's first sip results in taste formation.

For the moment, let us grant that the taste which is formed in a case like this is brute. Although pre-identification with taste is absent, other kinds of relevant value judgements are present. It seems to me that Jerry could only have not taken his sip by acting in a fashion that contradicted his value judgement that he ought to find out what Diet Coke tastes like, or that he ought to drink it just because that's what he wants to do. Such contradiction is not directly related to taste. It is, however, obviously an incident of self-infliction of cost. Were it identical in every regard except the structure of its relation to taste, Cohen would say that it could not reasonably be expected of Jerry. If this kind of self-infliction is unreasonable where the judgement endorses the taste I do not see any reason why it is less unreasonable where the judgement endorses something else that can only be realized by performing an action that may or will result in taste formation. There is a slight causal difference but no moral difference: in both types of case we require individuals 'to accept an alienation from what is deep in them' if they are not to suffer a welfare deficit. On this natural reading of Cohen, he appears to base compensation on a morally arbitrary distinction.

Suppose, then, that we take a more liberal reading of Cohen. Here we describe a taste such as Jerry's – one that is not pre-identified with, but that could have been avoided only at the cost of violating otherwise independent value judgements – as an *indirect judgemental taste*. The resulting *broad* sense of judgemental taste, encompassing both indirect judgemental taste and *direct judgemental taste* (instances of which are pre-identified with), is somewhat strained as a construal of Cohen, given that it includes 'taste that does not track a judgment of the value of its object'.[24] But it – and the corresponding *narrow* construal of brute taste – sits far more comfortably with Cohen's moral argument that it is unreasonable to expect persons to contradict their value judgements. In this case, it looks like there is nothing morally arbitrary about compensating for chosen judgemental taste but not for chosen brute taste. But the revised position also radically limits the occurrence of chosen brute taste (that is, a chosen taste that could have been avoided at no self-inflicted cost). Usually a taste must be either unchosen or endorsed, somewhere along the line, by valuational judgement; in the odd case where it is both unendorsed and, in some sense, chosen, compensation is still appropriate.

This is shown in two more kinds of cases. We might suppose that Jerry has no pre-identification with Diet Coke but that he is a 'diceman' – one who makes his choices in a random fashion – and, when ordering his drinks, Diet Coke's number comes up. Or we might suppose that, while Jerry's action might look like it could be explained as either experimental or wilfully random, he is simply acting on impulse. In each case we again suppose that the first sip results in taste formation.

When presented with cases like Diceman Jerry, it is tempting to think that chosen narrow brute taste might ride in on the back of uncertainty about outcomes. The unexpected results of random but deliberate action may appear to be chosen without there having been any question of identification. It is therefore important to note that the actual likelihood of the taste arising from the action, and the individual's perception of this likelihood, are quite irrelevant to the question of whether the taste is (indirectly) judgemental. All that matters is that the individual could not have performed otherwise without contradicting his own judgement. Even if the individual thought there was no possibility of taste formation, and it was in fact a million to one shot, that taste would be fully judgemental on account of the clear causal link between it, the action, and the endorsement of the action.

Both this point and the more general point about the infrequency with which chosen narrow brute taste can occur is illustrated well in the Diceman Jerry case. Diceman Jerry's taste is, I will allow, chosen and not *itself* pre-identified with. But the endorsement of running one's life on the roll of a dice is clearly a value judgement. That pre-identification with randomizing is, in this instance, bound up with the taste. Even though the link between Diceman Jerry's taste and his judgement is indirect and fortuitous, his taste is judgemental, for he could have declined the option of drinking Diet Coke only by alienating himself from his own judgement. This causal relationship is all that is required to show that the taste is not brute in the narrow sense.

The final, impulsive case faces the initial worry that no taste formed in this way could be chosen. But I am willing to grant, for the sake of argument, that choice may be present here. This issue aside, impulsive action appears to present the best opportunity for non-compensable chosen brute taste to arise. Even so, Jerry's behaviour is presumably explainable in one of two ways, and neither of these will do. Firstly, there may be a value judgement even further back in the causal chain than in the earlier two cases. This judgement may direct Jerry to act spontaneously and without regard to consequences. This case is not relevantly different from that of the self-defined free spirit. As before, the taste can be treated as non-compensable only if we demand that Jerry alienate himself from his judgement. On the alternative reading of Cohen, the taste is, again, not brute. Secondly, and more interestingly, Jerry may be following no value judgement whatsoever. He may by nature be an extremely impetuous person. It may have never crossed his mind that acting in a more considered way is a viable option. This is the one kind of case where the more liberal reading of Cohen can, like the more straightforward construal, identify chosen brute (that is, unendorsed) taste. But the common denial of compensation in both instances is morally arbitrary. If it is unreasonable to expect someone to act against their valuational judgement, it is, if anything, more unreasonable to expect someone to act against their natural temperament, where no reasons for such behavioural modification have even been entertained. The complete absence of valuational judgement makes it inappropriate to punish (or reward) in this case as one might were a full moral agent involved. Even if we allow that there is choice, there is not responsibility.

4. Accommodating Valuational Judgement

The basic problem we have so far encountered is that one can choose to undergo a course of action that may result in the acquisition of a taste only where one holds value judgements that recommend that course of action. A taste of this kind is an indirect judgemental taste. One can avoid this conclusion only by failing to acknowledge the cost involved in acting contrary to value judgements that are only indirectly linked to the acquisition of the taste (for example, ones recommending 'taste testing' or spontaneity). This is precisely what Cohen does on the more natural reading mentioned above. But I can see no moral justification for such a position. Indeed, it seems to run counter to the unreasonableness-of-expecting-self-imposed-costs justification with which Cohen attempts to support his stance. If, on the other hand, we work with the more liberally interpreted senses of brute and judgemental taste, chosen brute taste can be held only by the impulsive. So interpreted, Cohen's position is either, again, morally arbitrary (if we penalize purely impulsive behaviour) or virtually normatively identical with equality of welfare. In the latter case, it makes conceptual distinctions (between brute and judgemental taste, and between chosen and unchosen taste) that equality of welfare does not, but the only normatively relevant combination (chosen brute taste) is all but impossible since non-purely impulsive chosen brute tastes are reclassified as indirect judgemental tastes.

I say 'all but impossible' because there is one special case where it may appear that Cohen could still reasonably deny compensation for expensive taste. This is the case of *costlessly removable expensive taste*. Whether it was initially chosen or not, Cohen denies compensation for expensive tastes which can be removed at no expense – which is to say not only that the tastes are not *presently* identified with, but also that there are no 'incidental' costs that are unrelated to the identification itself. Equality of welfare would even compensate in the case where an individual with such a taste obstinately refused to remove it.

The absence of present identification marks these tastes as brute in the sense that was rejected in section 2 above. The absence of incidental costs is much the more demanding of the two requirements mentioned in the previous paragraph. Even where a taste is disidenti-fied with, there will almost always be some financial expenditure, lost time, or other inconvenience involved in schooling oneself out of it that results in a welfare loss. As costlessly removable expensive tastes are little more than a possibility, the space between the broad judgemental taste view and equality of welfare is barely a sliver.

The rarity of costlessly removable expensive tastes is not the most significant problem they present for Cohen's position. The refusal to compensate for these tastes is morally suspect for reasons that are very much parallel to those that applied to the natural reading of Cohen (where judgemental taste was narrowly construed). A deliber-ate failure to remove a taste, even where there is no cost involved, presumably itself involves valuational judgement. We might again ask why it is unreasonable to ask people to act against their value judge-ments in some cases, but not in others.

Someone endorsing compensation for judgemental taste in either the narrow sense (admitting direct judgemental tastes only) or broad sense (admitting both direct and indirect judgemental tastes) faces an unpalatable choice. They could treat the value judgements that oppose costless removal of expensive tastes as the basis for compen-sation for those tastes (either because the judgements are necessarily tied up with judgemental taste or for independent reasons). Or they could refuse compensation, in which case their moral consistency is in doubt, given the original justification for compensation for expensive judgemental tastes.

The argument that expensive judgemental taste should not be penalized has some intuitive support. But consistent endorsement of what appears to be its key premise – that it is wrong to penalize persons for choices that are required by their valuational judgement – commits Cohen to more than he acknowledges. For the premise to be consistently endorsed, both the broad construal of judgemental taste and compensation for costlessly removable expensive tastes that are not removed are required. This treatment of tastes is identical to that of equality of welfare, even if the justification is different.[25]

As I believe that equality of welfare's complete insensitivity to indi-vidual responsibility is morally implausible, I feel that Cohen's version of egalitarian justice has now drifted into dangerous territory. I will not here, however, attempt to defend responsibility sensitivity or offer specific grounds for rejecting an equality of welfare-type response to the problem of valuational judgement.[26] But it is worth noting that Cohen still appears determined to put distance between his account and equality of welfare.[27] If the arguments presented here have helped to clarify the size of that distance and, in particular, the moral difficulties that are involved in retaining it, they would for those reasons alone have some significance. At any rate, Cohen's proposal cannot qualify as luck egalitarian.

It seems to me that there may be a less hazardous way of endorsing the premise that it is wrong for persons to be disadvantaged by valuational judgement-endorsed acts. On one prominent construal of equal opportunity for welfare, which Cohen has consistently endorsed, a disadvantage such as an expensive taste is non-compensable only where the holder has *genuinely* chosen it – that is, where she is *responsible* for it in a deep, metaphysically valid way.[28] The appropriate distribution is dependent on which account of free will and determinism is correct and on facts particular to each case. The presence or absence of pre-identification, or of other, less direct value judgements that have resulted in taste formation (such as those of dicemen), are candidates for relevant particular facts. It might be thought that, although a history of valuational judgement is not grounds for assuming full non-responsibility, it may diminish an individual's responsibility for developing their taste. As the strength of the value judgements – and the degrees of difficulty and pain involved in acting contrary to them – increase, so responsibility decreases.

We might, then, hold that Cohen's discomfort with the position he took in 'Currency' is based on a failure to appreciate the full range of considerations that responsibility may take into account. The complaint is really with certain prevalent conceptions of responsibility and related concepts, such as choice, which fail to recognize the significant role of valuational judgement. That a person is acting on valuational judgement is not typically taken to be a factor in favour of their case for compensation – Dworkin for one thinks quite the opposite. Once the argument shifts to this level there appears to be little problem with the position Cohen took in 'Currency'. One gets the outcome of compensating for valuational judgement-based tastes by combining conventional equal opportunity for welfare with a particular account of responsibility.

5. The Bad-Price-Luck Argument

The argument of the preceding sections shows that the alternative account of compensation for taste Cohen now offers is actually not much of an alternative to the original triadic choice between equality of welfare, equality of resources, and equal opportunity for welfare, as it amounts to little more than the first of these. I will now move on to focus on the dispute between welfare egalitarians, meaning those who endorse equal opportunity for welfare (equality of welfare will be mentioned only in passing), and resource egalitarians. Responsibility will become relevant again only in section 10. Until then, my main concern will be with working out when compensation for taste is due, provided that whatever responsibility requirements there are have been met.

As we saw in the previous chapter, Cohen overstates equality of resources' divergence from equal opportunity for welfare, particularly in characterizing it as an objectivist theory. I now hope to show that Dworkin also misrepresents the relationship between equality of resources and equal opportunity for welfare, although his misrepresentation takes a radically opposed shape – that of describing the welfare egalitarian's position in such a way that he should have no reason to oppose equality of resources. I will also claim that persons may reasonably feel disadvantaged, yet be denied compensation on Dworkin's scheme.

Dworkin proposes to offer compensation for those tastes and only those tastes with which the holder disidentifies.[29] One of his main arguments against the position he thought Cohen took in 'Currency' is roughly as follows. Equality of resources has at its heart the distinction between, on the one hand, a person and her ambitions, and on the other, the circumstances that advance or hinder the fulfilment of those ambitions.[30] Preferred expensive tastes cannot qualify for compensation, for such tastes, unlike handicaps and cravings, cannot be depicted as unfortunate circumstances.[31] To treat such tastes as a burden is to treat individuals as divorced from their personalities in a way that is inconsistent with ordinary ethical experience.[32]

Both Cohen and Dworkin recognize that, whatever its merits, this argument can only count against compensation for bad preference luck. The advocate of compensation for bad price luck will be unshaken by them, for he can note that the cost of steaks (see fact 6) is unambiguously an obstacle to the fulfilment of Steve's ambitions. There would be nothing self-alienating about him describing *that* as a burden.[33] Even someone who accepts Dworkin's distinction between personality and circumstances therefore has no reason as yet to reject the proposed compensation. The case that, without compensation, some persons are penalized for their brute bad luck of having tastes that are expensive to satisfy remains intact.

In his latest reply to Cohen, Dworkin remarks that he had previously 'emphasized what I took to be Cohen's bad-preference-luck argument because many other critics of my views about equality have pursued a similar argument, and because I thought that version of the bad-luck argument, for all its faults, much stronger than his bad-price-luck version, which is not even yet an argument'.[34] His counter-argument uses the following example. Imagine that A and B hold identical resources, and that A has a cheap taste for rock while B has an expensive taste for opera. B wishes that his taste was cheaper, but nevertheless identifies with it, and would refuse the pill to eradicate it. He therefore suffers from bad price luck, though not from bad preference luck. Should B be allowed to 'wave his magic wand', and receive compensation from A for his expensive taste? Dworkin makes this comment on that proposal:

> That would make A's well-being less and B's well-being greater than each now is. So the transfer could seem justified, even to someone who aims at equality of well-being, only if B were now worse off than A now is. But B doesn't believe that he is worse off than A, and could not honestly claim to be . . . Indeed, no one, including A, might think that B is worse off than A. So no reason has yet been offered, even to welfare egalitarians, to explain why the transfer would be just.[35]

Is it really the case that B does not think himself worse off than A? We have been given no reason to think so. Dworkin's belief to the contrary is apparently based on the fact that B wishes to keep his taste. But this shows only that he thinks himself better off with it, not that he thinks that anyone else is better off with it. It is perfectly possible for someone to think that what is good for them is not good for another. Suppose, for example, that B's love of opera was instilled in him as a child by his father, who detested rock music. It is perfectly possible for B to be reflective enough to realize the source of his taste, and also that not all persons were subject to the same formative influences as he. Furthermore, if he is a certain common kind of relativist about value, he may believe that, for persons subject to other influences (such as A, whose father bombarded him with the Beatles and the Rolling Stones throughout his childhood), other tastes are appropriate. Finally, if he believes that, in their right place, all musical tastes are equally valuable, and that welfare has any non-instrumental value for persons whatsoever, he will believe that A is better off than him, for his taste is of equal value and his welfare is higher.[36]

A further illicit move is completed in the penultimate sentence of the passage quoted above. This move is that from 'B doesn't believe he is worse off than A' to 'even welfare egalitarians do not believe that B is worse off than A'. The former in no way implies the latter. Most of the familiar accounts of welfare give an individual's overall comparative assessment of their standing no constitutive role whatsoever, let alone the sole constitutive role that Dworkin's argument requires. Accounts based on pleasure, enjoyment, preference satisfaction, and informed preference satisfaction all imply a series of 'micro' measurements that are then summed to arrive at an overall assessment of individual welfare. Individuals rarely take all, or even most, of the objects of measurements of any of the main accounts of welfare into account when comparing their situations with those of other individuals. Even if we assume that by 'is worse off' B means 'has lower welfare', that still leaves B's particular conception of welfare unspecified, and it may well not be the right one, or even a recognizable one. A lay person can hardly be expected to hold the right account of welfare when there is nothing like philosophical agreement on which account that is. And even if B does subscribe to the right account, he may well be subject to information constraints that prevent him from making correct assessments of welfare levels. For these kinds of reasons the gap between individuals' assessments and equality of (opportunity for) welfare's assessment will more often than not be different in practice as well as in principle. Even if B thought himself better off than A, and A also thought B better off, B could still have less welfare on any or all of the accounts mentioned above. This is because individuals do not judge their own and others' welfare in these ways and, even if they did, they would very often get it wrong.

It is not necessarily the case that B thinks A in an equal or worse-off position than himself. And even if B did think himself better off than A, equality (of opportunity) for welfare could, on any of the usual understandings of welfare, offer a justification for compensation. Whether the bad-price-luck argument is ultimately successful or not, its general shape is plausible.

The discussion of the previous chapter and of this section should have clarified what the dispute between equality of resources and equal opportunity for welfare is *not* about. Contrary to Cohen's urging, the choice is not between taking welfare into account, and not taking it into account at all. Contrary to Dworkin's implication, the choice is not between compensating B when he is not, on any account, disadvantaged, and denying such compensation. What, then, *is* in dispute?

Dworkin says that, for the bad-price-luck argument to work, Cohen must first define a conception of welfare that shows B to be worse off than A even when both have the same wealth.[37] As I have suggested, this stage is traversed easily enough by many, if not all, welfare egalitarians; indeed, Bentham would have had little difficulty with it two centuries ago. The second stage, Dworkin says, is to 'provide some reason to think that justice requires that A and B be equal in welfare defined in *that* way, in spite of the fact that B himself rejects that way of defining his overall welfare; in spite of the fact, that is, that B does not think himself worse off than A all things considered'.[38]

As a description of the argument needed by someone who endorses equality of welfare, this is strictly speaking true[39] and, when so stated, the task before the welfare egalitarian may appear daunting. But Dworkin's description is also somewhat one-sided. I see no reason for thinking that the burden of proof lies with the welfarist. For the matter to be resolved in his favour, Dworkin must prove that (dis) identification is a more morally plausible ground on which to assess claims for compensation than welfare levels. I would suggest that Dworkin has not as yet provided any such proof. To see this we must first take a closer look at welfare.

6. *Welfare*

Dworkin often writes that one cannot assess welfare egalitarians' claims without knowing which conception of welfare is in use. This is, he asserts, 'because equality of welfare has gained whatever appeal it has precisely by remaining abstract and therefore ambiguous: the ideal loses its appeal whenever a particular conception of welfare is specified, which presumably explains why those who defend it rarely attempt any such specification'.[40] Although the definition of a welfare assessment (as opposed, say, to resource assessment) is itself a contentious issue, L. W. Sumner's description seems adequate: 'Welfare assessments concern what we may call the prudential value of a life, namely how well it is going *for the individual whose life it is.*'[41] An individual's welfare is what is ultimately or non-instrumentally good for her. One useful understanding of an individual's welfare is as what one should want insofar as one rationally cares about her.[42]

Given how compelling equal opportunity for how-well-each-individual's-life-is-going-for-them sounds to the luck egalitarian, one might be forgiven for thinking that Dworkin is mistaken, and that it is only *wrong* accounts of welfare that render equal opportunity for welfare deeply unattractive. While I broadly agree with this thought I will, nevertheless, seek to insulate equal opportunity for welfare from Dworkin's charge by specifying a particular conception of welfare. I am not sure that it is the right one but it should suffice for the purposes of the present argument.

Philosophical accounts of welfare are conventionally classified as being either subjective or objective. Objective theories set a welfare subject's level of welfare on grounds that are independent of their consciousness. The most popular approach here is an 'objective list' of goods that constitute welfare. For instance, Aristotelians' lists are composed of those things that perfect human nature as that is variously described.[43] Subjective theories, by contrast, conceive welfare as being mind dependent.[44] Desire theory, the economist's favoured account of welfare, falls into this category.[45] According to this theory, an individual's welfare level rises each time one of her desires is fulfilled. Each form of desire theory seems to give rise to compelling counterexamples, however, some of which we will encounter in due course.

The classical hedonistic theories of Jeremy Bentham, John Stuart Mill, and Henry Sidgwick are traditionally viewed as subjective. It is arguable, however, that they are actually objective list theories, with the items on the lists being the particular sensations or feeling tones that are identified as being pleasurable.[46] Imagine that a particular individual's brain scans revealed that when she was dehydrated to a certain extent, thirst satisfaction produced more pleasure than book reading. This is all the classical hedonist needs to know to say that, in such cases, thirst satisfaction promoted that individual's welfare. But suppose we can also look at the relevant individual's self-endorsed priorities and that, in some cases where she was dehydrated to the stated extent, she very much preferred to read. If she chooses to read in one such instance, it would be strange for her or anybody else (even someone who would view such pain negatively) to say that her life has, *from her perspective*, become worse.

The most plausible conceptions of welfare are, in my view, strongly subjective.[47] It seems implausible to suggest that it makes no difference how a welfare subject anticipates and responds to particular instances of the sensations of pleasure and pain. Similarly, I do not see how thriving interpersonal relationships, a successful career, and other typical components of objective-list welfare advance a person's well-being where, abnormally, they bring only suffering and regret to the supposed beneficiary.[48] Much more can, of course, be said on objective accounts of welfare.[49] But my main intention here is to define welfare in such a way that equal opportunity for welfare is a plausible, or even preferable, alternative to equality of resources. A full examination of each conception of welfare is not possible here. In section 11 I will consider some objectivist counter-arguments.

The account of welfare I will propose is indisputably subjective.[50] I will suggest that the hedonist shift his attention from sensations of pleasure and pain to the attitudes and feelings they may give rise to.[51] I begin by discussing and, where necessary, extending two contemporary theories of welfare, enjoyment theory and happiness theory, that make these moves. I then identify problems with these theories and propose an affective state account of welfare which appears to overcome them.[52]

7. Enjoyment Theory

Suppose that two women are in labour in a hospital that has no supply of painkillers. The first is appalled at the standard of care and finds the pain intolerable, but the second views the pain as a natural and positive part of child birth and would have declined painkillers anyway. Both women experience identical sensations of pain. The classical hedonist will therefore describe their welfare levels as identical. This seems implausible; the circumstances of the two women are not equivalent. Given the possibility of cases such as these, an *attitudinal* approach would give us a far more intuitively sound account of welfare. It will recognize the important differences between typical and atypical responses to pleasure and pain, and be sensitive to the varying degrees of different individuals' positive and negative responses to the same pleasures and pains.

The closest theory to classical hedonism that embodies this shift is *enjoyment theory*. On this theory, positive affective responses are referred to as instances of *enjoyment*. Enjoyment's negative counterpart is *suffering*; the term is used without the usual connotation of severity, so that even the mildest negative response is an instance of suffering. A life that is going well is one with more enjoyment than suffering. On the enjoyment theorist's taxonomy, pleasures are that group of sensations (broadly construed) that typically – but not always – give rise to enjoyment, while pains are that group of sensations that typically give rise to suffering.[53]

But what is meant by positive and negative responses in the

definition of enjoyment? These notions are vaguer than they might appear. Perhaps the most obvious way to understand them is as merely expressive: positive and negative responses to a mouthful of pie amount to 'hurrah for the pie' and 'boo to the pie' respectively. But this does not explain very much; we are bound to want an answer to the questions 'why hurrah?' and 'why boo?'

My answer to this question is to focus on the affective response of *desire formation*: an experience is enjoyable insofar as it makes the welfare subject want its continuation.[54] An experience is a source of suffering where desires for its cessation arise as a result of it. Desire is manifestly playing a major role here, but there is still clear conceptual space between enjoyment theory and desire theory. On the desire-formation conception, enjoyment is constituted by the formation of desires for an experience's continuation that have arisen owing to the experience. For me to be enjoying my reading of a book I need only form the desire to continue reading it. My welfare will increase as that desire arises; desire satisfaction does not come into the equation.

The emphasis on desire *formation* enables this account to circumvent a number of complications found with satisfaction-based accounts. There is no motive for the enjoyment theorist to focus on *informed or ideal desires* as the content of the desires is not itself important. If I am playing table football (foosball), and inadvisedly form the desire to continue playing all day long, it is of no consequence to the enjoyment theorist that that desire is uninformed. Indeed, the extent of my passion very much suggests that *so far* the game has increased my welfare. Now suppose that I really do play table football all day in spite of the fact that, after an hour or so, I have become weary of the game. This demonstrates that, for enjoyment theory, there is no problem associated with *disappointing desires* – those whose fulfilment counts as welfare enhancing in spite of their actual unpleasantness simply because we wanted to undergo them.[55] Likewise, *distant desires* – preferences for states of affairs that have no impact on our experience because of their currently remote temporal and/or spatial location – are no source of embarrassment for the enjoyment theorist.[56] If, in my initial enthusiasm, I had desired that people would one day play table football on Pluto, it is implausible that, if this actually occurs in the year 3000, my life consequently goes (or, rather, will have gone) better. Nor, finally, will experiences that we manifestly find unpleasant nevertheless count as themselves welfare enhancing because we want to undergo them either as a means to an end or in the hope that we will eventually start to enjoy them.[57] Suppose I play golf, in spite of a continuing dislike of the activity, in the hope that I will 'get into it' along the way. Here I have a pre-existing *second-order desire* which may make me carry on playing, but it seems reasonable to say that its ongoing satisfaction does not itself further my welfare.

Desire theory can be modified to meet some of these cases but it is debatable whether it can be modified to meet all of them without disfiguring the theory beyond recognition. The general strategy taken by desire theorists is to restrict the range of desires that are admitted. One may attempt to meet the problem posed by distant desires by restricting focus to those desires that are personal,[58] or to those that have an impact on the welfare subject's consciousness.[59] Though I think the latter of these does the job, it does constitute a watering down of desire theory's key intuition – that individuals' welfare is promoted when they get what they want.

Krister Bykvist's response to the problem of disappointing desires is that the satisfaction of such desires may coincide with both the frustration of existing desires for fulfilment (in work, play, etc.) and the generation of now-for-now desires to end the disappointing experience.[60] Hence the fulfilment of disappointing desires 'need not make me better off *on the whole*'.[61] But this is not enough. Even if desire theory can say that my long game of table football was, all things considered, a source of ill-fare, it still measures the fulfilment of the disappointing desire as a source of welfare. But, even if we abstract from the content of my other desires (for a fulfilling game, or to end *this* game), it is hard to see any way in which that fulfilment has made my life go better. At best it has not itself made things any worse for me.

The desire theorist can only really cope with the problems posed by disappointing desires and second-order desires by imposing further restrictions on which desires count. This seems rather ad hoc; it is hard to identify any underlying rationale, other than the desperate attempt to track intuitions. Perhaps the counter-intuitiveness of certain desires being welfare enhancing derives from their unpleasantness (whether in terms of pleasure, enjoyment, or happiness). One may well conclude that such cases suggest that desire fulfilment does not itself ultimately matter. At any rate, the discomfort of desire theory, when faced with such cases, contrasts starkly with the ease with which enjoyment theory copes with such cases on account of the latter's indifference to the satisfaction of preferences.

There may, however, seem to be a temporal problem with

enjoyment theory. Let us break up each experience into a series of 'moments', by which is meant the smallest noticeable unit of time. As enjoyment refers to experience-*continuation* desires ('continuation desires' hereafter) it can arise only after the first moment of an experience. But many instances of enjoyment may seem to occur at the instant that the experience starts. There is, I take it, always a reaction time, however, no matter how small. I include even those desires that arise within a small fraction of a second of the moment of the experience occurring. Thus, the first moment of experience needs to have ended for enjoyment to arise but the experience itself need not, and often will not, have ended.

Allow us briefly to contrast the enjoyment theory, so conceived, with two other theories. A desire theorist would look at desire-continuation desires but also desires for experience continuation or commencement that have not arisen from experiences and desires that do not refer to experience at all but rather states of the world. More significantly, her measure of how well someone's life is going is how well their desires are being *satisfied*. Contrariwise, the enjoyment theorist looks to certain kinds of desires themselves as proof of enjoyment. Satisfying those desires may lead to more enjoyment but, equally, it may not. If it does, it is because it precipitates the formation of new continuation desires. Thus on enjoyment theory, desire satisfaction has only contingent value. Again, the greatest enjoyment contrasts with (and is further away from the greatest desire satisfaction than) what R. M. Hare designates '"greatest happiness", in the restricted sense used by some utilitarians', that is, 'the maximal satisfaction of now-for-now and then-for-then preferences'.[62] The formative conception of enjoyment utilitarianism would recommend maximal *formation* of *continuation desires* – that is, a subclass of now-for-now and of then-for-then preferences – and would aim to provide the conditions – an appropriate matching of sensations to particular welfare subjects – for such formation.[63]

So clarified, the formative conception of enjoyment should be clear. But is it adequate? It may be suggested that this conception of enjoyment is too narrow in referring only to continuation desires. Suppose that I have been looking forward to going to a cricket match for a very long time without ever having been to one. We might say that I have an experience-commencement desire (for short, a commencement desire), that is, I want the experience of watching a cricket match. One day I finally go to a game and find the experience highly enjoyable (in the everyday sense). I believe that this enjoyment is partly because of my pre-existing commencement desire and partly because of the day's gripping play, on account of which I formed a continuation desire. I enthusiastically tell a friend that 'it was everything I hoped for, and then some; you should go some day'; but she replies 'I have no desire to watch cricket, so I don't think I would enjoy it as much as you did; in fact, I don't think I would enjoy it at all.' I take her at her word. Is it not, then, the case that the motivational view is too narrow, telling me that I enjoyed the experience only as much as is shown by my continuation desires when, in fact, I enjoyed it as much as is shown by both these and my commencement desire?

We must answer this question in the negative. Let us begin our answer by looking at the genesis of commencement desires. As was implied above, the starting point of enjoyment theory is response, specifically attitudinal response, to something. The presence of an experience-commencement desire before I have even entered the cricket ground is patently not a case of response to the cricket match. To be sure, this may well be a response to something else, such as my conclusion, on having seen cricket on television, that it would be exciting, or my having perceived that there was some prestige attached to having been to a cricket match. In some cases, such as the latter, the response would not commonly be one of enjoyment either on the account given here – there can be no desire to continue the activity for it has not commenced – or intuitively – it would be strange to report that one took enjoyment in noticing the social standing of those who had attended a game of a sport to which you were indifferent. In other cases, such as the former, matters are confused by a blurring of the line between commencement desires and continuation desires. Yet it is clear enough that the connection between watching the television and watching at the match is significantly stronger than that between perceiving the prestige and watching at the match – the former pair is the same kind of experience in a way the latter pair is not.

It makes sense, then, to talk of the television-formed commencement desire as constitutive of enjoyment in a similar way as the match-formed continuation desire is; the only difference is one of degree. But the commencement desire indicates that I enjoyed watching cricket on television, not that I enjoyed watching the match. In terms of enjoyment, that the desire gets satisfied when I go to the match does not of itself register. That desire satisfaction would, after all, have been quite consistent with my being disappointed by the actual experience. In the cricket counterexample, it is vital that the satisfaction of the desire gives rise to a continuation desire. If it did not, there would not even be a prima facie counterexample, for I would not cite the commencement desire as part of my enjoyment. This all suggests that intuitions coincide with the view that the formation of continuation desires is foundational; the 'enjoyment value' of commencement desires is contingent on either their satisfaction giving rise to continuation desires or on a blurring of lines between experiences making them tantamount to commencement desires.

8. Happiness Theory

Both classical hedonism and enjoyment theory might be described as *reductionist*, in the sense that they give an individual's welfare level as nothing more than the sum of numerous discrete units of welfare and ill-fare.[64] The person with the greatest welfare is simply that man who has the greatest net pleasure or enjoyment (pleasure minus pain or enjoyment minus suffering). *Happiness theory*, by contrast, is *holistic*: it invites us to view the present state of one's life as something other than the sum of its parts. In Elizabeth Telfer's formulation, happiness is 'a state of being pleased with one's life as a whole'.[65] A happiness theorist equates individuals' welfare levels with their levels of happiness, while their levels of happiness are defined as their levels of *life satisfaction*.[66] In discovering welfare levels, the happiness theorist will be interested in truthful answers to questions such as 'How do you feel about your life as a whole?'

An individual's level of life satisfaction need not, and usually will not, directly correlate to levels of enjoyment or suffering, far less pleasure and pain. A person who has recently lost their fortune may be made no happier in this sense whatsoever by even quite substantial enjoyments. A person who has found romantic love for the first time may remain equally satisfied – indeed, elated – with the state of their life when some other aspect of their life changes from being a source of enjoyment to a source of suffering. Note that this has the consequence that, were we to adopt happiness as our measure of welfare, there could in principle be cases where we are indifferent to bringing about enjoyment or preventing suffering even where no happiness cost is involved.

The life-satisfaction conception of happiness can be illuminatingly contrasted with two alternative conceptions of happiness.[67] First, although we are interested in the subject's feelings towards their 'life as a whole', we do not require an assessment of the entire chronology of their life. 'Life as a whole' is used to highlight the fact that the subject is being asked about their feelings regarding the present overall state of their life, with all its divisions – work life, social life, family life, and so on – having whatever significance for that subject that they do.[68] Human psychology being what it is, reference to past events and our feelings about them is an inevitable part of the process of answering the question. As a general rule people who view their personal history positively will be happier at any given time than those who view it negatively. But the relation between the overall happiness or goodness or any other value of the individual's personal history and their present happiness is something that varies from individual to individual. There can be startling exceptions to the general rule. Consider Calamity Jane, who led a very happy life, only to be hit by a personal tragedy that left her filled with sorrow; far from being any consolation, the contrast presented by the memories of the good times only rubs salt into the wound. Or take Reformed Roy, who has, by his own lights, made terrible mistakes over most of his life of such a magnitude that he cannot hope to make the overall history of his life a good or happy one. Yet Roy has made drastic changes in recent years that leave him with a positive view of his life as a whole (that is, in all its parts) *as it is now*; indeed, part of his satisfaction derives from his belief that he has bettered himself. Furthermore, we all have first-person experience of less drastic divergences between history and present satisfaction, simply because recent events and feelings tend to influence our present life satisfaction more than 'ancient history'.

The present-life and life-history conceptions are demonstrably not the same thing. But why favour the former over the latter? Of the two, it is the only plausible welfare candidate by virtue of being the kind of life satisfaction that relates to how well a person's life *is* going for them. Life-history satisfaction is relevant to well-being, but only insofar as it contributes to present-life satisfaction. For some people, 'personal historists', that contribution may be decisive but, for many, it will not be; and even personal historists have no sound reason to complain about the measure of present-life satisfaction for it can accommodate their historism.[69] If we want to be able to meet the demand that we can compare subjects' current welfare levels, the present-life account is clearly preferable for the simple reason that it recognizes that, for most people (though not personal historists), Roy's life is going better than Jane's.

The second contrast relates to the type of judgement about one's present-life satisfaction that we are seeking. When someone says they are satisfied with their life they are, in a certain sense, talking about a feeling. But that feeling has to be differentiated from the current *mood* the subject is in.[70] It would strike us as strange to say that a generally depressed person is satisfied with their life as a whole just because, on the particular day we encounter them, they are unusually in a positive frame of mind (perhaps for no discernible reason; perhaps because they have won £100 pounds on the lottery – the first time they have ever won anything). The problem is not only that we encountered them on an atypical day. If we encountered them every day for a month, and on one of those they were in a good mood, and on the others depressed, it would still be odd for us to say that on the one day they were satisfied with their life as a whole. Were we to ask our depressed person if they were satisfied with their life as a whole even on their good day they might say 'no'.[71] What we are looking for, then, is the subject's *settled* and *considered* view of their level of life satisfaction.[72] Being satisfied with one's life involves an element of *emotion*, but also an element of *judgement*: an individual is asked to take all relevant considerations into account and then express a feeling about those considerations, not about the narrow range of thoughts they happen to be having at any given time.[73]

The affective and judgemental aspects of life-satisfaction assessments both profoundly influence the recorded welfare level. The affective aspect means that the recorded welfare level may vary from day to day with moods. It is therefore necessary to arrive at a settled view by looking at a range of days. (Perhaps meaningful changes in mood occur not over days but over hours or parts of days or even over weeks. But I will not go into this issue.) It is clear, I think, that this way of arriving at a settled level of life satisfaction is sensitive to intrapersonal variations in moods. There is, as a minimum, a relationship of interdependency between moods and life satisfaction. It makes sense to say both 'I'm in a good mood at the moment because I'm satisfied with my life' and 'she's dissatisfied with her life at the moment because she's in a bad mood'. It would be rare, indeed, to find someone who was almost always in a bad mood yet was satisfied with their life. Indeed, it is sometimes suggested that there is no clear distinction between good moods and feelings of life satisfaction.[74] The rationale for considering life satisfaction over a range of days is simply that that is what is required to give a temporally balanced account of moods and of life satisfaction.

The judgemental aspect of the assessment makes happiness more sensitive to personal history than it might otherwise have been. But a considered assessment of present-life satisfaction will still usually be a very different thing from a considered assessment of life history, as the reflections of Jane and Roy in the earlier example would suggest.

9. An Affective-State Account of Welfare

I will now argue that neither enjoyment theory nor happiness theory is a satisfactory theory of welfare. A better account of welfare would draw on the strengths of both theories while minimizing its exposure to their weaknesses. Such an account will be described shortly but it is first necessary to attend briefly to the weaknesses of the theories presented thus far.

The most obvious weakness of enjoyment theory is the way it deals with *addiction*.[75] The definition of an enjoyable experience given above was an experience that gave rise to desires for its continuation. On the face of it, experiences of heroin use that left the user with a dependency would therefore qualify as an excellent source of welfare according to the enjoyment theorist. But we do not think that the heroin addict's life is going well; quite the contrary. Enjoyment theorists could, of course, stick to their guns and claim that our beliefs here are reliant upon rival conceptions of welfare that have been shown to have their own weaknesses. But I do not think that any amount of reflection is likely to change our minds, in which case enjoyment theory appears to be at odds with our bottom-line intuition. There may be another way out, however. We might start with the observation that severely harmful addictions, such as heroin, tend to be largely physiological. Even when addictive experiences give rise to desires, those desires often have a physiological basis. There is some promise, then, in the suggestion that physiologically determined continuation desires could be discounted to the effect that heroin use becomes a poor source of enjoyment. To be sure, some continuation-desire formation, such as those resulting directly from drug-induced 'highs', may still slip through the net. But such formation may well be evidence of welfare promotion; the problem is just that this benefit is outweighed by the costs of addiction. In sum, though worrying, I do not think that the problem of addiction is sufficient grounds for rejecting enjoyment theory.

A more serious weakness of enjoyment theory is what I have described as its reductionism. As has been mentioned, there is no neat correlation between the level of enjoyment a person experiences and their level of life satisfaction. Furthermore, there is also indeterminacy in the relationship between enjoyments and the kind of unreflective life satisfaction that is perhaps indistinguishable from mood. The criticism here may seem dangerously close to being a simple counter-assertion of happiness theory. But life satisfaction, whether reflective or not, is, on the face of it, very much a matter of welfare. To the subjectivist at least, the question of whether the welfare subject herself thinks her life is going well is surely relevant to the question of whether her life is actually going well.[76] Her calculation may take into account something essential to her good that is not quantifiable in terms of enjoyment.

Happiness theory's main weakness is the excessive *reflectiveness* it demands of welfare subjects. This makes the theory all but impossible to extend beyond humans, which raises doubts about its adequacy given that many non-human animals are uncontroversially welfare subjects. More seriously, it appears less than satisfactory when applied to humans. The problem is that the happiness theorist's interest in considered life-satisfaction reports is too narrow. An enjoyment or a good mood *can* make someone's life *better* even if, were they to stop and think about it, they would not say that it made them more *satisfied* with their life.[77] Equally, suffering and bad moods can decrease the prudential value of a life without changing the welfare subject's assessments of its present state. If I am waiting at an airport for several hours, it is good for me if I can get a decent coffee, a comfortable seat, and something to read, and bad for me if I cannot. But such things are not likely to affect my reflective beliefs about how well my life is going. This contrast is possible as people are not constantly conducting a critical evaluation of their lives; in fact, any kind of life assessment is unusual. Given this, the indifference of the happiness theorist to promoting non-happiness-related enjoyment is unacceptable.

On the one hand, we have an excessively reductionist conception of welfare; on the other, we have an excessively reflective conception. I believe that a better account of welfare would take the spontaneity possible with enjoyment theory's measure of welfare and combine it with happiness theory's holism. It is very hard to see how the former theory might be united with holism, other than by merely confederating it with a holistic theory. For example, we might place enjoyment theory and happiness theory on the same footing, and define welfare as some composite of enjoyment and happiness. While this is not an unattractive option, it does retain the weaknesses of both theories, only mitigated in each case by the extent to which the opposed theory holds sway.

We might hope to do better than this slightly uncomfortable compromise. We might start by observing that some degree of spontaneity is compatible with happiness theory. This can be achieved simply by dropping the requirement that the welfare subject's life-satisfaction report be based on considered judgement. The researcher might ask 'How do you feel about your life as a whole?' without insisting that the response be a settled one or that all relevant facts are taken into account. I rather suspect, however, that such a question inevitably provokes the welfare subject into taking a considered view. An individual's 'life as a whole' is inevitably connected to personal history (although, as is suggested by my earlier argument, the extent of this connection varies from person to person). And as soon as people start thinking about personal history they start being reflective.

I think there is a better way of injecting spontaneity into happiness theory. Instead of asking 'How do you feel about your life as a whole?', we should just ask something like 'How are you feeling?' Here our focus has moved from present life satisfaction to *present mood*. The kind of question we ask makes only a minimal demand for reflection by the welfare subject as it does not invite her to revisit her past. For that reason it admits a broader range of considerations than the present life-satisfaction account of happiness. In particular, an individual's reported mood is far more likely to be affected by (recent) enjoyment and suffering than her reported life satisfaction. If I am generally depressed but I have just had an enjoyable day watching cricket and someone asks me 'How do you feel about your life as a whole?' my answer will be much the same as the previous day when I was struggling on the golf course. But if someone asks me 'How are you feeling?' there will be a difference in the answer I give on the two days. This is quite appropriate as the cricket has, in its own small way, made my life go better. It is also likely that my response on both days will be influenced by my general depression: my good mood will be checked and my bad mood exaggerated. This demonstrates that some holism has been retained, as one would hope, although it is not the full-blown holism of the life-satisfaction variant of happiness theory.

The present-mood account of welfare belongs to the school of happiness theories known as *affective state* theories. Although these are often used by empirical researchers, virtually no philosophers endorse them even as theories of happiness.[78] They are even less popular as theories of welfare. It is worth emphasizing, however, that the space between this particular affective-state theory and the life-satisfaction

71

account is not great. As I mentioned, a life-satisfaction assessment included elements of both emotion and judgement. This is true also of a present-mood assessment but the balance has shifted towards the affective state. The continuity between the two schools of happiness theory is unsurprising given the possibility that present-life satisfaction and mood are similarly continuous. Both are concerned with how things feel from the inside, but present mood minimizes the inappropriate influence of that concern on the feeling itself: it makes welfare less a question of how one feels, all things considered, and more a question of how one feels, *simpliciter.*

10. Equal Opportunity for Present Mood

The life-satisfaction account of welfare discussed earlier appears to be the same as what Dworkin names *overall success*, meaning an individual's overall level of success in leading a valuable life, as she judges it.[79] Dworkin offers a counter-argument against overall-success egalitarianism which is, *mutatis mutandis*, equally applicable to the present-mood account of welfare. Suppose Jack and Jill hold equal resources and have similar natural endowments, occupational success, and day-to-day enjoyments:

> But Jack (who has been much influenced by genre painting) thinks that any ordinary life fully engaged in projects is of value, while Jill (perhaps because she has taken Nietzsche to heart) is much more demanding . . . If each is asked to assess the overall value of his or her own life, Jack would rate his high and Jill hers low. But there is surely no reason in that fact for transferring resources from Jack to Jill provided only that Jill would then rate her life, while still of little overall success, a bit higher.[80]

Dworkin appears to assume that nobody would be prepared to accept such redistribution, and spends the remainder of his analysis of overall success cutting off various welfarist escape routes from it. To make the objection applicable to present-mood egalitarianism we need only add that Jack is generally in a good mood and Jill in a bad one. This is certainly believable. But I am afraid that I see nothing counter-intuitive in the resource-transfer proposal, except the idea of redistributing something without reference to responsibility (see the next paragraph). Dworkin offers no help in pinpointing the problem with overall success, other than this remark, made in the process of blocking the aforesaid escape routes: 'the differences between Jack and Jill we have noticed are still differences in their beliefs but not differences in their lives'.[81] This remark, given its context, simply assumes that justice is about something other than beliefs (resources, one supposes) but overall success assumes the opposite. If Jack believes his life to be going well and Jill believes her life is going badly then egalitarian justice has, contrary to Dworkin's assertion, been given a plausible reason to transfer resources from the former to the latter. If, consequently, Jack always has a spring in his stride but Jill always gets out the wrong side of bed, that is also plausible grounds for redistribution – indeed, for the reasons given earlier, more powerful grounds.

Of course, if Jill is responsible for cultivating her mindset (as is likely given the possible source that has been identified), then we may believe that the level of compensation she receives should be less than full (and perhaps zero). But that suggests only that we ought to distribute in a responsibility-sensitive fashion. It says nothing whatsoever about the conception of welfare itself. In this regard luck egalitarianism and present mood appear to be a good fit.

As we have not found anything wrong with the conception of equal opportunity for welfare implied by the present-mood account of welfare, the following welfarist luck-egalitarian chain of thought may appear plausible. With their equal resources, but unequal expensiveness of taste, A can secure better moods than B. B is therefore entitled to welfare-egalitarian compensation. If B's taste is unchosen, as it may well be, equal opportunity for welfare will also recommend that he be compensated.

In addition, note that, although B does not disprefer his taste,[82] he may well be unhappy about the fact that it is more than averagely expensive. He may also believe that the expense of his taste (though not the taste itself) leaves him disadvantaged relative to A (see above). B may even think that he would want to swap places with A, were it only the case that A's taste was as appropriate for him as it was for A (recall his special kind of value relativism). A may, of course, agree that B suffers a comparative disadvantage, and an unfair one at that, yet feel that it's his good luck that equality of resources does not recognize this. B is therefore clearly unfairly disadvantaged relative to A on all accounts (that of the welfare-egalitarian observer and that of A and B) other than Dworkin's, and this despite the fact that B identifies with the taste that is the source of his disadvantage. For all of Dworkin's arguments, compensation for unchosen welfare disadvantages is plausible, and will compensate in many cases that equality of resources would overlook.

11. Equal Access to Advantage

Cohen accepts that equal opportunity for welfare is an advance upon earlier egalitarian currencies of justice but still believes it falls short of capturing everything that it needs to. He instead puts forward *equality of access to advantage*. The change to 'access' from Arneson's 'opportunity' is purely semantic.[83] The important difference is in the object of equal access: welfare or advantage. Advantage includes but, crucially, is not limited to, welfare: thus equal access to advantage 'corrects for inequalities to which equal opportunity for welfare is insensitive'.[84] Cohen feels he 'cannot say, in a pleasingly systematic way, exactly what should count as an advantage' but maintains that '[w]hat does appear clear is that resource deficiencies and welfare deficiencies are distinct types of disadvantage'.[85] His argument for readmitting resources to the egalitarian's considerations proceeds by presenting two counterexamples to Arneson's criterion. Let us consider these in turn.

The first counterexample, as Cohen admits, 'exploit[s] to the hilt . . . the heterogeneity of its conception of advantage'.[86] Cohen uses Dworkin's example of Jude who has 'cheap expensive tastes'.[87] They are cheap as he needs fewer resources than others for the same level of welfare, but expensive as he requires even those few resources (rather than fewer still) for that level of welfare because he has cultivated an expensive taste for bullfighting. Cohen argues that Jude should be given more resources to indulge his expensive taste than equal opportunity for welfare permits, though less than equality of resources allows: 'I see no manifest injustice in Jude's getting the funds he needs to travel to Spain. He then still has fewer resources than others, and only the same welfare, so equality of access to advantage cannot say, on that basis, that he is overpaid.' [88]

I find it hard to see how this counterexample can work as an argument for equality of access to advantage. Cohen claims that 'unlike either Dworkin's theory or Arneson's, mine explains why both gross underresourcing and gross "underwelfaring" (despite, respectively, a decent welfare level and a decent resource bundle) look wrong'.[89] But these only both look wrong and, indeed, only both look like 'under-phenomena' when one assumes equality of access to advantage or some pre-theoretical equivalent. In fact, if we take seriously Cohen's argument that people should be held responsible for how they develop their tastes, there isn't anything wrong in Kim, who has expensive tastes that are nevertheless cheaper owing to her own efforts than they naturally were, having more resources *and* more welfare than Jude. Luck egalitarians will be unresponsive to the fact that Kim's tastes are still more expensive than Jude's as that is entirely attributable to the brute luck of their native tastes. Where nature has been unkind to Kim, it has been kind to Jude; and where Kim has been prudent, Jude has been imprudent. It is therefore 'nobody else's business to pick up the tab' for the latter's extravagance.[90] If there are relevant countervailing considerations here, Cohen doesn't present an argument for them but merely begs the question.

What Cohen needs, then, is an independent argument for resources that does not contradict his earlier endorsement of responsibility sensitivity. This is what his second counterexample seeks to provide. Consider a paralysed man who needs an expensive wheelchair in order to be mobile:

> Egalitarians will be disposed to recommend that he be given one. And they will be so disposed before they have asked about the welfare level to which the man's paralysis reduces him . . . They propose compensation for the disability *as such*, and not, or not only, for its deleterious welfare effects. Insofar as we can distinguish compensation for resource deficiency from compensation for welfare deficiency, the first appears to enjoy independent egalitarian favor.[91]

Here a lot relies upon *why* egalitarians provide the wheelchair 'before they have asked about the welfare level'. Obviously it is not enough for Cohen's case for them to do so because they assume that the paralysed person has a less than equal opportunity for welfare (perhaps because paralysed persons tend to have a less than equal opportunity and it is too costly to find out if this is so in each case). Egalitarians have to provide the wheelchair, or compensation generally, on the grounds of resource deficiency, regardless of any considerations of welfare however that is conceived. Roemer suggests that Cohen's case that this is so rests on 'undefended intuition'.[92] Still, let us explore the arguments that might be presented in defence of this intuition.

The case cannot be made in the straightforward way Cohen wants to make it. Suppose that Emma and Fiona share identical opportunities for welfare but Emma is disabled while Fiona is not. Why should Emma receive more than Fiona? Cohen claims that she is compensated for the disability '*as such*'. But it is not in principle sensible to give compensation for something just because it looks like a disadvantage (of course, this may be unavoidable in practice). Perhaps the assumption is that this kind of disability is something that the disabled person would rather not have. But some disabled people, for example many of the deaf, do not have this view of their disability. They may feel it opens up valuable new opportunities, particularly in disabled subcultures, that are not open to the able-bodied. I see no reason for ruling this out in the case under discussion. Perhaps Cohen would intend to compensate the 'identifying disabled' anyway. It seems prima facie peculiar, however, to compensate people for something which they are glad or (at worst) indifferent about. Leaving welfare considerations aside, that compensation would presumably have to be either arbitrary or rest on some dubious notion that the able-bodied were somehow objectively better off than the disabled in terms of resources. It is very hard to see how such a notion could be defended in non-circular fashion.[93] Certainly, the prejudices of certain members of the able-bodied population would be a weak grounding. In the absence of such a notion, Emma, if we stipulate further that she does not view her disability negatively, would, so far as we can tell, get everything Fiona gets, plus compensation. The egalitarian can surely put society's resources to better use.

There are four likely responses to this line of reasoning. First, it might be said that the wheelchair is only *offered* to the paralysed individual, and it is up to her to accept it or to turn it down. Thus, no compensation would be wasted on satisfied Emma as she would (we hope) reject the offer of a wheelchair she didn't feel she needed. This seems plausible only in cases where non-fungible medical treatment or aids are being offered. If fungible goods are offered – such as money, or even medicine or aids that have a market value – Emma will again not feel disadvantaged compared to Fiona, yet get compensation. More seriously, the question about why we are offering compensation to Emma but not to Fiona in the first place remains. If we are to grant that Emma and Fiona cannot be differentiated on some objective criterion of personal resources – as I have urged they cannot – it is arbitrary to make compensation available to one but not to the other.

Second, it might be claimed that the argument from intuition works in the most obvious cases because *nobody*, including the disabled, can object that, say, being paralysed without a wheelchair is not a disadvantage. Cohen's case requires merely that in some instances resources are unambiguously relevant. The implications of this argument, however, are counter-intuitive. For a disability to be deserving of resource compensation on this account, there must be unanimity over its disadvantageous nature. But this implies that those disabilities over which there is not unanimity – such as deafness – do not grant their bearers any entitlement to resource compensation. Indeed, it would take just one 'queer fellow' who considers paralysis a blessing for that disability to be denied compensation as well.[94] I submit that insofar as egalitarians are committed to compensating the deaf and the paralysed before considering welfare, they do so irrespective of whether someone can be found who would not call such persons disadvantaged. Thus, this possible response confounds the intuition which it purports to be an elaboration of.

Third, it might be thought that the notion that the able-bodied are objectively better off is not at all dubious, for however satisfied a disabled person may be with her disability, she still bears greater costs in living her life than the able-bodied owing to the way in which society is organized. Such costs can, indeed, be objectively quantified – clearly someone who needs a wheelchair in order to be mobile faces greater costs in performing a wide range of activities. But I think the fallacy of this objection can be shown by asking when these costs arise. On the one hand, these costs might arise in the course of fulfilling *her* preferences and ambitions; on the other hand, they might arise in the course of fulfilling preferences and ambitions *generally* – not necessarily hers. In the former instance, I think there is, indeed, a case for compensation but not for reasons to do with objective resources. I do not see how the latter instance presents any independent case for compensation. Why should anyone be compensated for the greater cost of doing something when that activity forms no part of her ambition? The jump from objective cost to objective disadvantage is too great where those costs do not actually arise in the course of an individual's life, and do not set the scope of that individual's ambitions.

This final qualification, however, leads us into the final response. This is the suggestion that disabled persons' preferences, being formed under conditions of limited opportunity, should not be taken at face value and instead treated as adaptive preferences – that is, we face the problem of 'sour grapes'.[95] I find such an argument unconvincing. Note that, for Cohen's position to be supported in this way, we must stipulate that *all* disabled persons' preferences that approve of their disability should be disregarded as adaptive – for otherwise Cohen is left recommending unwarranted compensation to some persons. To do this in a non-question-begging manner is a tremendously tall order. In fact, I believe that we can never sensibly class a set of preferences as adaptive in the compensation-entitling sense. To be sure, if a disabled person is satisfied with their disability and experiences average levels of welfare – in my favoured formulation, has averagely good moods – that is very likely to be because her preferences and ambitions have adapted to her circumstances. But an equivalent process of adaptation routinely occurs with the non-disabled. I am satisfied with my sub-standard ten-pin-bowling ability simply because I am used to it, and (in part, consequently) bowling does not figure as a prominent part of my life. That is just how ambitions work. We do not compensate in the latter case, and I do not see how Cohen can do so non-arbitrarily in the former.

Of course, equal opportunity for welfare will give us grounds for compensating a disabled person if her welfare levels are lower than the average and she is not responsible for this. But this requires no illegitimate assumptions about the attractiveness or value of her particular physical circumstances. This also reminds us that this compensation for bad price luck is not made conditional in the unacceptable way that envy-test equality's compensation was found to be in Chapter 1. Equal opportunity for welfare does not deny compensation to persons who would not trade their bundle of goods for another's bundle of goods on the grounds that they are not prepared to sacrifice some significant personal characteristic (here, a disability).

12. Concluding Remarks

This chapter defends a conception of equal opportunity for welfare that refuses to identify individual characteristics as compensable or non-compensable on the basis of any features other than their welfare expensiveness and their genuine chosenness. The case for this conception is plausible in its general design, and can be successfully combined with an affective-state account of welfare that tells us all we need to know about advantage levels. Equal opportunity for present mood appears to capture the luck-egalitarian objective better than any of its rivals.

Notes

1 Dworkin 1981.
2 Cohen 1989; Arneson 1989; Roemer 1996.
3 For presentational convenience I assume throughout this chapter that chosen tastes are ones which the holder is responsible for holding and that unchosen tastes are ones which the holder is not responsible for holding. Those who are unhappy with this are directed to replace ref-

erences to '(un)chosen tastes' with 'tastes for which the holder is (not) responsible'.

4   Although this difference of terminology is superficial, there is a deeper difference in the two theorists' positions because Cohen actually endorsed equal access to *advantage,* where advantage included both welfare and resources; see Cohen 1989, 907, 916–21. The main argument does for the moment set this difference aside, as Cohen allows (Cohen 2004, 4). Equal access to advantage is the focus of section 11, below.

5   Arneson 1989, 86.

6   It seems anomalous that Arneson lists (3) alongside (1) and (2) as a circumstance of effectively equivalent options. My options are not effectively equivalent to yours where the options are the same but you have developed your knowledge of the options and abilities to use them far more effectively. It rather seems to be one form of equal opportunity for welfare in the extended sense, the other form being that which Arneson treats as typical (non-equivalent options which are not offset by variations in negotiating abilities).

7   Arneson 1989, 86.

8   Cohen 2004.

9   Cohen 1989, 923; cf. 920.

10   Cohen 2004, 7.

11   Dworkin 2004, 344.

12   This is also suggested in one place in 'Currency' (Cohen 1989, 927). But Cohen introduces this thought as one of a number of additional comments on Dworkin's position that come after his main argument against it. Despite Cohen's protestations, it is far from 'abundantly clear' that his main concern was always with expensiveness of taste rather than taste itself, and the only textual support he offers is the passage cited above.

13   Dworkin 2004, 344.

14   See Cohen 2004, 12, 14.

15   Cohen 1989, 923; cf. 920.

16   Cohen 2004, 7.

17   Cohen 2004, 7.

18   Cohen 2004, 7. See also Price 1999.

19   Cohen 2004, 7. A note makes it clear that 'standardly' means only 'barring the special case where people *welcome* the fact that their taste is expensive' (Cohen 2004, 27 n.13).

20   Cohen strongly hints that those who develop expensive tastes for snobbish reasons or who unsuccessfully gamble that they will be able to afford them should be denied compensation (Cohen 2004, 12, 14, 20–1). But given that such tastes are patently based on valuational judgement, and that Cohen mentions no reasons for denying

compensation in these cases of judgemental taste but not others, I find this puzzling (see Dworkin 2004, 347).

21 Dworkin said something similar about Cohen's position in 'Currency': 'that supposedly different ideal (equal opportunity for welfare) turns out to be equality of welfare under a different name' (Dworkin 2000: 286). The argument for this claim is based upon the thought that all tastes are unchosen (and therefore compensable on Cohen's scheme) as they are themselves the result of uncultivated second-order tastes; see note 25 below. My argument, by contrast, accepts that some kinds of tastes can be chosen.

22 See note 4 above and section 11.

23 See Cohen 2004, 21.

24 Cohen 2004, 8.

25 Cohen holds that, even if all expensive tastes were unchosen in the way Dworkin suggests (see note 21 above), and therefore compensable according to equal opportunity for welfare, there would still remain a difference of principle between that theory and equality of welfare; see Chapter 5, note 48. It is worth noting that the present situation is very different from that described here, because Cohen has provided a reason for providing compensation for all expensive tastes, *even if they are chosen*.

26 I say a little more in a longer version of the present argument; see Knight 2009a.

27 Cohen 2004, 19–21.

28 See 5.4.

29 Dworkin 2000, 82–3.

30 Dworkin 2000, 322–3.

31 Dworkin 2000, 81–2; see also 69–70.

32 Dworkin 2000, 289–90; see also 323–4.

33 Cohen 2004, 11.

34 Dworkin 2004, 345.

35 Dworkin 2004, 345.

36 It might be claimed that the kind of value relativism I have furnished B with is inconsistent with the ordinary ethical experience that Dworkin appeals to. I doubt that this is true – I think that many people really do believe that there are 'different strokes for different folks', and that those 'strokes' that are different from their own are not without value. But what would be proven even were this an unusual attitude to take towards value? Suppose only a handful of people value things this way: what possible grounds are there for justice, let alone *egalitarian* justice, to ignore *their* ethical experience? Of course, these uncomfortable thoughts would be avoided were this value relativism not only very unusual but actually non-existent, but I think it quite impossible to show that. In any case, even were this stitch of my argument undone

altogether, I would have only to drop my proposition that B may view himself as disadvantaged relative to A. The welfare egalitarian argument may fare better with this proposition, but it remains coherent without it.

37 Dworkin 2004, 345.

38 Dworkin 2004, 345, original emphasis.

39 It is not, of course, an accurate description of the task before the advocate of equal opportunity for welfare. She must rather provide some reason to think that justice requires that A and B be equal in welfare, except where one of them has performed more responsibly than the other.

40 Dworkin 2000, 285. See also Dworkin 2000, ch. 1; Dworkin 2004, 341–2, 346. It should be kept in mind that Dworkin refuses to distinguish between equality of welfare and equal opportunity for welfare; see note 21 above.

41 Sumner 1996, 20, original emphasis; see also Arneson 2000c, 503. The term 'prudential value of a life' originated in Griffin 1986.

42 See Darwall 2002.

43 See Aristotle 1954; Finnis 1980; Nussbaum 1988; 1990; Hurka 1993; Gert 1998; Arneson 2000c.

44 This is a narrower definition of subjective theories than is sometimes offered; see Sumner 1996; Sobel 1997.

45 Influential desire-based accounts include those of John C. Harsanyi (1982), R. M. Hare (1981, ch. 5), and Joseph Raz (1986, ch. 12). Whether James Griffin (1986, chs. 1 and 2) should be added to this list is a moot point; see Sumner 2000 and Griffin 2000.

46 See Sumner 1996, ch. 4. The most celebrated statements of classical hedonism are Bentham 1970; Mill 1969; Sidgwick 1962. Contemporary proponents of this view include Goldstein (1980; 1989) and Tännsjö (1998).

47 See Sumner 1996.

48 For a contrasting view see Bower 1998, 311.

49 Richard Brandt suggested in 1979 that objectivism about welfare 'seems to be obsolete'; see Brandt 1979, 246. That has not stopped a considerable literature developing since then, a small sample of which is given in note 43 above.

50 I will not here consider the plausible suggestion that subjective theories should be subject to some objective constraints to protect welfare subjects from such possibilities as the experience machine; see Nozick 1974. It is sometimes suggested that even the use of hypothetical informed preferences that is common in desire theory renders a theory of welfare objective; see Schwartz 1982, 197. It should be noted that both Dworkin's version of equality of resources and envy-test equality may face similar difficulties to subjective accounts of welfare on account of the large subjective input they require.

51 In L. W. Sumner's terms, this would be a shift from internalism to externalism; see Sumner 1996, ch. 4.
52 Brandt 1979, 246.
53 Cf. Ryle 1949: 109. Pain and suffering are used to mark the sensation/affection distinction in Tatarkiewicz 1976, ch. 8; Hare 1981, 93; Cassell 1982; Cassell 1991. This distinction is extended to pleasure and enjoyment in Sumner 1996, 108.
54 Brandt 1979, esp. 38–42; 1982. Note, however, that Brandt's terminology is somewhat different. Brandt's view has been described as 'virtually Benthamite in its focus on the elements of pleasure and pain' (Scarre 1996, 136). But this interpretation ignores Brandt's concern with responses, which places him in the enjoyment theorist camp rather than the Benthamite (i.e. classical hedonist) one.
55 See Sumner 1996, ch. 5.
56 See Brandt 1979, 147; Parfit 1984, 494; 1982, 177; Temkin 1993, 270; Sumner 1996, ch. 5; Tännsjö 1998, ch. 6.
57 For a presentation of this type of problem, and a different way around it, see Warner 1987, ch. 4.
58 Krister Byvist suggests that the fulfilment of posthumous desires that are personal – i.e. 'directed at facts about me and my life' – may have an impact on welfare: 'Things that happen to me after my death, e.g., what happens to my dead body, are things that happen in my life in the sense of being part of my *life-story* or *history* . . . Note also that in this case it is not excluded that my life is made better when the posthumous satisfaction occurs, since the satisfaction may be part of my life.' (2002, 485, 481, original emphasis) But it is counter-intuitive to suggest that my life *itself* goes better if I am buried as I wish. My life story may, in some sense, go better, but that is only insofar as my life story is construed as being about things connected to, but other than, my life.
59 See Haslett 1990, 79–81; Goldsworthy 1992, 6; Sumner 1996, 125–8.
60 Bykvist 2002, 486–7. For the definition of now-for-now, now-for-then, and then-for-then preferences see Hare 1981, 101–2.
61 Bykvist 2002, 486, emphasis added.
62 Hare 1981, p. 103. Hare adds to the description in the text: 'The happiest man is then, in this sense, the man who most has, at all times, what he prefers to have *at those times*.' (original emphasis) As the text suggests, the view Hare describes (without endorsing) seems to lie between enjoyment theory and desire theory – like both of them it is subjective and aggregative, like enjoyment theory it excludes now-for-then preferences, and like desire theory it aims to satisfy (the remaining) preferences.
63 In view of the roles of desire, preference, satisfaction, and formation suggested in the last two paragraphs, we might do better to talk not of

desire or preference utilitarianism but, with J. J. C. Smart, 'satisfaction utilitarianism'; see Smart 1978. But I will stick with convention.

64　Haybron 2001, 502.

65　Telfer 1980, 8. Similar accounts appear in Montague 1967 and Benditt 1974. Compare Robin Barrow's definition: 'Happiness involves a sense of being at one with the world, of thinking that things are as one would have them be.' (Barrow 1991, 68) Provided that 'thinking that things are as one would have them' is intended to mean something like thinking that *on the whole the things that matter to me* are as one would have them, Barrow's and Telfer's definitions come to much the same. But Barrow's definition is much too strong if he intends to mean that, in order to be happy, one must think either that all things one cares about are as one would have them be, or that on the whole things (even things I am close to indifferent about) are as one would have them be. A person can evidently be happy where she believes either that some of the things she cares strongly about are not as she wishes or where most of the things she cares very little about are not as she wishes.

66　That life satisfaction equates with happiness is not universally accepted. The most common view among philosophers is the classical hedonist's theory that an individual's level of happiness is just the sum of units of pleasure and pain. An equally reductionist theory of happiness is obviously also available to enjoyment theorists. See also the comments on affective state theory below.

67　There are other uses of 'happy' that are not especially interesting for our purposes for they do not present alternative candidates for welfare; see Tatarkiewicz 1976, ch. 1; Lloyd Thomas 1968, 97–104; Telfer 1980, ch. 1; Sumner 1996, 143–5. The one exception is mood: see the discussion in the text below.

68　Contrastingly, Robert Nozick restricts use of 'life as a whole' to the life-history kind of satisfaction, describing present-life satisfaction as 'feeling your life is good now'; see Nozick 1989, 108–13. Other writers do not distinguish clearly between the two. Telfer, for example, mentions both the phrases 'He had a happy life' and 'At last he has found happiness' in her portrayal of 'happiness in life' (Telfer 1980, 2).

69　I borrow the term 'historist' from Karl Popper's term for the view that our historical situation defines our opinions; see Popper 1966.

70　Telfer 1980, 1–2; Nozick 1989, 114.

71　See Warner 1987, 17.

72　Sumner 1996, 155.

73　See Sumner 1996, 145–7.

74　Sumner 1996, 147. For a contrasting view, see Telfer 1980, 11–12.

75　Some forms of desire theory also have difficulties coping with addiction; see Parfit 1984, 497.

76 'As William James once remarked, whether a life is worth living depends on the *liver.*' (Bykvist 2002, 475, original emphasis; see James 1956, 32)
77 Of course, it does not follow from this that even the most superficial enjoyments contribute to *happiness*; quite the contrary. See Haybron 2001, 505–6.
78 Daniel M. Haybron is one such philosopher; see Haybron 2000, 215; 2001.
79 See Dworkin 2000, 32–42. Overall success or life satisfaction is offered as an account of happiness in much of the literature on the topic; see Tatarkiewicz 1976, ch. 2; Telfer 1980, ch. 1; Nozick 1989, ch. 10. L. W. Sumner proposes that welfare is 'authentic happiness', i.e. informed and autonomous life satisfaction; see Sumner 1996, ch. 6. Although some such objective constraints on overall success may be necessary for it to offer a satisfactory account of welfare, they (together with various technical matters) are unnecessary complications in the present context.
80 Dworkin 2000, 36.
81 Dworkin 2000, 38.
82 On what Dworkin feels is its most plausible account, overall success refers only to 'personal preferences', i.e. a person's preferences about their own experiences and circumstances. Where some of B's strongest preferences are excluded for this reason, he is likely to identify with a taste that embodies them even though it fails to contribute to his overall success. For instance, B may think that 'it's what my father would have wanted' is a conclusive reason for continuing to identify with his taste for the opera, quite regardless of whether that taste, or even the knowledge that his tastes are as his father would have wanted, would contribute to his well-being or his anything else; his overriding concern may be with his father's memory.
83 Cohen is unhappy that in common usage 'equal opportunity' may be consistent with variations in individuals' ability to *use* opportunities; see Cohen 1989, 916–17. Arneson is quite clear that it is not merely opportunities in this sense that should be equalised but also individuals' abilities to use them; see Arneson 1989, 85–6. Thus equal opportunity in Arneson's slightly idiosyncratic usage (which I will follow) amounts to Cohen's equal access.
84 Cohen 1989, 916.
85 Cohen 1989, 920–1.
86 Cohen 1989, 925 n.36.
87 Dworkin 1981, 239–40.
88 Cohen 1989, 925.
89 Cohen 1989, 925.
90 The quote is from a different context, Cohen 1989, 923.

91 Cohen 1989, 917–18, original emphasis.
92 Roemer 1996, 274.
93 Cf. Roemer 1996, 275.
94 See Van Parijs 1995, 77–9.
95 See Elster 1982; Sen 1987; Arneson 2000c.

Part 2

Luck Egalitarianism as an Account of Equality

3

Substantive Equality

---

1. Introductory Remarks

It should be clear from the discussion in the previous Part of this book that there are several ways in which one might try to realize luck egalitarianism, some of which are more successful than others. The scope of this chapter is considerably broader, extending far beyond responsibility-sensitive egalitarianism to encompass the nature of egalitarianism itself. The primary purpose of this is to provide a framework for establishing whether luck egalitarianism really qualifies as a theory of equality in any substantial sense. As we shall see in the next chapter, this has been disputed by many writers. The discussion of egalitarianism here will prepare the ground for the later specific assessments of the various arguments that have been put forward by these writers. Our first task is a largely *descriptive* one: how do we identify a theory of distributive justice as being egalitarian? Answering this question is a more complicated undertaking than one might imagine.

The most basic feature of equality is probably its *comparative* or *relative* character.[1] Whether equality, in whatever regard, holds or not is a matter of whether a particular state of affairs holds *between* two or more entities. Where those entities are persons – as they will be in all cases considered here – equality of x is a state of affairs in which all persons hold the same (amount of) x. Theories which aim to justify such a situation, or one which is as close an approximation of it as is possible, are, in a weak sense, egalitarian. Often this egalitarianism-as-equality-of-x is supplemented with the demand that, where decisions affecting persons are made, each person is accorded *equal concern and respect*.[2] All are worthy of consideration, and all are to be treated as equals.

The demand that theories or principles of justice be egalitarian in these senses is not empty. Some possible and actual theories and principles fail to meet this demand.[3] The principle that William be given more x than Mary is clearly non-egalitarian. Similarly, theories that insist that members of one group – be they whites, or Christians, or men, or the middle class – be given more x than another group are excluded by the minimal egalitarian demand, unless this inequality is justified as a means to the end of equalizing something else. Even if we state that we are treating all people equally who are equal in the relevant respect, where that respect is possession of light skin colour, we are not treating all with equal concern and respect, because some persons are excluded from consideration. In general, the suggestions that some persons are entitled to more than others, or that some are to be disregarded altogether, are ruled out. If a state were to act on such ideas it would fail to recognize the impartiality that is implied by equality,[4] and perhaps even by justice itself.[5]

Nevertheless, the stated definitions of equality and egalitarianism do not get us very far. The suggestion that everyone should be equal in some respect is uncontroversial until the relevant respect is specified. Very few would dispute that persons should be treated equally, or that all legitimate claims should be taken into account, whoever might make them.[6] As Amartya Sen notes, 'every normative theory of social arrangement that has at all stood the test of time seems to demand equality of *something* – something that is regarded as particularly important in that theory'.[7] All the most familiar theories of justice would qualify as egalitarian in this weak sense, including some which are typically viewed as rivals to egalitarianism.[8] Utilitarianism, for instance, has 'an insistence on equal weights on everyone's utility gains in the utilitarian objective function', while right libertarianism offers 'equality of libertarian rights – no one has any more right to liberty than anyone else'.[9] Utilitarians and libertarians equally distribute particular sets of rights whose value to particular individuals varies with natural, social, and personal circumstances. Any definition which describes such theories as egalitarian appears to be too weak to be descriptively adequate. We need more discriminating ways of identifying egalitarian theories if we wish to avoid Bernard Williams's conclusion that 'when the statement of equality ceases to claim more than is warranted, it rather rapidly reaches the point where it claims less than is interesting'.[10]

In this chapter I will suggest how *substantively* egalitarian theories might be distinguished from those theories which are merely weakly, or uninterestingly, egalitarian. In each of the next three sections I will set out a condition for substantive egalitarianism. The three conditions are, I believe, individually necessary and jointly sufficient for substantive egalitarianism. In two subsequent sections I examine whether two arguably egalitarian approaches to justice can satisfy the three conditions. A concluding section remarks on some of the findings and suggests some ways in which the three conditions reflect intuitive notions of equality.

Each of the conditions has made previous appearances in the literature on equality. But some parts of that literature have remained quite detached from others. Indeed, while close relatives of the first condition have been debated in law reviews, it may seem quite alien to political philosophers. According to the view advanced in this chapter, this is a particularly unfortunate state of affairs, because it is maintained that the key aspects of our egalitarian intuitions are explained by the combination of the first condition with the staples of political theory that are the second and third conditions.

2. *Treating Like Cases Alike*

The starting point for my presentation of the first condition for egalitarianism may appear less than promising. A quarter of a century ago, Peter Westen published an article aiming 'to establish two propositions':

> (1) that statements of equality logically entail (and necessarily collapse into) simpler statements of rights; and (2) that the additional step of transforming simple statements of rights into statements of equality not only involves unnecessary work but also engenders profound conceptual confusion. Equality, therefore, is an idea that should be banished from moral and legal discourse as an explanatory norm.[11]

By 'equality', Westen meant 'the proposition in law and morals that "people who are alike should be treated alike" and its correlate, "people who are unalike should be treated unalike"'.[12] This proposition is, I think, implied by the weaker sense of equality mentioned in the previous section. One cannot be treating persons with equal concern and respect if one refuses to acknowledge that, in relevantly similar cases, each person should receive the same treatment. Equality of x cannot be secured where the bases on which x is given to different people vary interpersonally.

Given the fit between Westen's sense of equality and my weak sense of equality, it is unsurprising that the former is not much help in identifying substantively egalitarian theories. The ambiguity inherent in x – is it welfare? or is it some complex set of libertarian rights? – is transferred into the notions of (un)alikeness and treatment in Westen's formulation. The substantive content of a theory depends on which features of persons it takes to be *relevantly* alike and unalike and what it takes to be the appropriate responses to such features.[13] As Westen's proposition (1) emphasizes, this content may be stated quite simply in terms of individual rights; the egalitarian form itself tells us nothing.

More recently, Christopher Peters has claimed that Westen overlooked 'true prescriptive equality [which] is the principle that *the bare fact that a person has been treated in a certain way is a reason in itself for treating another, identically positioned person in an identical way*'.[14] This differs from Westen's definition of equality by focusing on the actual treatment that a person (or a group of persons) has received, and treating *exactly that* as a reason for treating another person (or group of persons) in a certain way, rather than simply stating that all members of a certain class *ought to* receive certain treatment. We treat likes alike *because* they are alike, rather than for some other reason (typically to do with individual rights) that may be established without any need to look at the relative treatment of different persons. In this way, true prescriptive equality 'supplies a substantive, comparative treatment rule to apply apart from any non-comparative treatment rule that applies in a given case'.[15]

My proposed first condition for a theory or principle to count as substantively egalitarian is derived from Peters's true prescriptive equality.

> *First Condition: the theory or principle considers the bare fact that a person is in certain circumstances to be a conclusive reason for placing another relevantly identically positioned person in the same circumstances, except where this conflicts with other similarly conclusive reasons arising from the circumstances of other persons, in which case a compromise must be reached.*

The simplest example of a conflict between 'similarly conclusive reasons' would be if William and Mary are relevantly identically positioned, and they are circumstanced differently. This generates a reason both for Mary to be circumstanced as William is, and for William to be circumstanced as Mary is. The appropriate compromise is a straightforward matter, or at least is if the circumstances are quantifiable – each receives the mean of the two sets of circumstances. This treatment can be extended to cases involving more than two persons readily enough.

More complex cases of conflict involve some persons who are relevantly identically positioned and some persons who are not relevantly identically positioned. The circumstances of each of the relevantly identically positioned persons provide a reason for each of the other relevantly identically positioned persons to be identically circumstanced, as described above. There is, however, the added complication that these circumstances, as a minimum, must be less favourable than those enjoyed by any persons occupying a higher relevant position, and more favourable than those enjoyed by any persons occupying a lower relevant position. Accounts of equality that describe relevant positions cardinally (not merely ordinally) might further specify the extent to which the circumstances of those occupying each particular higher position should be better than those occupying each particular lower position. The first condition therefore allows for the Aristotelian kind of equality, according to which 'there is proportion between the things distributed and those to whom they are distributed'.[16] Of course, the condition does not presume that justice is proportionate in this way. It just says that, *if* the theory in question does identify more than one relevant position for people to occupy, equality requires a certain kind of relationship between those positions and the circumstances persons face.

The first condition for substantive equality incorporates the insight behind the principle of true prescriptive equality – it treats likes alike because they are alike. It captures the intrinsically (that is, not merely contingently) comparative nature of egalitarian justice by basing each person's treatment on that received by other persons. But it is, as the name suggests, a condition that may be met by a theory or a principle instead of a principle itself. It differs from Peters's prescriptive equality in three other important ways.

First, it makes it explicit that the positions of the persons under consideration need only be *relevantly* identical in order to trigger the stated response – the fact that Mary is a woman and William is a man, or that that the two have different shoe sizes, need not affect how they are treated by the substantive egalitarian. The relevant positions are identified by the theory itself. Relevantly identically positioned persons are persons with identical entitlements according to that theory. Entitlements may depend on the empirical situation, since many theories give rights to certain things only where certain material conditions hold.

Second, it explicitly extends the area of reference beyond *prior treatment by the first person*. It may be substantively egalitarian to place Mary in certain circumstances because relevantly identically positioned William is in those circumstances no matter how William got into those circumstances. It makes no difference whether William *was* treated in a certain way or *is* being treated in a certain way; nor does it matter whether that treatment came from the first person (in distributive justice this means the state or other distributive body) or from some other party, or if it has not resulted from something properly described as 'treatment' at all, but rather from a 'doing of nature'. This final possibility accounts for the reference to 'circumstances' rather than 'treatment'. The key contrast between circumstances (concerning the physical and/or mental conditions facing a person) and relevant positions (concerning entitlements) remains much the same as that between treatments and positions under true prescriptive equality. A person's treatment or circumstance is not a matter of how they are positioned, morally speaking, but is rather concerned with their real-world situation.

The final difference between the first condition and true prescriptive equality is perhaps the most significant. This is the way the former takes the circumstances of one person as *sufficient* grounds for placing another relevantly identically positioned person in the same circumstances, excepting conflicts with other grounds of circumstance. Peters, by contrast, is quite clear that someone who is egalitarian in his sense treats the reason generated by prior treatment as potentially overridable.[17] The change here is required to remove the possibility of essentially non-substantively egalitarian hybrid theories counting as substantively egalitarian simply because they have some minor comparative component. Consider, for example, the theory that social utility ought to be maximized but that, in the event of two courses of action producing the same utility, that which produces the most equality (in the sense of the circumstances of persons being extended to relevantly identically positioned persons) should be selected. Where the reason offered by others' circumstances can be less than conclusive, any theory which states that, '*all things being equal*, the particular circumstances of a person must be matched by the circumstances of other relevantly identically positioned persons', would count as egalitarian, even if 'things' were rarely or never 'equal' in the way required by that theory, and even if in the vast majority of cases the theory was manifestly inegalitarian.

Despite his innovation, Peters draws conclusions that are similar to Westen's: 'even nontautological equality unavoidably butts up against emptiness – inescapably becomes merely an aspect of some wholly non-egalitarian norm – or, where it cannot be said certainly to be empty, collapses into incoherence'.[18] Can such an apparently flawed principle really be used, in revised form, to do the work I want it to do? I think so. This is not on account of the revisions I have suggested, but rather on a divergence between the perspective shared by Westen and Peters and that which we ought to take.

Both Westen's and Peters's conclusions seem to be shaped by a legalistic presupposition that, where a norm might be stated in comparative (usually, egalitarian) terms, or in terms of non-comparative rights, it is the latter that is to be preferred; the egalitarian statement 'necessarily collapses into' a statement of rights. In the cases in which Peters claims that his form of equality is empty, the reasons offered are that it does not offer reasons that are independent of non-egalitarian justice.[19] But non-egalitarian justice is defined in such a broad way that it includes many typically egalitarian norms, simply rendered in terms of rights. For instance, it is considered non-egalitarian to state that two ill people, Smith and Jones, are each entitled to 75 out of 150 available units of medicine, where the justification can be explained in terms of their identical individual claims.[20] Westen and Peters argue that equality itself – the bare relative positions of different persons – does not add any normative value to a form of treatment (such as a distribution). Whether this is true or not is irrelevant to the descriptive task of identifying which theories are substantively egalitarian; it is not, of course, irrelevant to our broader concerns – far from it.[21] Likewise, for present purposes, little rides on the fact that we can describe recognizably egalitarian norms in non-egalitarian ways. Although, contrary to Westen's proposition (2), it will surely often be as simple and clear (or even simpler and clearer) to state such norms in egalitarian terms rather than in rights terms – that is, as 'equality of x', rather than as 'each has a right to the total x divided by the number of persons' – either way is valid. The question is, how do we recognize them as egalitarian in the first place? True prescriptive equality gives us part of the answer to this question.

To see how the first condition can help us start to distinguish between egalitarian and non-egalitarian theories and principles, consider equality of welfare, utilitarianism, and libertarianism. Suppose William holds a certain level of welfare and Mary holds a different level of welfare (that is, they are each in certain differing circumstances). Equality of welfare weighs the demand that Mary holds William's level of welfare precisely because he holds that level of welfare against the demand that William holds Mary's level of welfare precisely because she holds that level of welfare. It satisfies the first condition, for it makes persons' circumstances entirely dependent upon the circumstances of relevantly identically positioned persons – and for equality of welfare, this means the circumstances of all persons, since all have rights to an equal amount of welfare. But neither utilitarianism nor libertarianism satisfies the condition, for neither of them takes persons' circumstances to be grounds for placing relevantly identically positioned persons in identical circumstances. In both cases, two persons may be relevantly identically positioned – that is, have identical rights as the situation is such that each unit of their utility contributes to the social calculus in the same way (utilitarianism) or their historical entitlements are identical (libertarianism) – and therefore be entitled to identical circumstances. *But the circumstances due to each person are fundamentally independent of the circumstances the others are in.* The circumstances of other persons do not enter the libertarian moral calculus at all, and only enter the utilitarian's moral calculations instrumentally. Mary would receive the same treatment whether or not William existed, provided that the background facts (to do with social utility and historical entitlement) stayed the same. They are treated alike only because they are alike in terms of relevant position, not because they are alike in their circumstances. Similarly, when persons are treated unalike, this is solely on account of their differing relevant positions. Mary's and William's circumstances will directly reflect their individual abilities to convert resources into utility, or the set of libertarian rights each has acquired. They will have nothing directly to do with each other's circumstances.

Now it may be objected that the first condition for substantive equality would permit some evidently unjust policies.[22] Suppose that, in treating William, we violated his basic rights, without even so much as a justification from utility maximization or other consequentialist considerations. To make this vivid, suppose that we have falsely imprisoned and tortured him, for our own obscure reasons, or for no reason at all. Surely egalitarian justice does not give any support to the demand that we treat Mary likewise, just because that is how we treated William.

Egalitarian justice makes no such demand. As indicated at the outset, the first condition for substantive egalitarianism is necessary but not sufficient. It reflects the inherently comparative nature of egalitarian justice, and nothing else about it. But there is more than this to substantive equality. In particular, the third condition specifies which circumstances are appropriate bases for the future circumstances of others. Suffice to say, our treatment of William would not qualify. First, however, we must turn to the second condition.

3. Full and Equal Consideration

The first condition for egalitarianism helps to filter out some theories and principles of distributive justice theories that are (at least intuitively) non-egalitarian. But as we have just seen, satisfaction of the first condition is insufficient grounds for calling a theory or principle egalitarian. Consider the following principles:

(a) equality of welfare *among men*;
(b) equality of welfare *among men*, equality of welfare *among women, higher levels of welfare for men*.

Both (a) and (b) are substantively egalitarian if the first condition is the only condition for substantive egalitarianism. The fact that a man/woman holds a certain amount of welfare is treated as grounds for another man/woman (that is, someone who is relevantly identically positioned on account of gender and age) holding that level of welfare, the fact that the second man/woman holds a certain amount of welfare is treated as grounds for the first man/woman holding that level of welfare, and so on, until a compromise is reached. (a) admits no other reasons, while (b) adds that, since men occupy higher relevant positions, their circumstances should be better than women's, as the first condition allows. But neither principle can sensibly be thought to be substantively egalitarian. If, as we are assuming, either might be the sole distributive principle for a society, it could give rise to many instances of significant social inequality. In the case of (a), there would be no limit to the inequality, in any dimension, between men and women, or between women and women. (b) deals with this latter problem, but not the first; it also adds a particularly grievous intergender inequality. In neither case is any justification for these particular types of (possible) inequality presented, and none presents itself. At least one further necessary condition for substantive egalitarianism is needed.

A candidate is suggested by the weak egalitarianism mentioned in the opening of the chapter. There it was noted that such egalitarianism is strong enough to ensure that all persons are considered, and that none is of more concern than others. In other words, it ensures *full and equal consideration*. But the italicized portions of (a) and (b) implicitly disregard or disadvantage all persons who do not meet certain less than compelling criteria. An obvious solution therefore presents itself.

Second condition: the theory or principle can be stated as 'equality of x *for all persons', making no explicit or implicit exclusion of persons or individuals and showing no greater concern and respect for some rather than others.*

The second condition recognizes simple equality of welfare as egalitarian while ruling against the two more discriminatory formulations. But the first and second conditions together are still insufficiently demanding. Consider another principle:

(c) equality of *hair colour.*

This principle satisfies the first condition as it considers persons' circumstances (here = hair colour) to be sufficient conditions for relevantly identically positioned persons (here = any other person) to be in those circumstances (here = have that hair colour). It satisfies the second condition as it does not place limits on which individuals or groups the equality is to hold between. The trivial nature of that equality, however, makes a mockery of the principle's claim to be egalitarian. With (a) and (b) we found that many notable social inequalities would go unaddressed; with (c), *all* major inequalities are ignored.

One response to this problem which naturally presents itself is to focus on those equalities which seem *valuable.* Egalitarians are not concerned with just any kind of inequality; rather, they 'are concerned with how *bad* a situation's inequality is'.[23] This enables us to cope with principles like (c) which, if taken as the sole distributive principle for a society, are inegalitarian by virtue of the triviality of the equality they secure. But while this is part of the solution, it cannot be the whole of it. Reconsider right libertarianism which pursues equality of rights to appropriate unowned resources, to retain all profits from free trade, and so forth. Insofar as it pursues equality, it does so in a dimension which is not considered particularly important by egalitarians; indeed, they may consider these kinds of rights to be pernicious given likely economic and social conditions. But the right libertarian may genuinely believe that he is pursuing equality in that dimension which is most valuable.

Two variations on this initial suggestion also fail, but in telling ways. The first holds that the initial suggestion was insufficiently demanding, in allowing a variety of different equalities all to count as substantively egalitarian. Ronald Dworkin states that 'it is necessary to state, more exactly than is commonly done, what form of equality is finally important'.[24] But this approach faces two fatal objections. First, it is far too exacting. We are, I think, quite convinced that there is more than one substantively egalitarian theory – equality of income, of resources, and of welfare are all clearly identifiable as theories (or groupings of theories) of equality, whatever else they might be. If it turned out that, say, welfare as I construe it (that is, as present mood) was the most valuable thing that could be equalized, it would not follow that that was the only substantive equality to be had. It might be a *better* theory of equality than the others on offer but it seems to abuse the language to describe it as the only theory that achieves substantive equality, and to thereby describe the others as egalitarian in the same kind of way that right libertarianism or utilitarianism are. Second, it actually aggravates the problem that gave rise to it in the first place. Suppose that it turns out that equality of libertarian rights was, after all, the most valuable kind of equality – which is just to say that it is more important that people have these kinds of 'rights' respected than other kinds of 'rights' (rights to equal welfare, for instance). It is patently absurd thereby to suggest that right libertarianism is the only theory of substantive equality, and that the various varieties of equality of outcome are actually *less* egalitarian than it is. I do not see how this kind of result can be ruled out without knowing all that there is really worth knowing about distributive justice; but we ought to be able to identify egalitarian theories even without such extraordinary knowledge.

The second variation on the 'valuable equalities' suggestion seeks to limit both the kinds of value and the type and pattern of distribution that are admissible in egalitarian theories. The examples of typically egalitarian theories mentioned so far all put the spotlight on how well off (in some regard) people end up. In particular, they might be interpreted as attempting, with varying success, to equalize a certain conception of *individual prudential value* – that is, to make each individual's life go just as well as every other individual's life.[25] We might say, then, that substantively egalitarian theories are *prudential outcome egalitarian*, or at least try to be so (income may not be a particularly good measure of prudential value, but equality of income may be a genuine attempt to approximate prudential-outcome egalitarianism). Faced with this new requirement, the libertarianism which we have been trying to exclude from our definition falls at the first hurdle – it focuses on historical events (usually individuals' actions) rather than end states.[26] Utilitarianism is an end-state theory, and focuses on prudential value (utility), but the desired end state is not one of equalization.

So far so good. Unfortunately, the new requirement allows far too little to count as substantive equality. Often, committed egalitarians will favour a situation of increased prudential-outcome inequality. This reflects the fact that they have a broader range of concerns than the new requirement permits. To see this, consider the case of professional baseball players. Suppose that, at a certain point in time, the two largest racial groups of players were not, on the average, equally paid. The question is this: is this prudential-outcome inequality – where one racial group of players is advantaged relative to others – a sufficient ground, *and* the sole ground, for a substantive egalitarian to oppose this distribution?[27] Definitely not. Many other factors are relevant. I will mention three possible scenarios that bring out a few of them. In the first case, suppose that we know that the sole source for the inequality is the fact that the better-paid group performs, on the average, more effectively than the other – that they are more productive. This may go at least some way to justifying the inequality. In the second case, suppose that both groups have an identical level of performance, and that we know that the source of the disadvantaged group's disadvantage is the blatant racial discrimination that they are subject to (to give an extreme example, that the teams place a salary cap on one group's players that is lower than the minimum salary for the other group). Or, alternatively, suppose that there are no official discriminatory policies, but that one group's players are more marketable than the other group's owing to the racism of fans, and that results in the income inequality. Would the existence of such circumstances really make no difference whatsoever to the egalitarians' response to the situation? The egalitarian may well oppose this distribution more strongly than in a case where the distribution is the result of non-racially influenced market forces.

Finally, let us bring together the considerations the first two cases highlight with a real-world example.[28] In 1970 the average black Major League baseball player earned more than the average white player. The average black player of a certain level of productivity (as measured by performance averages), however, actually earned less than the average white player of the same level of production. It appears, then, that 'blacks, on the average, earn less than whites of equal ability'.[29] This led some to suggest 'that widespread racial discrimination still exists in baseball, and that this racism becomes clear only when salaries are compared *at each level of performance*'.[30] I do not think that the substantive egalitarian is compelled to demand an equal distribution of prudential outcome in this case, where black players have not only outperformed their white counterparts, but outperformed them so much that, despite evidence of continuing racism (whether it be on the part of the teams or fans), they have managed to surpass them in salary terms. In cases like this, the would-be substantive egalitarian may find her intuition that there is more to a distribution than equal prudential outcome supported in a number of ways. She may think that, to some extent, productivity or merit should themselves be rewarded,[31] or (more plausibly, in my view)[32] that they are a useful rough guide to other things which are not equally spread among the population – desert and, of course, responsibility may be particularly significant considerations here.

4. The Object of Egalitarian Concern

Much can be learned from the shortfalls of the three versions of the view that substantive egalitarians seek to secure equality of those things which seem valuable. The first variation is both too weak, in potentially admitting what are at heart non-egalitarian theories, and too strong, in requiring a theory to be the best account of *justice* to count as a theory of *equality* (and remember, we are not even trying to define *good* theories of equality here!). The second variation is much too narrow, in reducing substantive equality to one particularly obvious kind of substantive equality. In the end, I think the original version comes closest to succeeding, in making equality something worth caring about. The problem is just that it is not something worth caring about *for egalitarians in particular.*

These final points are the most significant. But I do not think there is any 'quick fix' for the problem posed by cases of type (c). The objection to it is just that it is not worth caring about. But there seems to be no unproblematical way of filtering unworthy entries to the formula 'equality of *x*' in the pleasingly formal way that the first and second conditions filter the particular non-egalitarian elements that they tackle. It is, I think, necessary to adopt a final condition for a theory or principle to count as egalitarian that leaves more scope to intuition.

> *Third condition: the theory or principle pursues equality in a dimension that is valuable to egalitarians.*

This condition is vaguer than the others, but necessarily so. We have seen that we have to accept a variety of theories as egalitarian, and I think one of their distinguishing features has to be that they pursue a type of equality that is valuable – but not necessarily *most valuable* – to egalitarians. It may strike the reader that there is an obvious circularity here: what I am really saying, it might be alleged, is that substantive-egalitarian theories are those which pursue sub-stantive equalities. But that would be an inaccurate description. In the first place, observe that this condition has been adopted precisely because theories which equalize substantively are, paradoxically, neither uniquely, nor even necessarily, egalitarian in the required sense. Those theories that equalize prudential value are only one kind of substantive egalitarian theory, while those that equalize all-things-considered value need not be substantive egalitarian at all. A substantively egalitarian theory must equalize a particular kind of value – an *egalitarian* kind of value. In this way, the egalitarianism of substantive egalitarianism comes in both in the pattern of distribu-tion and in what is distributed. It also must be reiterated that this is not supposed to be a sufficient condition for substantive egalitarian-ism. It is to be used alongside the first two conditions which we have seen can narrow down the range of candidate theories. Later it will be shown that some positions, which may be appear to be substantively egalitarian and which many people assume are consonant with the usual understandings of egalitarianism, are ruled out by the first con-dition. First, however, let me say a little about 'usual' understandings of equality and egalitarianism.

In philosophical and in non-philosophical discourse, 'equality' is used to refer to something (an idea or a practice, for instance) which stands in a certain relation to the work of particular prominent writers and to particular social arrangements (which have more often than not been influenced by those writers). Jeremy Waldron puts the point quite succinctly:

> 'Equality', like 'liberty' and 'fraternity', is a shorthand slogan but not an abbreviation. It evokes a particular range of moral considerations and a particular set of complex arguments, and it does that, not by virtue of its meaning, but because every political theorist is familiar with a tradition of argumentation in and around certain texts and doctrines and knows that colleagues can be alerted to the possible relevance of that tradition by using that simple word.[33]

A substantively egalitarian theory is characterized by giving an answer to the question, 'equality of what?', that falls within a certain range of the possible answers. As is shown by imaginary principles, such as (c), and also by established theories, such as right libertarian-ism (with their particular complex understandings of what it means

102

to treat persons as equals), the x in equality of x cannot be just any-thing if that theory is to be egalitarian. The position of this range is informed both by the history of moral and political thought and by contemporary scholarship. Any claim that Nozickian historical entitlement was substantively egalitarian, or even as egalitarian as equality of welfare, simply in virtue of its formal structure, would not be taken seriously by the vast majority of philosophers, including Nozick himself.[34] That theory belongs firmly to a different tradition, one which is opposed to the egalitarian tradition.[35] Realizing equality in one regard will destroy equality in another, and these equalities hold different levels of significance within different traditions. Which of these equalities seem really to matter to the egalitarian?

The kind of comprehensive egalitarian theory of distributive justice which is most familiar to members of the general public is economic equality. Equality of income and equality of wealth are the best-known theories in this field, and two of the simplest. But these theories and their close relatives have little currency as fundamental objectives with political philosophers, for the simple reason that money is not, after all, what matters; or at least, not all that matters. Some people can *do* more with a given amount of money than other people. According to philosophers, the exemplary egalitarian theo-ries are equality of resources (construed quite broadly) and equality of welfare. Of the two, a given philosopher will choose that theory which accords with their own view about whether it is resources or welfare which are the appropriate objects of distribution. It is highly likely, of course, that equality of income would lead to greater equal-ity of welfare or that equality of wealth would lead to greater equal-ity of resources than present distributive regimes would, but even this instrumental value is diminished where we might bring about patterns of distribution that are tailored to the needs of the more complex equalities.

The point of this is not to dispute the substantively egalitarian nature of economic egalitarianism, even as an account of what justice ultimately requires. Income and wealth are fields in which equalization is both valuable – though not, as philosophers note, most valuable – and valuable in an egalitarian way – in a way that, say, right libertar-ian rights are not. Undoubtedly, a large part of the explanation here is the prudential value that can be realized with money. But that is not the whole part. Economic egalitarians usually hold individuals at least partially responsible for what they do with their money. Wealth egalitarianism is not usually construed as requiring that equality of wealth holds at every moment of time, regardless of choices – if I win at the dog track, the resulting inequality is likely to hold long enough that I will have time to spend my winnings. Income egalitarianism certainly would not step in if I lost my money at the track, whereas a welfare egalitarian government would do, assuming, as is likely, that my welfare will drop as a result of my actions. The dispute here really is an intramural one: the choice is not between substantive egalitarianism and something else, but between two different kinds of substantive egalitarianism.

I say all this on the assumption that the theories in question satisfy the first two conditions for substantive egalitarianism. As already shown, this is true of welfare egalitarianism, and the same demonstration could easily be extended to economic egalitarianism. These are paradigmatic theories of equality, even if they are not ultimately the best theories of equality, all things considered. If equality of resources is construed as a kind of halfway house between these other two theories – it equalizes a range of goods such as basic liberties, income, wealth, basic opportunities, and perhaps talents – it qualifies just as easily. Someone who proposed to equalize Rawlsian social primary goods would fall into this category although this is not what John Rawls himself suggests.[36] In each of these cases, the circumstances of persons set the entitlements of relevantly identically positioned persons, all are considered to be relevantly identically positioned, and hence none are favoured or excluded. If equality of resources is construed as either of the complicated Dworkinian formulations examined at length in Chapter 1, things are much less straightforward. The same is true of equal opportunity for welfare- and similar-luck-egalitarian positions, though for different reasons. Furthermore, these complexities are not limited to elaborate philosophical theories. Some social policies, that are more commonplace (in discussion, at least) than even the most familiar comprehensive egalitarian theories, appear to be far less obviously egalitarian than popular opinion might hold. Let us begin with the last of these topics.

5. Application to Prioritarianism

In contemporary developed countries there is consensus that there should be a certain minimum level of income, education, and health care for all persons. People who wish to set these minimum levels at significantly higher levels than those that presently exist are popularly known as left wingers, social democrats, or (in the United States) liberals. Let us call this view 'contemporary egalitarianism'. Now consider the following social policies:

1. Where the levels of income, education, and health care of the worst off can be increased by making a disproportionately larger increase in the levels of income, education, and health care of the better off, make these changes.
2. All things being equal, increase the levels of income, education, and health care of the better off.
3. Where the levels of income, education, and healthcare of the worst off reach a certain level that is still below the average level, maximize the total levels of income, education, and health care.

Each of these policies is quite consistent with the defining attitude of a contemporary egalitarian (assuming that the 'certain level' in [3] is appropriate). One may even adopt contemporary egalitarianism and *all* of these strategies. I will not speculate about how common this might be, but I am sure that each of these views is held by some people who are contemporary egalitarians. With equal certainty, I can say that each of these strategies is inconsistent with equality of income, with equality of education, and with equality of health care. This is simply because each strategy promotes (or, in the case of [3], may promote) inequality in the specified fields – it increases the percentage difference in income, education, and health care levels between the better off and the worst off.[37] Contemporary egalitarianism is consistent with such strategies because it does not distribute equally the goods in question. Income, education, and health care are distributed without reference to the comparative positions of persons.[38] The main focus is on the absolute amounts of these goods that find their way into the hands of the worst off.

If contemporary egalitarians are not egalitarian by virtue of demanding equality in the dimensions with which they are explicitly concerned, how might the characterization of them as egalitarian be explained? It might just be that it is mistaken. Perhaps people are just generally confused about the different strategies available to the left. If the characterization is not mistaken, it might reflect the fact that these persons endorse equality in some other dimension – welfare, say – and simply endorse the policies that are supportive of that goal that have the best chance of political acceptance. The most interesting possibility, though, is that their focus on the absolute position of the worst off is fundamentally egalitarian in a broader sense.

This last possibility might be fleshed out with any of several distributive principles. The most famous of these is Rawls's 'difference principle' which combines a focus on 'relevant social positions' (rather than individuals) with a *maximin* strategy, thereby maximizing the condition of the worst-off group.[39] The closely related *leximin* strategy maximizes the condition of the worst-off group (or, alternatively, person), then maximizes the condition of the next worse-off group (or person), and so on.[40] The radical priority to the worse off granted by leximinism may be restrained by some kind of utilitarian or other maximising principle, such that the commitments to the worse off and to the overall good are both conditional. This *limited priority* strategy would imply that, though an improvement for the worse off is always more weighty than an equivalent improvement for the better off, a minor gain for the worse off may be outweighed by a larger gain for the better off.[41] Finally, a *sufficiency* strategy would ensure that the worst off held a certain minimum of whatever it is that is being distributed, but would say nothing once this minimum had been secured.[42]

Each of these positions is consistent with the bare statement of contemporary egalitarianism and with (1) and (2). Sufficiency is consistent with (3) while maximin, leximin, and limited priority are not. This reflects the fact that the last three strategies, as forms of prioritarianism, always grant some priority to the worst off, whereas sufficiency is a different kind of principle altogether – one which makes the priority to the worst off conditional. Of the two kinds of principle, the case for sufficiency as a form of egalitarianism is much weaker; indeed, its advocates typically present it as an alternative to egalitarianism.[43] Furthermore, the one criticism of prioritarianism-as-egalitarianism that I will present is, *mutatis mutandis*, applicable to sufficientarianism.

The general form of prioritarianism might be described in this way: moral value, ranging from 0 (no value) to 1 (most value), is assigned to each unit of whatever it is that is being distributed. Maximin is 'binary', in the sense that the only values will be 0 and 1. Units held by the worst off have absolute value; units held by those who do not fall into this category have no independent moral value (although they may be required to improve the position of the worst off). Limited priority, by contrast, will make full use of the range from 0 to 1, with the exception of 0 itself. Moral value is assigned to every unit, with the specific value of each unit being proportional to how badly off its bearer is: the worse off the bearer, the greater the value. For all prioritarian principles, the best distribution is that which yields the highest moral value. (Leximin is a bit more complicated as it would need a series of calculations. The first of these would be exactly the same as maximin's calculation; thereafter maximin's binary model would be followed, but with absolute value being given to improvements for the *worse* off rather than for the *worst* off.) Individuals would then have rights to whatever units they have under the optimum prioritarian distribution.

Many writers have supposed that prioritarianism is one form of egalitarianism, or even *the* kind of egalitarianism worth caring about. This latter supposition is particularly common in economics where maximin and leximin are often taken to be the standard egalitarian strategies.[44] This is no doubt linked to the commonplace acceptance of the Pareto principle (the view that a change improves a distribution where someone benefits and no one loses out) in economics.[45] But several philosophers have held similar beliefs. While Thomas Nagel allows that the difference principle is less egalitarian than a principle which would prohibit inequalities even if they benefited the worst off, he mentions a 'very strong egalitarian principle . . . which is constructed by adding to the general value of improvement a condition of priority to the worst off'.[46] Such a principle may not be strong enough to satisfy 'pure impartiality', which 'is intrinsically egalitarian . . . in the sense of favoring the worse off over the better off'.[47] Rawls himself is more cautious, suggesting that 'the difference principle is a strongly egalitarian conception in the sense that unless there is a distribution that makes both persons better off (limiting ourselves to the two-person case for simplicity), an equal distribution is to be preferred'.[48] He adds that this principle achieves some but not all of the objectives of the more obviously egalitarian principle of redress.[49] Even so, G. A. Cohen has suggested that the so-called 'Pareto argument' for the difference principle 'has often proved irresistible even to people of egalitarian outlook', and that its 'persuasive power . . . has helped to drive authentic egalitarianism, of an old-fashioned, uncompromising kind, out of contemporary political philosophy'.[50] However many of these theorists continue to describe themselves as egalitarians, it seems clear that prioritarianism is at the least such an attraction to those of an egalitarian persuasion that it is worth asking whether it is itself a form of egalitarianism.

How well does prioritarianism meet the three conditions for egalitarianism? I will start with the second condition: *the theory or principle can be stated as 'equality of x for all persons', making no explicit or implicit exclusion of persons or individuals and showing no greater concern and respect for some rather than others.* This can be done easily enough by the prioritarian: 'equality of *rights to whatever they would receive under the best prioritarian distribution* for all persons'. No individuals are excluded or picked out for especially good or bad treatment.

Next, the third condition: *the theory or principle pursues equality in a dimension that is valuable to egalitarians.* As just noted, the prioritarian's favoured dimension of equality is prioritarian rights. As I have loosely characterized it, prioritarianism does not actually specify *what* is to be distributed according to these rights. But this is no ground for thinking that it fails to meet the condition. The space that is left open can be filled in in any way. It is, furthermore, typically filled in with just the kind of individual prudential value that I have said egalitarians are largely concerned about. The Rawlsian maximining of income and wealth is one kind of prudential-value prioritarianism; other kinds may involve welfare or a broader conception of resources (Rawls himself thinks that income and wealth are only a subgroup of social primary goods, which are themselves a subgroup of primary goods).

Two hurdles may seem to remain in the way of prioritarianism satisfying the third condition. First, and as already observed, prudential value is not the only thing that egalitarians care about. Although this is true, we have already accepted as egalitarian some theories that only refer to prudential value, such as equality of resources and equality of welfare. Such theories are egalitarian even if they do not say all there is to be said about egalitarianism. Furthermore, there is little difficulty in building other considerations into the prioritarian's conception of moral value.[51] These can, in principle, be tailored exactly to reflect egalitarian values, whatever those may be.

Second, it might be observed that no form of prioritarianism distributes whatever it is that it distributes in an egalitarian fashion. It is, like libertarianism or utilitarianism, egalitarian only in the sense that it equally distributes a certain package of rights – a package of rights that is inegalitarian in content. There is some truth in this objection but it does not tell the whole story. While the objective of prioritarianism is explicitly to distribute in non-egalitarian fashion, that is insufficient grounds for saying that it does not actually achieve equality in a space that is valuable to egalitarians. As noted above, some have refused to distinguish between equality and priority for the worst off as objectives, and many egalitarians have been moved to accept prioritarianism. The kind of egalitarian value that is of importance here is, I must reiterate, fairly loose, and defined largely by practice and tradition. Prioritarianism is a view of fairly recent vintage, having only really been examined and advocated as an alternative view to egalitarianism in the last twenty years or so.[52] Before then, egalitarianism largely subsumed it: prioritarian concerns were treated as a kind of egalitarian concern. As the discussion of contemporary egalitarianism at the start of this section might suggest, prioritarianism might better – or at least more directly – explain many views that go under the label 'egalitarian'. The same could hardly be said of libertarianism. Utilitarianism would fare better than libertarianism here, but largely on account of empirical factors such as diminishing marginal utility and envy.[53] Its refusal to give any special precedence to the claims of the worse off places it at odds with egalitarian attitudes in many cases. Although the kind of precedence to the worse off or worst off that prioritarianism gives may, in the case of limited priority, be less than total, and in any case concerns their absolute position rather than their relative position, the fact that it gives precedence puts it much more in line with underlying egalitarian values. For this reason, the rights that prioritarianism assigns on an equal basis may plausibly be valuable to egalitarians.

This is enough, I believe, to suggest that prioritarianism satisfies the third condition. But the first condition is another matter altogether. This is the condition: *the theory or principle considers the bare fact that a person is in certain circumstances to be a conclusive reason for placing another relevantly identically positioned person in the same circumstances, except where this conflicts with other similarly conclusive reasons arising from the circumstances of other persons, in which case a compromise must be reached.* Imagine that, this time, William and Mary hold certain amounts of whatever our favoured prudential value is (that is, they are in certain differing circumstances), and that they are relevantly identically positioned. Since William and Mary are relevantly identically positioned, prioritarianism of whatever stripe obviously requires that they be identically circumstanced. *But the reasons for this have nothing to do with William's and Mary's circumstances.* Prioritarianism treats likes (that is, those with equal potential under present conditions for furthering priority-weighted welfare) alike but it does not treat likes alike because of their alikeness of circumstance.

In the case of simple prioritarianism, where it is the case either that priority to the worst/worse off is the only value (maximin and leximin) or it is supplemented with overall prudential value (limited

prioritarianism), the circumstances of relevantly identically positioned individuals do not matter at all when deciding how to treat
somebody. All that matters is the position of the individual relative
to *everybody else* – whether they are the worst or worse off or not
– and how treating the individual in certain ways will affect the
overall picture – whether the worst or worse off are benefited. Simple
prioritarianism treats William in exactly the same way whether
Mary is rich, poor, happy, or depressed, except insofar as Mary's
circumstances happen to affect the condition of the worst or worse
off (which may be Mary or William).

It is true that the more complex kind of prioritarianism that admits
further kinds of moral value may treat Mary's circumstances as relevant to establishing the appropriate circumstances for William. For
instance, part of their being relevantly identically positioned could be
their having behaved equally responsibly. As we shall see in the next
section, where two individuals are equally responsible, and distributions reward the responsible, the circumstances of each individual
can become relevant to establishing the other's entitlement. But with
complex prioritarianism, these kinds of considerations are not conclusive, as the first condition requires. There will sometimes be the
potential for prudential value gains that can be achieved only through
circumstancing persons in ways that do not reflect responsibility or
other non-prudential values. Such circumstancings will fail to correspond to the circumstances of other persons. Although a reason
for basing persons' circumstances on those of relevantly identically
positioned persons may be present in one of the component values
of complex prioritarianism, the fact that complex prioritarianism as
a whole takes that reason to be conditional means that that theory
cannot satisfy the first condition for egalitarianism.

6. Application to Luck Egalitarianism

This section addresses the main issue for the broader project: whether
luck egalitarianism can really count as an egalitarian theory. I will
begin with a brief discussion of Dworkinian equality of resources,
which may be construed as a form of luck egalitarianism. The standard form of luck egalitarianism, equality of opportunity for prudential value (or equal opportunity, as I will sometimes call it), will then
be examined at some length. In both cases the focal point will be the
three conditions for substantive egalitarianism.

As observed in Chapter 1, Dworkinian equality of resources comes in three forms: the official hypothetical insurance-market version, and two unofficial envy-test versions, one of which builds in responsibility considerations. The official version falls at the first hurdle. The appropriate circumstances for any given person are not based on the circumstances of relevantly identically or non-identically positioned persons; rather, they are based on the fact that they are part of the optimal expected outcome for the average member of society in conditions of limited information. The second condition creates no problems – equality of resources (in the particular sense intended) is extended to all persons. The third condition is, however, problematic. The equality of rights that is created is similar to that under utilitarianism, being set on the basis of maximizing assumptions; this dimension may well not be considered valuable enough by egalitarians. In any case, given its failure to meet the first condition, official equality of resources is not substantively egalitarian.

The first of the two unofficial versions of equality of resources, 'envy-test equality', fares little better. Suppose that William's circumstances differ from those of Mary, who is relevantly identically positioned (that is, that they are due the same resources under an envy-free distribution). There is, according to envy-test equality, a reason for placing Mary in William's circumstances, and a reason for placing William in Mary's circumstances. But that reason does not concern either person's circumstances. Mary's circumstances could improve without William's entitlement changing since one need not prefer to have more of anything rather than less.[54] But the second condition is met whether or not responsibility is involved as equality of resources (as construed here) holds between all persons. The third condition is, I think, less obviously troublesome for envy-test equality than it is for the official variant, as the maximizing tendency of the latter is not present in the former. It may face difficulties, however, on account of the problem introduced in 1.8. This same problem may also be connected to envy-test equality's failure to meet the first condition.[55]

Responsibility-sensitive envy-test equality cannot satisfy the first condition, satisfies the second one, and may or may not satisfy the third one. The reasons for this are almost exactly the same as for envy-test equality, the sole difference being that the reference to responsibility may or may not create extra problems regarding the third condition. Relevant considerations are given in the discussion of equality of opportunity that follows.

With the failure of responsibility-sensitive envy-test equality to meet the first condition, luck egalitarianism's claim to be egalitarian rests with equality of opportunity. The first condition, though the bane of several theories, including prioritarianism and every kind of Dworkinian equality of resources, creates no difficulties for this theory. Suppose that William holds a certain amount of whatever our favoured prudential value is, that Mary holds a different amount, and that they are relevantly identically positioned (that is, that William and Mary have conducted themselves equally responsibly). Unlike any form of prioritarianism, equality of opportunity takes Mary's being in those circumstances as grounds for putting William in those circumstances, and vice versa. The circumstances of a third person who is more responsible or less responsible than William and Mary would also be relevant, were such a person present. Whether or not that is the case, individuals' entitlements are entirely dependent upon the circumstances of other persons. In spite of its reference to responsibility, equality of opportunity meets the first condition just as effortlessly as outcome-egalitarian ideals such as equality of welfare.

The second condition is also met comfortably by equality of opportunity. It guarantees equality of opportunity for all persons, and shows no person any more concern than any other.

The third condition is a more complicated matter. My favoured formulation of prudential value is the present-mood conception of welfare but some other conception of welfare, or some conception of resources, would also function perfectly well for present purposes because these are all things of sufficient importance to egalitarians. The complication comes in, however, because prudential value is not to be distributed in strictly equal fashion, but rather proportionately – specifically, in a responsibility-sensitive fashion. This commitment to responsibility may appear to cut into equality. It might be thought that, wherever the two come into conflict, it must be equality that yields; that is, wherever one person acts more responsibly than another, inequality is established.

Although in one sense correct, I believe that this is to oversimplify the situation. For one thing, we have seen that some weak notion of equality is at the heart of virtually every account of justice, and that there is little difficulty in describing theories we would usually think of as alternatives to egalitarianism in terms of equality. Equal outcomes may be upset by responsibility sensitivity but that is not sufficient grounds for saying that equality is compromised, for equality in one dimension almost always requires inequality in others. The question is whether a decrease in outcome equality is an acceptable price for the egalitarian to pay for increasing the responsibilitarian version of equal treatment.

As has been hinted already, I think egalitarianism is itself often construed as involving considerations of responsibility. We do not typically view real-world equal opportunity as a rival to equality but rather as one conception of equality (which may, of course, conflict with rival conceptions). If a first child makes the genuine choice to eat her apple while a second chooses to save hers for later, and a parent then divides the remaining apple between the children, the second child can, one would think, sensibly complain of being treated not only unfairly but *unequally*. There is perhaps some substantive idea of equality that recommends considerations of attributive responsibility.

Unsurprisingly, many (at least nominally) egalitarian critics of luck egalitarianism feel that the benefit afforded by its association with responsibility is illusory. Many arguments of this type will be discussed in subsequent chapters. Here I will refer to two that I think actually suggest that responsibility is, at the very least, compatible with egalitarianism.

In the first case, the reasons for this have been alluded to in section 3 above, but are particularly well illustrated by a critic's counterexample. Timothy Hinton has this to say about the apartheid regime formerly found in South Africa: 'What made the system evil, surely, was the way that black people were forced to live . . . The evil did not consist in the fact that the color of one's skin is largely a matter of brute luck.' [56] If black people had (somehow) freely chosen to be oppressed, 'that would surely not ameliorate the evil of the unequal conditions that they would have to endure'.[57] But the biggest part of the evil surely is that the disadvantages suffered by the black population are disadvantages for which they are not responsible. Contrast an apartheid-era township with a settlement identical to it in every regard except for the fact that the subordinated population have all committed serious crimes for which they are, by their presence in the penal colony, paying the pre-established penalty. It is an affront to justice to suggest that the two cases are equivalent: here at least attributive responsibility matters.

If egalitarianism suggests that the township and the penal colony are equally morally wrong I think the sensible conclusion to reach would be that egalitarianism should be rejected. But I do not think that this is actually what egalitarianism suggests. Egalitarianism is certainly not committed to that claim, even if it may be consistent with it (as I think must be allowed if outcome egalitarianism is to count as egalitarian). The moral difference between the township and the penal colony can be identified as a difference of equality – specifically, as a difference in equality of opportunity. Provided a society has reasonably just laws, most egalitarians would not have much time for someone who had committed a serious offence and then complained that he was being treated unequally. They would be much more sympathetic to the complaint of someone who was being treated unequally on the basis of their skin colour and/or the status of their family. This is because there is an inequality of opportunity in the second case but no inequality of opportunity in the first. As we shall see later in this book, if the inequality between an irresponsible person (such as an offender) and averagely responsible members of society was very extreme – and in particular, if basic needs are going unmet or suffering exceeds certain levels – the egalitarian may then start to be concerned by it. But even if the egalitarian's concern here is directly related to end-state equality – rather than to the absolute position of the negligent or malicious person – it is clear that that is not all there is to her thinking, and that something else plays a very significant role in it.

It might still be denied that it is specifically responsibility that is doing the work here. This is where the second criticism comes in. As we have seen, equal opportunity insists that inequalities in the presence of a history of equivalent exercises of attributive responsibility are unjust but that differential attributive responsibility-based inequalities are not. Samuel Scheffler writes that

> [i]t is far from clear that, in this generalized form, this claim enjoys widespread intuitive support. The more common or intuitive view, I believe, is that the fairness or unfairness of differences in advantage resulting from, on the one hand, factors beyond people's control and, on the other, people's voluntary choices, is highly dependent on the prevailing social context and institutional setting.[58]

The argument is that luck egalitarianism fails to coincide with the 'social and political conception of equality'. Scheffler attempts to bring this out with regard to what we might call *differential natural endowment cases*. Consider, for example, how we think about occupational talent and success:

> [I]f I have a less successful career as a philosopher than you do because your superior philosophical gifts enable you to refute all my arguments,

then, contrary to what the generalized claim might lead us to expect, most people would not regard that as unfair. Nor would most think it unfair if a naturally gifted professional athlete were offered a more lucrative contract than his less talented teammate.[59]

The underlying idea here seems to be that some conception of productivity or merit is the 'something' that explains why egalitarians do not focus only on end states. In some cases responsibility and merit coincide but where they come apart it is merit that captures the egalitarian intuition.

Scheffler's examples are messy because it is probably difficult for the majority of the population to conceptualize cases where the difference in ability is purely a factor for which no one is responsible. Those who are successful in their fields have generally tried harder than the average, and this is reflected in a general scepticism about the importance of the 'gifts' that are central to Scheffler's examples. What the majority would say were they to accept the existence of clear-cut examples is pure speculation.

But suppose for the sake of argument that the majority of persons in existing societies would not side with the luck egalitarian if clear cut cases could be identified.[60] Even then the luck egalitarian need not be concerned. In the first place, the differential career success and income in the examples are, I hold, manifestly instances of substantial social inequality. I do not think that the majority would want to deny this, even if they wanted to defend these distributions. They might say, coherently enough, that there was justice but not equality. If an outcome is both unequal and derived from differential opportunities then there is no morally significant way in which it is equal – no part of our egalitarian intuitions recommend such an outcome. Luck egalitarianism is a theory of equality and responsibility, and it is no argument against its egalitarian (or, for that matter, responsibilitarian) credentials that it does not capture non-egalitarian (and non-responsibilitarian) principles. A principle of merit allows persons with unequal talents, which they maybe take no credit for, to exploit them for unequal rewards. Yet Scheffler characterizes his criticism as an egalitarian one.

More importantly, however, equal opportunity does not stand or fall with the volume of support for its dictates among the general public. Distributive justice is not a popularity contest – something Scheffler seems implicitly to concede when venturing the distinctly ivory-tower libertarian-assumption objection.[61] Even if the majority did claim that the philosopher and athlete cases reflected equality, that would not make it so. If most ancient Greeks or early twenti-eth-century southern-state Americans described the master–slave arrangement as one of equality that would not and should not satisfy egalitarians. The emphasis on merit in particular is woefully unreflec-tive, relying in large part on the scepticism about natural variations in ability (disabilities excepted) mentioned above and a confused notion of responsibility (with which it is often conflated). A sounder, fuller conception of responsibility, taken together with equality, reveals the natively untalented, with their disadvantages for which they are not responsible, to be the closest thing to slaves in developed countries in the twenty-first century. Little surprise, then, that the population of those countries sees no injustice in their treatment. Here luck egali-tarianism's anti-conservatism is especially evident.

7. Concluding Remarks

With a notable exception, the findings of this chapter coincide with my initial intuitions about egalitarianism. The positive findings regarding the substantive egalitarianism of the various forms of outcome egalitarianism and equality of opportunity, and the negative findings regarding the substantive egalitarianism of utilitarianism, right libertarianism, 'official' Dworkinian equality of resources, and prioritarianism all ring true. The one result which I would not have anticipated was the non-substantively egalitarian character of both the responsibility-sensitive and responsibility-insensitive variants of envy-test equality. These had, I thought, shown many of the signs of being strongly egalitarian. In particular, they have a tendency towards levelling down.

I am now comfortable with the idea that equality of resources is not substantively egalitarian. The true severity of the implications of the problem I mentioned in 1.8 – that envy-test equality actually fails to offer equivalent options – was not reflected by my initial intuitions. The levelling down present in envy-test equality is a different variety from that found in, say, equality of welfare, because it is dependent on continuing envy. Given non-equivalency of options, envy-test level-ling down may be a notably non-egalitarian example of the phenom-enon. The levelling down may not actually be penalizing the better off but rather those who experience no envy merely because they are unfortunate enough to have a meagre income and wealth together with expensive tastes in a society where the only hypothetical offers on the table are much better, except for the fact that they involve an unacceptable change of gender or fundamental, character-altering change of taste. Given the possibility of this kind of example, I think my initial intuition was mistaken.

In satisfying both of the first two conditions for substantive egalitarianism, equality of opportunity succeeds where utilitarianism, right libertarianism, prioritarianism, and three versions of Dworkinian equality of resources fail. The remarks at the end of the previous section do, I hope, give some plausibility to the suggestion that the equality pursued by luck egalitarians may be truly valuable in an egalitarian way. They are really only the beginning rather than the end of the assessment of luck egalitarian's ability to meet the third condition. This topic is pursued much further in the next chapter where luck egalitarianism's claim to be truly egalitarian is defended against a wide variety of challenges. Thus far, luck egalitarianism's claim to be substantively egalitarian looks to be strong, though certainly not beyond dispute.

I will conclude with a few remarks regarding the status of substantive egalitarianism and the three conditions. My intention is to capture our intuitive sense of those theories or principles that are properly worthy of the description 'egalitarian'. Further general specification is, I think, hard to give, given both the ubiquity of the rhetoric of equality[62] and the need to steer clear of merely offering a list of 'certified egalitarian' stances in advance. But a little can be said about the intuitive underpinnings of the three conditions.

The first condition captures something which I think is often assumed, but less often said, by egalitarians.[63] An egalitarian theory's distribution is one which is not only equal but also equal for *egalitarian reasons* – reasons, that is, to do with the intrinsic moral value of persons facing certain circumstances relative to others' circumstances. Utilitarians and others are keen to point out that their theories will, given plausible empirical conditions, return equal distributions but egalitarians have always been suspicious about the egalitarianism of such theories, even if such conditions were to hold. This condition explains that suspicion.

The second condition reflects the typically egalitarian notion of *inclusiveness*. The formal property of equality says nothing at all about which entities the equality should hold between. But egalitarians insist that all persons are to be considered, and considered equally, merely by virtue of their humanity. This universal and humanistic idea is incorporated in the second condition.

The third and final condition provides the space in which all the egalitarian values not accounted for by the first two conditions may be expressed. As such, little justification needs to be given for its intuitive importance. If the first two conditions describe the form of substantive equality, the third condition describes its substance. The relevant values may demand that persons have the means to live their lives, and/or that their lives are actually lived well; it may or may not make provision for responsibility or desert. This is roughly what Dennis McKerlie means when he discusses 'substantive equality in the conditions of people's lives: not just political equality, or equality in the sense of having the same set of basic rights, but equality with respect to the opportunities open to them, or the resources available to them, or in the quality of their lives themselves'.[64] The third condition allows debate over these issues to proceed, and for several satisfactory accounts to emerge. But I reserve the phrase 'substantive equality' for accounts which also meet the first two conditions, ensuring that the potentially vast scope of that debate stays in strictly egalitarian territory.

Notes

1　Flew 1981, 29, 59; Temkin 1993, 13; 2003, 62; but cf. Kagan 1999, 299.
2　Dworkin 1977, 180–2, 227, 272–3; 1978, 125.
3　See Waldron 1991, 1358–62.
4　See Sen 1992, 24; Kymlicka 1990, 4–5.
5　See Rawls 1999a, 112–18; Hare 1997, 219–21; Raz 1986, 218.
6　Rakowski 1991, 19.
7　Sen 1992, 12.
8　Dworkin 1977, 179–83; 1983; Nagel 1979, ch. 8; Sen 1992, ch. 1.
9　Sen 1992, 13.
10　Williams 1962, 111.
11　Westen 1982, 542.
12　Westen 1982, 539–40, footnote suppressed.
13　Westen 1990, 127.
14　Peters 1997, 1223, original emphasis. See also Peters 1996, 2062; Raz 1986, 225; Westen 1990, 74.
15　Peters 1997, 1224; see also Peters 1996, 2063–4.
16　Aristotle 1995, 103; see also Aristotle 1954, bk5, ch. 3.
17　Peters 1997, 1227.
18　Peters 1997, 1212.
19　The cases in which it 'collapses into incoherence' are (for our purposes) uninteresting cases involving infinite supply; see Peters 1997, 1245–54.

20 Peters 1997, 1232.
21 This issue is taken up in Chapter 6.
22 This was put to me by Jon Quong and, independently, by Richard Arneson.
23 Temkin 2003, 63.
24 Dworkin 1981, 185. Dworkin probably thinks that this is a necessary task for anyone who is interested in devising a theory of justice, as opposed to merely a task for the egalitarian, as he explicitly refuses to draw a distinction between egalitarianism and non-egalitarianism here.
25 On prudential value, see Chapter 2, note 41 and the attached text.
26 Nozick 1974, 150–5.
27 Of course, the egalitarian may well hold that the most arresting inequality concerning baseball players is the (undeservedly) huge economic inequality between them and the vast majority of the rest of the society. But that is a separate issue.
28 The case is from Scully 1974.
29 Scully 1974, 261.
30 Rae 1981, 9, original emphasis.
31 See Vlastos 1962.
32 See section 6 below.
33 Waldron 1991, 1352; see also Sen 1992, 16.
34 Nozick, of course, styles his theory as an alternative to patterned theories such as equality; see Nozick 1974, chs 7 and 8. A Nozickian might nevertheless present his theory as weakly egalitarian in the way I mentioned earlier, without thereby diminishing his commitment to historical entitlement.
35 Some theories – left libertarian theories – may be less wedded to the libertarian tradition – or more accurately, less wedded to particular interpretations of Lockean libertarianism; see, for example, Steiner 1994; Otsuka 2003. They might be viewed as drawing from the libertarian and from the egalitarian traditions. Nozick's theory obviously does not fall into this category. For discussion of left libertarianism, and its relation to egalitarianism, see Fried 2004; 2005; Vallentyne et al. 2005.
36 Rawls 1999a; 1996. Rawls would distribute some goods in a strictly egalitarian fashion and some in a broadly prioritarian fashion.
37 To simplify, I have presented the case as though there were two homogeneous groups. In such a case, the percentage difference is probably the appropriate measure of inequality; see Oppenheim 1970. In real world cases, where there are as many relevant positions as there are persons, measuring inequality is more complex. The gist of it is suggested by Rae et al.'s definition of 'relative equality' as meaning 'that one allocation is more nearly equal than another, by being more extensive or

more intensive or both' (Rae 1981, 106, emphasis suppressed). This is to be contrasted with 'absolute equality', by which is meant 'that every pair of individuals (or blocs) who are supposed to be equal at all are fully equal' (Rae 1981, 105, emphasis suppressed). In the definition of relative equality, 'more extensive' means involving more persons, while 'more intensive' means that, for a given pair of persons, absolute equality is more closely approximated. For further discussion of measures of inequality see Temkin 1993; Carter 2001.

38 See Flew 1981, 29–31.
39 Rawls 1999a; 1996.
40 Scanlon 1975, 197; Van Parijs 1995.
41 Weirich 1983; Nagel 1991, 68, 73; Parfit 1996. An alternative way of combining leximinism and utilitarianism is suggested by Vallentyne 2000.
42 Frankfurt 1988; Anderson 1999; Crisp 2003.
43 Frankfurt 1988; Crisp 2003. Elizabeth Anderson is unusual in presenting her sufficiency-based theory as egalitarian. This characterization is challenged in Knight 2005 and Chapter 4 below. My arguments suggest, among other things, that this form of sufficientarianism would not satisfy the third condition for substantive egalitarianism.
44 See Tungodden 2003.
45 The Pareto principle – or the 'principle of efficiency', as Rawls styles it – plays a key part in Rawlsian arguments for the difference principle. See Rawls 1999a, ch. 2; cf. Barry 1989, ch. 6; Kymlicka 1990, ch. 2; Cohen 1995; Shaw 1999. See also the Conclusion of this book.
46 Nagel 1979, 110; 1991, ch. 7.
47 Nagel 1991, 68–9.
48 Rawls 1999a, 65–6.
49 Rawls 1999a, 86–7.
50 Cohen 1995, 160. Note that Cohen construes the Pareto argument, 'as suggested by John Rawls and elaborated by Brian Barry', to encompass the move from equal opportunity to equality as well as the move from equality to the difference principle. Given that this first move is an argument for equality, I assume that Cohen thinks that it is the second move – involving a Pareto-optimal shift of attention from relativities to absolute conditions (and particularly those of the worst off) – that might make egalitarians rethink their position.
51 Richard Arneson, for example, incorporates responsibility considerations into a prioritarian view. I discuss this position in Chapter 6.
52 The earliest explicit discussions I am aware of are Weirich 1983 and McKerlie 1984.
53 Nagel 1979, 107; Hare 1997, 224–5.
54 An alternative way of understanding equality of resources also shows it to fail the first condition. Suppose the circumstances in question are the

presence or absence of envy. In that case, the fact that William envies someone else's resources is no reason for the resources of relevantly identically positioned Mary to be altered such that she envies someone. Even if William is envy free, the reason for making Mary envy free has nothing to do with William's envy freeness.

55 See the conclusion of this chapter.
56 Hinton 2001, 79.
57 Hinton 2001, 80.
58 Scheffler 2003a, 32–3, footnote suppressed; see also Scheffler 2005, 9–10.
59 Scheffler 2003a, 33.
60 For evidence of this and related discussion see Marshall et al. 1999; Swift 1999; Miller 1999.
61 See Knight 2006a, 176–7, and 5.4 below.
62 Westen 1982; 1990.
63 Cf. Peters 1997, 1224 n.30; Greenawalt 1997, 1268.
64 McKerlie 1996, 274.

4

Insult and Injury

1. Introductory Remarks

Despite its prominence and many internal disputes, luck egalitarianism had, until the late 1990s, failed to attract high-profile external criticism from an egalitarian perspective. This changed, however, with the publication of Elizabeth Anderson's thought-provoking article 'What Is the Point of Equality?'.[1] A fixed conviction of egalitarian justice is, in Ronald Dworkin's terms, that a government treats all its citizens with equal concern and respect.[2] Anderson arrestingly claims that luck egalitarianism fails to express equal concern and respect for individuals. Contemporary egalitarian philosophy is consequently not only objectionable to conservatives but embarrassing to egalitarians.

She is not alone in making these claims. Several writers have argued that the roles of equality and responsibility in luck egalitarianism are far more problematic than its proponents suppose. According to some there is nothing particularly egalitarian about rewarding those who act responsibly and penalizing those who act less responsibly. It is claimed that luck egalitarianism's dedication to full responsibility sensitivity makes a mockery of its supposed commitment to equality. That same dedication makes it frivolously redistribute in some cases and turn its back when its assistance is most in need. As we shall see, some have gone even further than Anderson, and suggested that the conservative opponents of social equality will welcome luck egalitarianism with open arms.

Two broad categories of reasons for these kinds of conclusions may be distinguished. In section 3 I will examine the charge that luck egalitarianism disrespects or insults both those it compensates and those who pay for the compensation. I will call this *the insult argument*. In sections 4 and 5 I will consider *the injury argument* – that is, the allegation that luck egalitarianism illegitimately abandons or injures either certain badly off individuals or society as a whole. I will maintain that the critics' arguments in some cases fail to apply accurately luck egalitarianism to matters of public policy, and in others fail to take into account the best luck-egalitarian stances. But there is one kind of injury argument that does challenge the luck-egalitarian commitment to combating unchosen inequalities, and another that requires some clarification of the theory. In sections 6 and 7 I consider what the practical effects of luck egalitarianism and Anderson's rival account of 'democratic equality' might be, and argue that the former is more in keeping with egalitarian ideals.

Before the discussion begins in earnest, it is necessary to say something about luck-egalitarian approaches to public policy. In the next section it will be shown that some types of morally plausible luck-egalitarian policies do not require access to personal information, and that those policies that do require such access need not be as impracticable as has been suggested. These issues of policy and matters of respect are inextricably bound together, since one form of the insult argument is that luck egalitarianism expresses disrespect on account of the actions required by collection of the required information. In the subsequent section we will see how well this form of the argument fares with these policy considerations in place, and whether a form of the argument that is independent of considerations of public policy and self-respect might be made to work.

2. *Information, Behaviour, and Groups*

On a purely luck-egalitarian distributive scheme (that is, one which admits no other distributive principles) those disadvantages that are *unfair* and, as such, compensation entitling are those for which the holder is not responsible. Any disadvantages for which the holder is responsible do not give rise to compensation. This reference to responsibility is the only fundamental difference between luck egalitarianism and outcome egalitarianism. No surprise, then, that luck egalitarianism's critics urge that it is a reference that lands it in hot water when it comes to application.

It must be allowed that the reference to responsibility is an added complication. But just how much of a complication? Marc Fleurbaey, a vehement opponent of luck egalitarianism (or, as he prefers, 'equal opportunity' or 'conservative egalitarianism'), attributes luck egalitarianism's feasibility problem to the fact that 'outcomes are more easily observed than causal factors'.[3] On the face of it, this comment appears to be more or less correct: one can much more easily identify, say, the poor than the prudent, or the disabled than the lazy.

Furthermore, luck egalitarianism's problem may seem even bigger than this suggests, for the luck egalitarian policy-maker requires information not only about causality but also, if she is to know who is advantaged and who is disadvantaged, about outcomes. In other words, someone proposing equal opportunity for x faces whatever informational difficulties someone proposing equality of x faces, plus those introduced by the reference to responsibility.

Consider this concrete example. Fleurbaey suggests the following policy implication of luck egalitarianism: 'Mecca pilgrims would have to declare the origin of their faith, and those who have converted to Islam knowing the cost of travel to Mecca would pay full fare.'[4] The general idea here is that persons who deliberately develop expensive beliefs and tastes are (on certain metaphysical assumptions) responsible for holding them, and should therefore bear the costs associated with them, whereas those who are not in this way responsible for their beliefs and tastes are entitled to have those costs met either by whoever is responsible for them or by society.[5] According to Fleurbaey, the procedure he describes for distinguishing between those who are and those who are not entitled to compensation 'is not only practicably impossible, but looks ethically questionable'.[6]

The first question to be asked is whether luck egalitarianism even recognizes that there is a case for compensation *in principle*. There is an interesting internal dispute among luck egalitarians here. As we have seen, Dworkin's equality of resources suggests that we discriminate among costs according to whether they form part of an overall package that the holder *identifies* with, that is, views as preferable to the packages held by others. In the case of religiously imposed costs, identification is almost certainly present, and so we are almost always dealing with ordinary expensive tastes, for which Dworkin rules out compensation. So it seems that Fleurbaey's practical objection would be inapplicable to equality of resources, but in a way that does not reflect well on that theory. It simply demands that the pilgrims pay for their fares regardless of whether their religiously imposed cost is rooted in choice or not.

Will Kymlicka has nevertheless sought to defend a Dworkinian view that provides support for 'group-differentiated rights' grounded in ethnic and national cultures. The key move here is to describe culture as something other than garden-variety expensive taste; it is 'the context within which we choose our ends, and come to see their value, and this is a precondition of self-respect, of the sense that one's ends are worth pursuing'.[7] G. A. Cohen, however, objects that this 'framework of choice' feature of ethnic or national culture is in fact common to a person's entire heritage. For instance, '[y]ou could not expect an individual to prepare food from scratch, with no dependence on culinary traditions'.[8] Support for expensive lifestyles appears then just as justifiable as support for expensive culture. Furthermore, Cohen argues that Kymlicka's absolute distinction between frameworks of choice and mere practices does not hold, 'for frameworks of choice may themselves be chosen, and particular choices may enfold sub-choices'.[9] You might, for example, distinguish within the 'food' framework of choice between the 'vegetarian' and 'carnalian' frameworks. Cohen argues that the framework/ practice distinction is a relative one, operating on a continuum of specificity of choice, and quite unsuited to the stark distributive role Kymlicka assigns to it.

It seems, then, that Kymlicka's key move cannot survive scrutiny, for there seems to be nothing about expensive tastes that are matters of culture, in Kymlicka's strong sense, that could possibly justify compensation for them without justifying compensation for all manner of other expensive tastes. In other words, we are back to the original choice between equality of resources and equal opportunity for welfare. As we have seen, equality of resources takes a hands-off approach to Fleurbaey's case, but what about equal opportunity for welfare? This provides the previously lacking basis for multicultural policies such as that under consideration, for, where it sees an unchosen welfare deficit (such as that suffered when a religious expense that could not have been avoided goes unmet, or met at personal cost), it sees grounds for compensation. I do not think that it is at all clear that this stance is unjust. Fleurbaey's moral objection appears to rest on the radical position that all religion-imposed costs of this kind should be met.[10] But this position is implausible. Should society really pay the airfare even if the religion was adopted precisely *because* it held the prospect of a free trip to the Middle East? Leaving aside this outlandish possibility, the injustice might issue from the attempt to meet any costs, or from the attempt to meet these particular costs. I do not see any good reason for thinking that a religious cost is something that a believer has to grin and bear, whatever the circumstances. And if we are going to discriminate among costs, it is reasonable to suggest that responsibility for them is morally relevant.[11]

The issue of feasibility is best addressed by stepping back from this particular example for the moment. There are, broadly speaking, two approaches open to the luck egalitarian. The first has at its core the observation that informational difficulties alone cannot sensibly be thought to be any grounds for rejecting a distributive principle. At worst, information shortfalls lead only to apparently luck-egalitarian policies resulting in de facto non-luck-egalitarian outcomes. If we think that some of these outcomes are bad then we are merely in agreement with luck egalitarians even if that judgement is grounded in a rival theory. Information is a purely empirical matter, and its shortfalls, however substantial, cannot undermine normative principles. It may well be, as Amartya Sen puts it in a different context, 'better to be vaguely right than to be precisely wrong'.[12]

This response is fine as far as it goes. But, unless it is backed up, luck egalitarianism runs the risk of becoming a mere philosophical curiosity. Most luck egalitarians, like political theorists in general, would sooner not see their theories confined to ivory towers. Yet that is precisely what the first response invites.

The second luck-egalitarian response is more ambitious in seeking to render luck egalitarianism applicable in practice. Even so, its starting point is the modest but necessary acceptance of the fact that we will rarely, if ever, achieve perfectly luck-egalitarian outcomes. Informational deficits are not the only reasons for this, but they are particularly prevalent ones. We simply have to do the best we can with whatever information is available at a reasonable cost (that is, a cost that does not cause more unfair inequality than may be redressed with the information). Provided that a policy results in there being fewer and less drastic unfair inequalities than all rival policies, it is the best policy.[13]

Next we may note there are reasons for thinking that the luck egalitarian is not in as bad a position as she may seem to be. In the first place, establishing equal outcomes is not quite as simple as one might imagine. Some, of course, prefer to measure outcome in terms of resources or social primary goods – call these persons resourcists for short.[14] In these cases, information is more easily acquired although there are still difficulties as some persons may make efforts to conceal their resource holdings either for personal gain (as in the case of some advantaged persons) or out of the fear of stigma (as in the case of some poor and some disabled persons). Those who define outcome in terms of welfare face some closely related problems.[15] But, on top of those, they must tackle an infamously intractable informational task. How exactly is one to measure such subjective measures of advantage as pleasure, happiness, or preference satisfaction? Clearly some outcome egalitarians will have to do more than merely count the poor and the disabled. Luck egalitarians are not committed to being welfarists, their position being defined by their responsibility sensitivity, and a resourcist luck egalitarian may well face fewer informational difficulties than a subjective-welfare outcome egalitarian.

More importantly, the policy objective of making distributions responsibility sensitive is not as hopeless as the critic would have one believe. Let us start with *information-based policies*, and return to the example of the Mecca pilgrims. Fleurbaey says that the luck-egalitarian policy he depicts is impracticable, and indeed it is. Asking the pilgrims the source of their religion is entirely possible. But members of this group may, of course, lie. The obvious solution to this problem is to do what government departments and private companies in liberal democracies already do when faced with the possibility of fraudulent claims – investigate. For instance, the history of an individual's attendance at a place of worship could be confirmed by a religious leader. There is no need to investigate every claim; sufficient checks and penalties for the risks of being caught to be generally viewed as outweighing the possible advantage may be sufficient for strongly (though not, of course, ideally) responsibility-sensitive outcomes to be secured. In the event that any such investigations were intrusive to the point that the cost imposed on the unfairly disadvantaged group outweighed the benefits, they would be abandoned in favour of other policies (see below).

It should go without saying that this kind of strategy may require a division of labour. Yet it has been suggested that luck-egalitarian health-care policy 'forces[s] health-care workers to temper their compassion with investigations and moral scrutiny of patients'.[16] But if service providers are also investigators, unfair disadvantages (for example, those resulting from a lack of health-care worker compassion) will often be unnecessarily generated. In such cases, luck egalitarianism recommends that the incompatible tasks are divided between different persons. There is no need for nurses or imams to be detectives as well.

More complex systems of information may achieve efficiency and reduce the need for investigation. Suppose that one must have acquired a certain characteristic (for example, being a Muslim) by the age of majority in order to be considered not responsible for the associated costs. Or better, that we administer several questionnaires between the point at which it appears, on the best available information, that individuals begin to be responsible and the point at which they appear to be fully responsible discounting responsibility more heavily the earlier the questionnaire. We may be able to make allowances for varying individual capabilities in a fairly cost-effective way by taking relevant test scores into account. For instance, we might start with the thought that we can reasonably hold individuals with above-average IQs responsible at an earlier age than those with below-average IQs. In the long run, customized tests, measuring whatever capabilities are necessary for responsibility, might be devised.

However we grade individual responsibility, we should be able to relate it to cost-imposing (and for that matter, benefit-bestowing) characteristics in most cases. For instance, although reliable information regarding individuals' religions and pastimes on their approach to adulthood is not presently available, this simply reflects the fact that such information does not presently have the potential to confer benefits. It would be fairly easy to make such records – after all, the United Kingdom's census does already gather information every ten years on, inter alia, the religion of every (reachable) adult in the country – and back them up with investigations where fraud is a problem. These records may also make it possible to extract future compensation from parents or from other persons who are responsible for cultivating expensive tastes in minors. Once the results are available, it would be a simple task for a civil servant or (preferably) computer to match claims for compensation against them, and issue the appropriate compensation or (in the case of fraud) penalty.

Note that there will very often be a delay between the possession and record of a characteristic and the emergence of the cost it imposes. For instance, the cost of a Muslim's first pilgrimage to Mecca occurs after both the religious belief itself and the record of it. As a consequence, it is often no easy matter to make a false claim that is even prima facie plausible. An adult convert claiming compensation for her pilgrimage could pass the formal requirement of being recorded as a Muslim when below the age of full responsibility only by her having had (or the responsible adult having had) the character and foresight to respond to questionnaires in that way when she did not actually have the appropriate belief. As it seems unlikely that many underage persons (or their parents) would be willing and able to do this, even discounting the possibility that their fraud is detected, the need for investigation is diminished.

I think that these informational techniques will quite often be efficient, in the sense of decreasing the overall level of unfair inequality. Where their intrusiveness or other effects actually increase the amount of unfair inequality, they should not be deployed.[17] Fortunately, the

128

luck egalitarian need not fall back on the first 'ivory tower' approach in all such cases.

Sometimes luck-egalitarian policies need not place so much weight on detailed personal information. Some policies, by their very nature, favour the prudent over the otherwise equally positioned negligent without any special need for periodic personal information gathering on a large scale. Where this is on account of the different actions taken by individuals, I will call these *behaviour-based policies*. Such policies will, of course, need access to some personal information – for instance, in the health-care example mentioned below, insurance documents may have to be produced – while information-based policies have clear incentive effects. The distinction is just a convenient way of describing policies that make greater or lesser demands for information gathering at the micro level. Often the excessive intrusiveness of policies at the information-intensive end of the continuum suggests that policies more towards the middle of the spectrum should be explored, and the information-based/behaviour-based policies distinction is a useful way of explaining such a shift of focus.

As we shall see later, the critics' focus has been on behaviour-based luck-egalitarian policies that would, in practice, have morally dubious consequences. A health policy that gives an equal opportunity to insure and denies assistance to uninsured accident victims is behaviour-based luck egalitarian, for this system ensures that persons' different actions (including actions regarding insurance) result in comparative advantages and disadvantages. Many reasonably feel that such a scheme is unjust in certain cases. But in most major public-policy areas there are no obvious reasons for objecting to behaviour-based luck-egalitarian schemes.[18] Indeed, many familiar policies fall into this category. The provision of low-skill, low-wage public-sector jobs favour those who are able-bodied, relatively untalented, but hard-working, while high-quality state provision of education and training, and especially increasing access to those who would otherwise lack skills, will prevent many unfair disadvantages from arising in the first place, because conscientious students will have a greater opportunity to prosper.[19] Existing equality-of-opportunity legislation regarding employment would also generally favour those who make greater efforts or better choices, especially where fairer background conditions than those currently prevalent in the world were adopted.

An important means towards such conditions would be a third kind of policy, which we might describe as *group based*. These rely even less on detailed personal information, and so are clustered at one end of a continuum that has information-based policies at the other end and behaviour-based policies around halfway. They pursue luck-egalitarian objectives by transferring assets to those groups which are on the whole unfairly disadvantaged, from those which are on the whole unfairly advantaged. Progressive income taxes, business tax, capital gains taxes, savings taxes, property taxes, and, most obviously, inheritance taxes would all work to limit the unfair advantages that are derived from variations in native talent, inherited wealth, and familial support. The proceeds could be spent on free health care, disability-allowances policies, or other schemes which primarily advantage groups with unfair disadvantages, but not in a way that could accurately be said to be contingent on the behaviour of the individual members. These policies pursue quite traditional objectives of the left, but they have a clear luck-egalitarian justification. Furthermore, they can operate with quite minimal information – perhaps no more than governments already hold – because they are not meant to be fine grained.

Other less familiar groups-based policies may be equally benign. If investigation of the origin of a cost-imposing religious belief is counterproductive in the way mentioned above, it may be appropriate to provide advantages to all believers, as a group that *tends* to be unfairly disadvantaged, not because it would be unjust to deny compensation regardless of the origin of the religion (as Fleurbaey appears to suggest), but rather because the injustice of denying compensation to the unfairly disadvantaged majority outweighs the injustice of providing compensation to the fairly disadvantaged minority. This compensation itself may also be counterproductive, at least in welfarist terms, where the believers view paying the full cost as a welcome religious sacrifice which the state should not deny them. In such cases, the luck egalitarian may, on the available evidence, decide that this identification with costs is sufficient to offset fully their usual disadvantaging character (the usual frustration of preferences or decreased happiness does not occur) in which case no further action is necessary, or alternatively that such offsetting is only partial or non-existent in which case group compensation in another form may be appropriate. For instance, a Muslim community may reject plane tickets but accept funding towards a new or improved mosque. This kind of approach may not have the potential for precision of certain information-based policies, but it does move distributions in a luck-egalitarian direction without running the risks associated with those policies. As we shall see in the next section, these risks have sometimes been taken to be very substantial indeed.

3. Respect

Anderson believes that luck egalitarianism insults individuals by distributing on the basis of paternalistic beliefs and attitudes of pity and envy, and by making intrusive and stigmatizing judgements about responsibility. To consider the charge of paternalism, more context is required. This will be provided in sections 4 and 6.2; the charge itself will be briefly discussed in the latter. The other charges will be assessed in this section, beginning with the claim that luck egalitarianism requires an unacceptable level of intrusion into people's lives. While most of the focus will be on the disadvantaged victims of bad brute luck, the alleged insult to the relatively lucky will be briefly considered at the close.

According to Anderson, luck egalitarianism, in compensating the disabled, the untalented, and the unattractive, *'raises private disdain to the status of officially recognized truth'*.[20] Sheer rhetoric aside,[21] two arguments are offered here. She says, firstly, that 'general knowledge of the grounds upon which citizens laid claim to special aid would be stigmatizing'.[22] Let us grant what is far from certain, that there is common knowledge of the grounds of compensation and that citizens are able to apply these criteria accurately enough to establish who gets compensation and why they get it. The sensible luck egalitarian's response is to take this into account when deciding whether and to what extent to compensate different groups of people. General judgements about the likely causes of stigmatization would have to be made, but these seem unobjectionable because their purpose is to prevent unnecessary stigmatization. If it is judged that the non-negligent worse off would be worse off still (in terms of whichever luck-egalitarian metric is favoured) were they to be compensated, then the compensation will be withheld. But the stigmatization may be part of a bundle of measures that, overall, improves the situation of the stigmatized individual and/or unfairly disadvantaged persons generally.[23] In the case of the ugly and socially awkward, it may well be the case that, by and large, the social stigma exceeds the benefits of compensation. If so, the government simply would not compensate these people. In the case of the disabled and the long-term unemployed the social stigma of compensation would often be outweighed by the benefits of compensation, which may allow far more fulfilling lives.

So, even if we grant the conditions of stigmatization, it is unclear how this adds up to an argument against a luck egalitarianism that is sensitive to the danger of stigmatization.

These points can be further amplified by considering a related objection to luck egalitarianism put forward by Jonathan Wolff. Wolff identifies three ways in which citizens' perception of their respect standing (the extent of others' respect for them) can be undermined: first, a failure of common courtesy; second, a failure of trust, particularly found where there is the implication of unfair personal gain; third, 'shameful revelation', where information is revealed that reduces respect standing. While observing that existing welfare systems often fail to extend common courtesy and trust to citizens, Wolff grants that a luck-egalitarian system need not do so.[24] He argues, however, 'that collecting the type of data required to implement an opportunity conception of fairness requires shameful revelation'.[25] Take the example of the claim for compensation of a person who is unemployed despite there being a favourable labour market:

> [T]hink how it must feel – how demeaning it must be – to have to admit to oneself and then convince others that one has not been able to secure a job, despite one's best efforts, at a time when others appear to gain employment with ease. This removes any last shred of dignity from those already in a very unfortunate position. If benefits were unconditional one could at least maintain the belief (and with it one's self-respect) that one was unemployed at least in part through choice, whether or not this belief would stand detailed examination . . .[26]

This criticism is undoubtedly more effective against resourcist luck egalitarians than it is against welfarist luck egalitarians.[27] Even if all unfair resource inequalities have been removed, a distribution remains unjust in egalitarian terms if other important aspects of people's lives remain unfairly unequal. Any theory of justice that is prepared completely to disregard how it actually feels for people to live their lives is, I believe, faulty; Wolff's example brings this out well enough. But given that the argument is directed against luck egalitarianism itself, it is only reasonable to ask how damaging it is to the more robust welfarist luck egalitarianism.

The answer is 'not very'. The fatal flaw of the criticism is its failure to account for the way in which welfare, on any plausible understanding, accommodates self-respect. Even where the value of self-respect is only instrumental, it is crucial nevertheless. People will almost always experience more pleasure, be happier, have their preferences better satisfied, and so on, when their respect standing has not been undermined in the ways Wolff describes. If, contrary to my view, it was felt that respect standing had been shown to trump welfare on any of the usual definitions, we could, in any case, redefine welfare in such a way that respect standing was a prominent component of it. Whether the value of respect standing is instrumental or constitutive, examples which are supposed to show a luck-egalitarian policy in conflict with equality and justice tend actually to show a policy with luck-egalitarian pretensions in conflict with equality, justice, and luck egalitarianism. If the policy Wolff describes has the effect of making the worst off even worse off in terms of welfare, and if we assume, reasonably enough, that many of the worst off are not responsible for their status, then it does not further luck-egalitarian objectives.[28]

Perhaps the root of the confusion is revealed by Wolff's assertion that 'no one can doubt that information about talent status will need to be collected'.[29] Luck egalitarians can have that doubt, for they are not information fetishists. The decision whether or not to collect data is based solely on whether doing so will further luck-egalitarian ends; as we have seen, sometimes it will not. Decision-makers face a familiar kind of conflict. A particular data-collection exercise might enable us to identify and alleviate some unfair disadvantages but might also, on account of its intrusiveness, deepen others. But there is no problem in principle of working out when the costs outweigh the benefits. A particularly relevant factor is the likely proportion of the unemployed who have no responsibility for their unemployment. The larger this group is, the greater the costs and the smaller the benefits of intrusive investigation, since more of the unfairly disadvantaged may have their self-respect undermined by investigation, and fewer instances of unwarranted compensation would go undetected without investigation.[30] There is, then, no question of 'fairness conflicted against itself' and no danger that 'it is impossible to generate a fair distribution'.[31] A fair distribution is just one in which the luck-egalitarian ideal is most closely approximated given real-world constraints, and data collection is just one means to this end.

If the choice before policy-makers was either intrusive pseudo-luck-egalitarian policies, such as that Wolff describes, or forgetting about luck egalitarianism altogether, they would often do better to go for the latter, even were they committed to luck-egalitarian objectives. But as I noted earlier, information-based policies are not the only explicitly luck-egalitarian option. In many cases, behaviour- or group-based luck-egalitarian policies can achieve the objectives more effectively than either information-based luck-egalitarian policies or policies with other motivations. In respect of Wolff's example, were no sufficiently efficient information-gathering techniques available (that is, all available techniques do at least as much harm as good), a combination of a New Deal-type scheme of low-paid (but not as low paid as benefits) public-sector (or public-sector supported) jobs, a scheme of taxes aimed at targeting inheritance- and native talent-derived wealth, and benefits for those who cannot work, would far more certainly redress unfair inequalities than policies that lack a luck-egalitarian motivation. Wolff's objection to luck egalitarianism is really an objection to information-based policies. Where it is valid in those terms, luck egalitarians can accommodate it.

Anderson puts the main emphasis on her second argument for the claim that luck egalitarianism 'raises private disdain to the status of officially recognized truth'. This argument would hold regardless of any practical considerations, because in this case the insulting nature of luck egalitarianism is more intrinsic than it merely having stigmatizing effects. The key contention is that luck egalitarianism

> can only express *pity* for its supposed beneficiaries . . . People lay claim to the resources of egalitarian distribution in virtue of their inferiority to others, not in virtue of their equality to others. Pity is incompatible with respecting the dignity of others.[32]

Two ideas, *inequality* and *pity*, seem to be conflated here. It is, of course, true that luck egalitarians grant resources or opportunities to people in virtue of their state being unequal in some regard to that of other people. If A holds fewer resources than B then there may be a strong case for distributing resources from B to A on the ground of that inequality (assuming that the choices of A and B are not substantially the cause of that inequality). This is detached from pity in two ways. First, the attitude of those from whom compensation for bad luck would come could hardly be further from superiority.[33] As David Sobel notes, a guiding thought would be something like 'there but for the grace of God go I'.[34] The basis for offering assistance 'is misfortune due to bad luck, so there is no basis here for holding oneself superior if one happens to have experienced good luck rather than bad, and to be in the position of helper rather than beneficiary'.[35] Contrast this with the attitude under other redistributive policies, which move resources from the prudent and hardworking to the negligent and lazy.

Second, it is in any case quite unnecessary to talk about the emotions of the more advantaged, as redistributive decisions are not made by them. They are made from the impartial perspective of the state, a perspective which represents the interests of all its citizens, advantaged and disadvantaged alike. Redistribution is performed out of respect for the fundamental equality of all persons that transcends the vagaries of particular unchosen circumstances. The recognition and tackling of inequalities in these circumstances are solely for the purpose of securing the fundamental equality of those individuals. This is a matter of justice, not pity.

In response to criticism of her article, Anderson has stated that compensating the less fortunate expresses superiority only when combined with either: (a) 'compensating for misfortunes that consist in the possession of personal qualities that others find repugnant or pathetic'; or (b) 'responsibility catering', making compensation conditional on proof that the claimant is not responsible for their plight.[36]

(a) is open to interpretation, and is either too strong or too weak. It is counter-intuitively strong if it is read as making all compensation for unfavourable personal qualities the expression of pity regardless of the motive for compensation. It is too weak to support Anderson's claims if read as saying that only that compensation which is issued on the grounds that the claimant holds what others believe to be pathetic characteristics expresses pity. Even Van Parijs's proposal of 'undominated diversity', which Anderson picks out for especially harsh treatment, avoids this interpretation of (a). On this scheme compensation is issued to B where 'A's internal endowment (a vector of talents) *dominates* B's internal endowment', and where domination occurs 'if and only if every person (given their conception of the good life) would prefer to have the former to the latter'.[37] Note that the unanimity required for dominance sets as a necessary condition of compensation that B *herself* favours A's endowments to her own. Hence B's 'misfortune' does not 'consist in the possession of personal qualities that others find repugnant or pathetic' but consists in the possession of endowments that others and she herself find unfavourable. Nevertheless, it might be thought that the fact that others' opinions play a role at all is insulting. It is crucial, then, that compensation is not issued to B because others judge her endowment as pathetic, but merely because it is not *preferred* by anyone given their conceptions of the good life. A person can hold a preference for their internal endowment over another's without viewing the other's endowment as repugnant or pathetic. A necessary condition of viewing an internal endowment as repugnant or pathetic is to have a very strong preference against having it. But this condition is not sufficient as it is possible for a person to have the strongest prefer- ence against having a certain internal endowment without holding the endowment to be repugnant or pathetic. For example, this might often be the case if persons compared their own endowments against those of persons of the opposite gender, as we saw in section 1.8. We need to say that certain *attitudes* beyond mere preference (however strong) are required in order for someone to believe an endowment to be repugnant or pathetic. Perhaps these attitudes would be based on beliefs about the objective or intersubjective value of various endow- ments. At any rate, such attitudes certainly *may* be present in some of the persons whose preferences establish undominated diversity. But undominated diversity does not express pity as defined by the weaker interpretation of (a) as it is the preferences, not the attitudes, that establish whether compensation should be forthcoming. This is even more obviously true of equality of resources and equal opportunity for welfare.

I find it hard to see how (b) expresses any objectionable superiority. Its intrusion into people's lives is similar to any insurance policy that asks its claimants not to lie.[38] If the claimant's claim is honest then there are no grounds for anyone to feel superior to them as their mis- fortune is unearned and could equally well have happened to anyone. If the claim is dishonest then the claimant cannot have any legitimate complaint with the procedure.

The flip side of Anderson's claim that luck egalitarians insult the disadvantaged by pitying them is her claim that the disadvantaged make their claim for redistribution from the advantaged in terms of *envy*. She is emboldened by the use by Dworkin and others of the 'envy test', which measures a fair distribution of resources as one in which no individual favours anyone else's bundle of resources to her own. Anderson states:

> Envy's thought is 'I want what you have'. It is hard to see how such wants can generate *obligations* on the part of the envied. To even offer one's own envy as a reason to the envied to satisfy one's desire is profoundly disrespectful.[39]

This may be true, but no luck egalitarian suggests that envy generates obligations. Dworkin avers that Anderson confuses the 'psychologi- cal and technical economic senses of "envy"'.[40] The latter sense, he says, indicates a preference for a good, while the former adds to this a feeling of entitlement to that good. This cut does not seem to be quite right, for one can envy without feeling entitled. I can envy your flashy new car while acknowledging that you can afford it only because you have worked harder than me your whole life. Nevertheless, it is patently untrue that luck egalitarians use envy itself to establish entitlements; those who use the envy test use it as a purely technical device that embodies an already accepted principle of justice. This principle of justice is equality which, on the luck egalitarian conception, requires that unchosen disadvantages are to be removed. This conception is quite independent of sociopsychological factors such as envy; whether anyone in actually existing society envies anyone else's share is an irrelevance.

4. Disadvantaging the Negligent

None of the claims that luck egalitarianism treats persons in an insulting manner appears to be well grounded, at least where welfare is the favoured conception of advantage. In this section and the next one we will see if the injury argument can offer more of a challenge.

As was noted in Chapter 1, Dworkin draws a distinction between *option luck* and *brute luck*. Option luck defines the consequences of gambles willingly taken in the full knowledge of their possible consequences. Brute luck defines the consequences of risks that were either unchosen, taken unwillingly, or taken without knowledge of their possible consequences. Dworkin argues that while equality requires inequalities resultant upon brute luck to be redressed, it does not require any such action to be taken in the case of option luck, provided the individuals in question had the opportunity to insure themselves against losses.[41] This is a view that has found favour among egalitarian thinkers.[42]

Anderson takes the effects this luck-egalitarian view justifies to be objectionable to the egalitarian on several counts. I will consider them in two broad categories. In this section I will present the first, which is 'the problem of *abandonment of negligent victims*' and related problems.[43] Suppose someone is offered the chance to insure against injury but chooses not to and is subsequently severely injured in an accident. Anderson says that the luck egalitarian refuses assistance even if that results in death. Similar cases concern those who choose to live in hazardous areas without insurance, and are consequently left homeless when nature devastates their homes, as well as those who undertake hazardous work without insurance, and are therefore denied medical treatment when they come to harm.[44] In each case the state has to decide whether to assist someone who is in great need but who is attributively responsible for that need.

Fleurbaey asks us to picture the case of Bert, who enjoys riding his motorbike without a crash helmet, and does so even though he knows the risks of doing so. Bert causes an accident which leaves him with an injury that will lead to his death unless he undergoes an expensive operation that, being uninsured, he cannot afford. Fleurbaey offers this commentary on the case:

> If you freely and deliberately make the slightest mistake that can put you in a very hazardous situation, a society complying with equal opportunity [for advantage, for example] will quietly let you die . . . It is not only whether Bert is responsible or not which matters, but also the amount of welfare loss he is about to suffer following his mistake. Admittedly, his punishment is indeed proportional to the degree of risk he has chosen, and he had envisioned the possible consequences of what he did and could have taken precautions against them. However, I believe that our ethical intuition may lead us to consider that the scale of penalties must not be so harsh.[45]

The obvious luck-egalitarian strategy in the face of negligent-victim cases is indeed the *hard-nosed response* anticipated by Anderson and Fleurbaey.[46] Its rationale might be developed a little further than they suggest, drawing on arguments parallel to those I ventured with regard to differential natural endowment cases in the previous chapter. The weight of popular opinion is neither here nor there as regards justice and, without it, the critic's 'ethical intuition' looks to be no better supported than the hard-nosed luck-egalitarian's intuition. To (over-)extend the analogy tentatively put forward in 3.6, are not negligent victims such as Bert the slave-masters of our age, extracting benefits (medical treatment) by acting improperly?

But I find such arguments unconvincing in negligent-victim cases. There is no epistemological confusion in this case parallel to that caused by the scepticism over differential natural endowments in the other case. To be sure, these common moral intuitions may still be mistaken but we have less reason to discount them. More to the point, I simply do not believe that justice permits the state to act as a 'Bad Samaritan'.[47] This is because basic needs are so important and, against that, the cost of satisfying them often small in moral terms. Assuming that the opportunity cost of performing Bert's operation is not too great, he should get it. To be sure, this is just a moral intuition but it is one that I do not believe luck egalitarianism can shake us out of.

The luck egalitarian may respond by denying that circumstances of the kind envisaged will occur, or are likely to occur. A simple way of doing this would be to stipulate that, as rational beings, individuals would not forego insurance in such circumstances when the consequences of doing so would be so catastrophic. But it may be rejoined that justice requires us to cope with people as they are, which is sometimes irrational. There would be no negligent-victim cases if everyone behaved responsibly but, if luck egalitarianism is viable only under such conditions, it is not very interesting.

Dworkin offers a more sophisticated response that seeks to show that the community would provide protection against such individual catastrophes. It turns on the claim that a good society would ensure that a public-health scheme was in place. He notes that 'a decent society strives to protect people against major mistakes they are very likely to reject'.[48] Of course, society could do this on an ad hoc basis, providing negligent victims with treatment as they appeared. But this is to invite free-riding from the negligent: 'when someone fails to buy any personal accident insurance, and is therefore unable to afford medical care when needed, costs are born by the rest of the community'.[49] The community would therefore prevent free-riding while treating all in need through a health scheme funded through taxation.[50]

Anderson attempts to resist this kind of reasoning by asserting that the kind of thinking that will not permit someone to die in the street however irresponsible they are is alien to luck egalitarians.[51] None of the theorists Anderson identifies as luck egalitarians, however, could fairly be said to hold this position. Aside from Dworkin's social-insurance scheme, Richard Arneson suggests that mandatory contributions to pension schemes are justified to prevent the imprudent suffering in old age, while Van Parijs advocates a minimum basic income which under most circumstances would prevent anyone from falling into dire straits.[52] These theorists are not only in principle open to the idea of protecting the would-be imprudent even when doing so breaches the demands of strict luck egalitarianism, but explicitly propose social policies that provide safety nets for such persons.

Rakowski and Roemer, on the other hand, seem to come close to the hard-line position that Anderson criticizes. As Anderson makes much of, Rakowski insists that, after a natural disaster, 'losses, as instances of nasty option luck, would be born solely by the owner, who might or might not have insured against such hazards'.[53] But it is clear that Rakowski is articulating the full implications of unbridled luck egalitarianism without taking a stand on whether or not it should sometimes be checked. Thus, he writes that '[t]here may be sound paternalistic reasons for not allowing people to dispense with health and accident insurance altogether'.[54]

Roemer proposes to establish the extent to which individual smokers who have developed lung cancer are responsible for their smoking.[55] Anderson claims that 'Roemer's plan leaves people vulnerable to such a deprivation of their capabilities that they cannot function as an equal.' [sic][56] This is an unsympathetic reading. Roemer proposes only 'to apply these ideas [about responsibility] to decide the amount that society should pay of a person's medical expenses'.[57] It is apparent that he is addressing the question of how medical expenses should be split between patient and state. Anderson's quite different question of what to do with individuals who are to some extent responsible for their lung cancer and who *cannot* pay the expenses attached to that responsibility is simply not considered. Anderson reads Roemer's answer to his question as an answer to her question. But there are good reasons to think that his answer would be different where the question changes from one about money to one about lives, because that change is morally significant.[58]

Anderson's first type of injury argument suggests that the imprudent should not be abandoned. But as this is not something any of her stated targets have proposed, her argument may appear to address positions held only by straw men. Yet it remains to be seen how far luck egalitarianism in pure form – construed as meaning, say, equal opportunity for welfare – is consistent with assisting negligent victims. It may be that the best-known luck egalitarians have always been willing to restrict the scope of responsibility sensitivity in certain areas.[59]

As we have already seen, Dworkin does not consider himself a luck egalitarian, and many aspects of his theory do not have very much to do with responsibility or equality. The argument for public health care mentioned a few paragraphs previously continues in this vein. In the first place, it assumes that a good society would assist negligent victims. This may not be particularly controversial, generally speaking, but it is not obvious how this is consistent with responsibility sensitivity. The connection between this assumption and the conclusion is the need to prevent free-riding. But luck egalitarianism does not give us any particular reason for opposing this type of free-riding. To the pure luck egalitarian, somebody's choice to pay somebody else's medical bills is a choice like any other. As such, it results in no wrong, regardless of whether it increases or decreases inequality.

Does this argument show that luck egalitarianism is inconsistent with any substantial system of public health care? Surely not. If the state makes health insurance compulsory by funding a public health service through taxation, there is not necessarily an inequality of health care nor, as regards health coverage, any differential exercise of responsibility.[60] There is therefore nothing in the principle of equal opportunity for welfare that requires persons to be given the choice to opt out of health insurance. Moreover, under a more laissez-faire system it cannot simply be assumed that individuals are responsible for their failure to arrange health insurance. There may be economic and psychological barriers which undermine non-insured persons' responsibility for their circumstances. Universal health care may be a much surer way of matching levels of health care to levels of responsibility. There is, at any rate, no reason to think that the advent of luck egalitarianism would leave persons in Bert's position to die.

Although excessively harsh treatment of negligent persons is not actually implied by pure luck egalitarianism, such treatment cannot be said to conflict with it. Luck egalitarianism is still in principle open to the charge of Bad Samaritanism.

5. Disadvantaging the Non-Negligent

The first of Anderson's objections to denying compensation to those with bad option luck focuses on the *extremity* or *disproportionality* of this position. The objection does not itself involve any doubt about luck egalitarianism's assessment of the persons in question as less deserving or less entitled to resources than others on account of their behaviour. It rather suggests that it is unreasonable to offer no protection whatsoever to certain persons, even if they are dis-praiseworthy. Given the limited scope of the objection in both theory (see the next chapter) and practice (see the next section), it does not threaten luck egalitarianism in any fundamental way.

Anderson's second type of objection to denying compensation for bad option luck is potentially more damaging, because it claims that luck egalitarianism punishes certain types of prudent or even laudable behaviour. Her most biting argument here concerns the *'vulnerability of dependent caretakers'*.[61] This highlights the supposed reliance of luck egalitarians on social systems that presume the male economic agent as the norm. As a result of this reliance,

Anderson claims that luck egalitarians treat those who choose to devote themselves to caring for children, the elderly, and the infirm, and who consequently command little or no market wage, on the same terms as those who choose to be lazy. This might mean either that a large group of people who work hard at a socially valuable job are pauperized, or that, in Van Parijs's case, they are provided with a level of income they could have secured without working at all.[62] Anderson writes: '[p]eople who want to avoid the vulnerabilities that attend dependent caretaking must therefore decide to care only for themselves. This is egalitarianism for egoists alone.'[63]

I think Anderson is right to say that luck egalitarianism, as it has been developed, has failed to come fully to terms with feminist critiques of markets. But I believe she moves too quickly to the conclusion that 'it is not clear whether luck egalitarians have any basis for remedying the injustices that attend [caretakers'] dependence on male wage earners'.[64] One way out for the luck egalitarian is to *regulate markets by social value*. Dworkin notes that '[t]here is no such thing as a "natural" market: we use "market" to designate a range of economic mechanisms all of them regulated and therefore defined in some way'.[65] He makes these comments in the context of refuting the view that someone with wealth-generating talent should be rewarded with whatever earnings the market allows; their scope is clearly not limited to a recommendation of checks on monopolistic practices and other purely capitalistic market regulations. I see no reason for thinking that luck egalitarians would be opposed to rewarding those who perform a socially valuable activity that is underpaid by the market with remuneration at a level above that set by the unregulated market.

The rationale for this regulation is provided by Anderson herself when she 'wonders how children and the infirm are to be cared for, with a system that offers so little protection for their caretakers against poverty and humiliation'.[66] She may be correct to urge against Rakowski that, in a market economy characterized by a division of labour, everyone is benefited by the next generation's development.[67] Public funding of care for the infirm could be justified in a similar way as health care, that is, by reference to the need to provide such care without rewarding free-riding. Given the social value of having children and having the infirm looked after by well-motivated caretakers, those caretakers are in a good position on a market regulated by social value. Obviously this market regulation would amount to a transfer of earnings from those with an income to caretakers. This apparent infringement of market choices is justified on the grounds that, without it, those persons performing socially valuable activities would be treated unequally. A society may pick out the choice to perform these socially valuable activities as one type of individual choice that it is prepared to subsidize. I think this is quite consistent with Dworkin's belief that 'people should pay the price of the life they lead, measured in what others give up in order that they can do so'.[68] The choice to be a caretaker is a choice that benefits society; without it, the cost of caring for children and the infirm would be born by society. This choice can therefore be rewarded on luck-egalitarian principles.

How, then, might luck egalitarians set the level of socially funded compensation for caretakers? Dworkinians might say that the risk of being abandoned as a caretaker is sufficient to warrant insurance on the hypothetical insurance market to ensure (via taxation) a certain level of income for caretakers above that paid to the unemployed. Welfarists could treat the choice to be a caretaker in the same way they treat uncultivated expensive tastes, providing compensation for any welfare deficit resulting from the choice. To be sure, wage earners will pick up a smaller pay packet in consequence of such measures, but this is also the result of all other redistributive measures. A valid complaint on this score would have to show that the redistribution is unjustified but Anderson, if she is to be consistent, is committed to the contrary view. Distributions remain sensitive to choice, as luck egalitarians demand, but the institutional background of those choices is modified in such a way as to reward worthy choices that would otherwise go unrewarded.

Anderson raises a valid point, then, in highlighting some luck egalitarians' bias towards unregulated market choices.[69] But her strong conclusion can be avoided when luck egalitarianism is flexible to the regulation of markets better to represent social value. Recognition of the components of social value requires no modification of the central ideas of luck egalitarianism, because the very young and the infirm are not responsible for their need for assistance, and are hence entitled. A further point of clarification is needed in the case of the former group, since luck egalitarianism is often explicitly formulated to avoid any discussion of them. Some principle giving value to procreation up to a certain level is needed to explain why parents (and mothers in particular) are not to be held responsible for all the costs associated with their children. Such a principle cannot really be drawn from either luck egalitarianism or egalitarianism generally, but nor is there any reason to think there will be any conflict here. I will not name a particular principle, but there are many that would serve perfectly well for present purposes.

A particular subcategory of dependent caretakers requires a different response from luck egalitarianism. The market regulation proposed above is premised on a requirement for dependent caretakers. While there will be some such requirement on a social level, it may be that there is no need for a particular individual (typically a woman) to care for a dependent. She may be wealthy enough to be able to afford to pay a well-qualified and motivated childminder or careworker, or it may be that society, laudably, provides such services without charge. Yet many women will nevertheless wish to handle the care of a dependant personally. Should society provide such women with financial and other assistance, even though it has no manifest need for their choice?

Andrew Mason argues that such 'career-sacrificing mothers' are, indeed, entitled to assistance on luck-egalitarian grounds. But why should their choice be treated differently from other choices? The answer is not, Mason holds, just the extensive socialization that forms the backdrop to the mother's decision. Socialization focusing on the norm that *parents* ought personally to look after their children would be insufficient grounds for saying there was injustice in parents bearing the cost of their child-rearing choices. Mason suggests that one of the ingredients of injustice in real-world career-sacrificing mother cases is 'the sexism of the norms which shape this process'.[70] It is this combination of socialization and *unjust* norms which generates the case for assistance, perhaps in the form of making recruitment and promotion procedures more favourable to those who look after their children.

It seems to me that Mason's argument is on the right track, but needs to be fleshed out a little further. Mason does not explain why norms of gender socialization such as 'mothers ought to personally look after their children' are unjust *according to luck egalitarianism in particular*. Any relevant injustice must issue from an inequality not arising from differential exercise of responsibility. Clearly, when we are talking about socialization at the early stages of life, there is plenty of potential for (relevantly) unchosen interpersonal variation, but the difficulty concerns the presence or absence of inequality. Perhaps for income and wealth egalitarians, it would seem obviously true that 'mothering norms' are disadvantaging, because they are likely (absent special state involvement) to result in an income or wealth disadvantage. But both the sophisticated luck-egalitarian theories discussed in Part 1 of this book are concerned with income and wealth only instrumentally (as things that might affect subjective resource or welfare levels), or perhaps in practice, as easily overridden proxies.

If we focus on equal opportunity for welfare in particular, it seems that two countervailing considerations in particular come into play: the possible welfare advantage for a mother derived from acting in accord with gender norms and spending time with her child, and the possible welfare disadvantage of counterpart 'breadwinning norms' among men, on account of the resulting loss of leisure time and stress. Now, there are also welfare disadvantages for the career-sacrificing mother deriving from the day-to-day inconveniences of child rearing, the loss of leisure time, and the (presumed) loss of earnings so, on balance, it seems that the mothering norm is probably disadvantaging and hence unjust. This extension of Mason's argument seems to yield similar conclusions to his original, but with a little less certainty, because the welfare effects of socialization are complex. The practical proposal of intervention in the labour market, to the benefit of career-sacrificing mothers (and others who choose to look after dependants) seems well grounded, and some disadvantage to employers and the rest of the labour force is justifiable. But the above argument suggests that there is a balance to be struck, since career-sacrificing mothers are not so surely or deeply disadvantaged relative to those who have chosen not to care for dependants that the latter's relative position can be disregarded.

Unlike the dependant caretakers arguments, other arguments for the position that luck egalitarianism injures the non-negligent do focus on those who suffer bad option luck. Anderson maintains that the victims of bad brute luck might be ignored, as an insurance scheme such as Dworkin's may offer no compensation to some congenitally disabled people:

> [P]eople who have an extremely rare but severe disability could be ineligible for special aid just because the chances of anyone suffering from it were so minute that it was *ex ante* rational for people not to purchase insurance against it.[71]

I must confess, I find this criticism perplexing. It is true that the likelihood of suffering a rare disease may be minute. But the rarer the disease, the cheaper the insurance. Thus, it would surely be rational to insure in these circumstances: the danger of contracting the disease may be tiny, but its effects would be disastrous were one uninsured, while the cost would be so infinitesimal that it would never be noticed.[72]

The final argument against luck egalitarianism to be considered in this section focuses on society as a whole rather than on the victims of any particular kind of luck. The argument, which is presented by Seana Shiffrin, has structural similarities to Wolff's argument discussed in section 3. In the new argument *autonomy*, in the sense of unfettered choice, plays a similar role to respect in Wolff's argument: 'Where the environment is permeated by cost-exaction and public spirited reminders that even many seemingly self-regarding acts have other-regarding effects, agents may feel constrained by the sense that everything they do has an impact on others and is subject to accounting'.[73] Where before, fairness was in conflict with respect, here it is in conflict with autonomy, for '[e]ven if this accounting is fair, the ubiquity of the message may nonetheless constrain or chill choice'.[74] Shiffrin recommends subsidization or accommodation of some activities in order to limit the cost-internalization that threatens everyone's freedom and their perceptions of being free. In short, '[t]he case for accommodation . . . provides some reason to reconsider a stringent commitment to . . . thoroughgoing choice sensitivity'.[75]

This argument, like several others, exposes a major weakness in resourcist luck egalitarianism. It shows that there is more to justice than resource distribution, for individual and social psychology could hypothetically be such that people did not feel free however large their resources holdings were.

That it works against welfarist luck egalitarianism is far less evident. Any plausible conception of welfare will give a major instrumental role to autonomy. People experience more pleasure, enjoy themselves more, are happier and more satisfied, and so on, when they do not feel constrained. Furthermore, if we take Shiffrin's concerns seriously, autonomy can be housed within welfare itself, in the same way as is possible with self-respect. In other words, welfare certainly tends to support autonomy and may give it a constitutive role. Welfarist luck egalitarianism is therefore very much alive to the psychological pressure that its focus on responsibility may put persons under, and policy may be adjusted accordingly.

Observe that any accommodating policies that are justified on welfarist luck-egalitarian grounds would not constitute any relaxation of responsibility sensitivity. The justification would simply be that, without accommodation, more unfair disadvantages will persist than with it, for the barriers to autonomy limit responsible individuals' welfare to such an extent that they are actually worse off relative to the non-responsible than they would be were there no attempt at advantaging them. Here there is no trade-off between luck-egalitarian fairness and autonomy: the former simply tells us how to distribute the latter (as one component of welfare).[76] Other justifications of accommodating policies may, of course, cut into luck-egalitarian objectives, but that would simply be because they invoke rival distributive principles. Shiffrin's concern is explicitly with the threat cost-internalization poses to 'the meaningfulness of the freedom that it is the aim of these [luck-egalitarian] theories to provide fair access to', but luck egalitarianism only endorses this aim, and any accommodation that might support it, insofar as this is necessary for ensuring that meaningful freedom levels correspond to levels of responsibility.[77] Luck-egalitarian accommodation would be targeted through, for instance, group-based policies that relax constraints on the actions of those who are unfairly disadvantaged, all things considered.

It remains to be added that Shiffrin appears to overstate the danger posed by cost-internalization under a responsibility-sensitive system. In all existing societies, persons are near constantly alert to the fact that their actions have effects on themselves and others, yet they are, I believe, more likely to be unfree owing to a lack of resources. If I am choosing whether to take the interesting job or the well-paid job, or whether to go on holiday or to give my money to charity, I am unlikely to be scared into unfreedom by the recognition that my choices have an impact upon my prospects, and those of others. But if I have no job options and no disposable income, my freedom may well be endangered. I see no reason why information- or behaviour-based policies need impose much more of a cost-internalization burden. Increased levels of data collection and the effects of responsibility-sensitive distribution itself may have some effect, but they are really just more of the same – many people are already subject to perform-ance reviews and performance-related pay, and many more are acutely aware of the fact that if they just worked harder they might secure a more lucrative career with which to support themselves and their families. Welfarist luck egalitarianism will in certain conditions recommend accommodation, but it is far from clear how often those conditions would hold.

It is an achievement of Anderson, Shiffrin, Wolff, and other critics that the significance of individuals' psychological make-up is unlikely to be overlooked. It is, however, equally possible to overemphasize its importance to the detriment of more traditional concerns. As Arneson notes, Wolff's proposal that justice consists in regard for both fairness and respect introduces what is from the welfarist's perspective 'illegitimate double-counting'.[78] I do not claim that such a conception of justice is theoretically flawed. But it is in urgent need of a powerful positive argument if it is to appear any more than the unfortunate upshot of a misunderstanding of the relationship between luck egalitarianism and public policy.

6. Luck Egalitarianism Applied

What, then, would luck-egalitarian policies actually mean for a society? Were luck egalitarians somehow to storm to power tomorrow, how would the social and economic structure of a developed country change? Will there really be more inequality (in the various senses that that term takes in political discourse)?

The answer to this final question is, I think, no. The contrary view is often built on shaky theoretical and empirical ground. Take one obvious instance of the former. It seems present in a complaint that Iris Marion Young makes of 'Dworkin and many other equality theorists':

> A large set of the causes of an unequal distribution of resources or unequal opportunities between individuals . . . is attributable neither to individual preferences and choices nor to luck or accident. Instead, the causes of many inequalities of resources or opportunities among individuals lie in social institutions, their rules and relations, and the decisions others make within them that affect the lives of the individuals compared'.[79]

It is true that many inequalities result from social institutions and their various effects. But so far as the luck egalitarian is concerned, however certain such institutions and effects may be, they count as bad luck for the disadvantaged individuals concerned (assuming that they did not personally create those institutions). For, in her terms, luck is just the inverse of responsibility.[80] Hence deliberately taken gambles that, by chance, turn out badly are not (the right kind of) bad luck but being under the control of a social institution that disadvantages you is bad luck and is, as such, compensation entitling.

Even where there is no sign of this error, some insist that luck egalitarianism is a recipe for inequality. Fleurbaey for one maintains that under it 'inequalities may be as large as one wants, because . . . there is nothing in this [luck-egalitarian] picture which precludes the coexistence of misery and outrageous wealth, the persistence of hierarchical social relations, and the reduction of some to the status of means to others' goals'.[81] He alleges that luck egalitarianism as usually conceived provides less assistance to the poor than 'minimal versions of the welfare state'.[82] Can this really be what egalitarianism is about? Elizabeth Anderson holds that luck egalitarianism's oversight is more drastic still: '[w]hat about inequalities of race, gender, class, and caste? Where are the victims of nationalist genocide, slavery, and ethnic subordination?'[83]

These remarks are clouded by some extremely dubious applications of luck egalitarianism. '[T]he persistence of hierarchical social relations' might be intended to mean that some form of hierarchy would reappear under luck egalitarianism, which cannot be denied (see below). But the phrase has clear overtones of social class. Yet the elimination of the intergenerational definition of life chances that continues to characterize all societies would be one of the very highest priorities of a luck-egalitarian policy-maker, for it is one of the most obvious sources of responsibility-insensitive inequalities, and of these one of the easiest to rectify. Even if some semblance of class persists for a while, and impoverished persons act less responsibly than the well-to-do, luck egalitarianism may all the same compensate the former where their actions are explained by their unfavourable education or upbringing.[84] For the same reasons, inequalities based on race, gender, and caste are equally obvious objects of luck-egalitarian concern, with the elimination of these categories – either outright or as (dis)advantage conferring – taking precedence. Can anyone imagine any more patent or grave causes of disadvantages not linked to responsibility than 'nationalist genocide, slavery, and ethnic subordination'? One could hardly choose better cases to bring out the attractions of luck egalitarianism!

Nicholas Barry has recently argued that very few real-world inequalities would slip through the luck-egalitarian net. He holds that individuals in existing societies cannot usually be held responsible for the major decisions they make in their lives on account of the limited and/or unequal options that most people face, and the shortage of information about the risks involved in taking those options.[85] Consider, for example, the case of individuals making career choices. These are 'compulsory gambles',[86] 'because future technological development and changes in demand will render some jobs obsolete'.[87] Barry holds that '[i]t does not seem fair to hold individuals responsible for their choices in such situations if they would rather not have made any decision at all'. For reasons such as these, the 'option luck category' would only really be practically useful '[i]n the more equal society that luck egalitarians envisage'.[88] For the time being, luck egalitarianism would seek to correct the vast majority of inequalities.

While Barry rightly draws attention to the important relationship between options and choices, he does not accurately describe the moral significance of the former for the latter. It is true that people in modern capitalist societies must gamble on one career or another, but the absence of a risk-free alternative does not preclude widespread judgements of responsibility. People still typically have the choice to pursue more or less risky career paths, and know they face that choice. If two persons of identical ability and potential make different career choices, and the first succeeds as a plumber while the second fails as an actor, it may be perfectly reasonable to hold these people responsible for their choices. If we suppose that, when making their choices, both persons were aware of the higher possible rewards and higher likelihood of failure associated with the second option, and that one of them decided that that gamble was worthwhile, there are not usually reasons to step in and compensate a competent risk-taking adult at the expense of more risk-averse persons. Of course, if we have good reason for believing that someone's career has not worked out as well as it might have done because of factors which were not foreseeable – there is a sudden and wholly unanticipated downturn in the demand for actors, say – compensation may be appropriate. Likewise, where similar investments pan out in spectacularly different fashions – Samuel Freeman mentions the example of two elderly couples, both of whom bought model homes in 1960, one in Palo Alto, the other in the Rust Belt[89] – some redistribution is appropriate since the scale of the changes in market conditions was not foreseeable. But career failures and poor investments are often attributable to factors, such as high competition for jobs or tough trading conditions, that it is reasonable to expect people to have taken into account.

Judgements of responsibility will also be appropriate where the initial options, and people's ability to choose between them and benefit from them, are unequal. This is obvious in the case of 'major overachievers' – persons with disadvantageous natural endowments, family backgrounds, and life options, who nevertheless secure more favourable outcomes through their efforts than those with preferable endowments, backgrounds, and options. But it applies in all kinds of cases. The luck egalitarian simply has to take the relative starting positions of different people into account when assessing their entitlements. The achievements of the initially disadvantaged will give entitlements to greater rewards than the equivalent achievements of the initially advantaged. Following this procedure would actually expand the inequalities between major overachievers and underachievers, since the former have achieved so much with so little. The general trend would be to decrease inequalities because so many of them are largely the consequences of unequal starts. But there would be no total equalization, and very many cases of continued or even expanded inequalities. Contrary to Barry's suggestion, the inequality of options does not make it inappropriate to distribute on the basis of responsibility in the majority of cases.

Some inequalities will, then, go unchecked. But once it is understood that they are not based on class, race, gender, or natural endowment, and that the upshot of unpredictable markets will be to some extent corrected for, I think they, and the hierarchies to which they are linked, are far less objectionable. Furthermore, the occurrence of major inequalities and hierarchies will be far less frequent. The most obvious sources of them, such as inherited economic and familial inequalities, will be systematically weakened or, ideally, eliminated altogether. To be sure, there will be some 'self-made millionaires' and, I suppose, some 'self-made paupers'. While I think there is some ground for egalitarian objection to such extremes, they are the exception rather than the rule, and may in any case be negated by particular interpretations of, or additions to, luck-egalitarian principles.[90] It is, in any case, apparent that a society run along luck-egalitarian lines would in all normal empirical conditions be considerably more equal, both in terms of resources and welfare, than contemporary societies.[91]

It is also worth noting that there is good reason to think that the nightmare scenario described by many opponents of luck egalitarianism, where someone has a very severe injury and no access to relatively inexpensive but vital health care on account of their irresponsibility, would *never actually happen* in an advanced industrial society ordered along luck-egalitarian lines. First, as noted previously, every advanced industrial society has a system of public health care in place, and luck egalitarianism gives, if anything, reasons for strengthening such systems. Second, it is fairly likely that even were such a system removed for some (non-luck-egalitarian) reason, charitable donations would cover all occurrences of negligent victims who could not pay their medical bills. Third, even given that responsibility is possible, doubts about individual responsibility will usually result in the provision of urgent treatment. Luck egalitarianism requires responsibility for outcomes, rather than mere responsibility for the choices that lead to those outcomes. Victims of lung cancer may be responsible for a choice (or a series of choices) to smoke but they are not responsible for their susceptibility to the disease.[92] Similarly, the seriously injured victims of road traffic accidents may sometimes be responsible for dangerous driving, but they will usually be comparatively unfortunate in that circumstances (road conditions, the behaviour of others, the innate tolerances of their bodies, the precise characters of the impacts their body suffered, and so on) meant that other dangerous drivers did not suffer such serious injuries.

Finally, even were there no public health care system, effective charity network, or local doubts about responsibility, the luck-egalitarian government would probably pay for every reasonably affordable and crucial treatment on account of doubts about responsibility itself. In the next chapter, I will argue that luck egalitarianism is best construed as being sensitive to the possibility that hard determinism or other sceptical positions on responsibility are true. Luck egalitarianism so conceived would view denying assistance a most unfavourable option even in the most seemingly obvious cases of irresponsible behaviour, on account of the chance that this denial may amount to the terrible wrong of imposing a very severe and easily prevented disadvantage on someone who is not responsible for that disadvantage. For these reasons, the practical difference between the basic needs-accommodating luck egalitarianism I describe in Chapter 6 and the conventional sort would be felt only where there was a highly improbable coincidence of certain empirical and metaphysical circumstances.

Much of the opposition to luck egalitarianism documented at the start of this section and earlier may not really be owing to its purely philosophical characteristics or even to what applying it to the letter would result in. Rather, the worry may be that, whatever luck egalitarianism *actually* requires, it may be used to support dubious social and political ends. To be specific, luck egalitarians, firstly, focus on philosophically interesting but politically irrelevant cases of distribution among individuals, taking the focus away from those significant social injustices that can actually be rectified; and secondly, justify some inequalities, encouraging political overextension. As we shall see, the first point leads into the second.

The problem, some may believe, is not that luck egalitarianism is in principle closed to undoing patently unjust social structures and practices but that it fails to accord such activity the central role it deserves. There is nothing philosophers like more than a good example, and the theorists of luck egalitarianism are no exception. Thus, they ponder what justice has to say about the claims of claret drinkers, bullfighters, gardeners, tennis players, music lovers, religious believers, fishermen, photographers, the incessantly happy, and the perpetually depressed (to name but a few).[93] This is not the traditional territory of social-justice campaigners. The focus in such cases on responsibility, choice, and luck has been marked as particularly misleading. Anne Philips claims that it encourages us to view

> [t]he cause of the bad luck [as] incidental. It no longer matters much whether it arose from genetic disorder, from racism or sexism, or the rules governing the inheritance of money; and since the cause of the bad luck is no longer the issue, there is less interest in identifying which ones are open to structural change.[94]

Luck egalitarianism has a formula for telling us what is wrong, but does not do a very good job of telling us how to put it right.

One reply to such worries is the counterpart to the 'ivory tower' strategy mentioned earlier in this chapter. We can start by accepting that, although luck egalitarianism 'possess[es] a normative programme, it is not based on an explanatory framework of any significance'.[95] Luck egalitarianism is intended only to be a general theory of distributive justice, not a detailed programme for social progression. Freeman argues that a conception of distributive justice must be concerned, as John Rawls is, with 'the specification of property rights and permissible economic relations, control of capital, limits on concentration of wealth, permissible uses of property . . .', things about which luck egalitarianism 'says nothing'.[96] But, taking a firm stance on such questions, in advance of considering empirical factors, is no more a requirement of a conception of distributive justice than is taking a firm stance on the metaphysics of responsibility. Division of intellectual labour allows that a conception of distributive justice is just concerned with principles for allocating benefits and burdens between persons, and it need not – indeed, had best not – give hostages to fortune by demanding a certain set of institutional arrangements, regardless of how these actually affect people.

That so much effort is expended on the philosophical exploration of luck egalitarianism's fine details, and so little mention made of the usual concerns of the left, does not mean that, once fully worked out, it cannot yield suitably egalitarian practical recommendations appropriate to each society. Some such recommendations have been mentioned above. Furthermore, it may be the case that, in practice, the luck egalitarian's interest in the plight of the claret-drinking, bullfighting types is minimal, given the costs associated with the invasive information gathering that may be required in these particular cases.[97] From a government's perspective, it is generally more difficult to tell if a taste in drink or a pastime is unchosen and disadvantaging than it is to tell if membership of a race, gender, or class meets these two criteria.

Nevertheless, it may be pressed that luck-egalitarian philosophers' emphasis on the theoretically most interesting but practically less significant elements of their work is itself harmful, for it may lead others to misconstrue or wilfully misrepresent the broad implications of their work. Fleurbaey makes this observation:

> In an era which witnesses a widening of the gap between the poorest countries and the affluent ones, and also of the gap between the poor and the rich in Western countries, egalitarian theorists have been mostly anxious to show that there may be substantial legitimate inequalities. It is not sure that by doing so they have managed to make equality a more acceptable goal, and egalitarianism a more respectable approach.[98]

This legitimizing tendency in egalitarian theorizing is not unique to luck egalitarians. As Fleurbaey notes, Rawls's famous difference principle has been deployed against egalitarian objectives.[99] Before the difference principle was known by that name, F. A. Hayek had argued that the position of the worst off was best improved by a capitalist economic system.[100] Is this whole move a political mistake? Does all talk of 'fair inequalities' give inequalities of all kinds a foot in the door?

This is a possibility. The adoption of certain luck-egalitarian policies in isolation from the rest of the programme could well increase social inequality. Wolff comments that, were policy-makers to read luck-egalitarian writings, they would probably come away with the message '[t]hat egalitarians, like, conservatives, now favour highly conditional welfare benefits. But in the real world this does not give us egalitarianism. Rather, it gives us Thatcherism, in which the poor are singled out for insulting levels of scrutiny.'[101] Some policy-makers may, indeed, draw these, and only these, conclusions; but if they do so, one must assume that they were conservatives to begin with. There are many other messages that the more egalitarian minded may be inclined to pick out.[102] The group-based policies mentioned earlier fall into this category, as do many information- and group-based policies – even the pilgrims' treatment would fall into this category if, as is likely, there would be no compensation under existing schemes.

These implications could have been foregrounded in luck-egalitarian writings but there is at least one good practical reason why they are not. For while everyone is anti-genocide and anti-slavery, and very many persons are opposed to inequalities based on class, race, and gender, outside of academia there are no advocates of compensation-for-unchosen-expensive-tastes, and compensation-for-less-than-average-talents has barely any more takers. Were luck egalitarians' efforts directed towards further increasing support for already popular projects they would have been wasted (except, perhaps, in forestalling academic criticism) in which case they may as well go where the argument takes them.

I accept the claim that luck egalitarianism has not made egalitarianism more respectable. But I believe that this is simply because it, like most theories of justice of twenty-five years' vintage, has attracted very little public interest. For the same reason it has done egalitarianism no harm. Yet, if my various arguments have been correct, luck egalitarianism may provide the theoretical underpinnings for progressive political programmes designed to remove those injustices that egalitarians really care about. These programmes need not be explicitly egalitarian. Indeed, in the political environment of developed countries, their proponents would doubtless do best to brand them as the moderate alternative to conservatism and the old-fashioned egalitarianism that has been so unpopular in recent decades. This is a more plausible and ingenuous strategy for luck egalitarianism, with its emphasis on both equality and individual responsibility, than it is for other egalitarian theories, which focus on the former to the exclusion of the latter. Political buzzwords, such as 'choice' and 'opportunity', appear in luck-egalitarian writings as frequently as they appear in politicians' speeches; moreover, the usage in the former setting is rarely, if ever, as strained as it is in the latter.[103] There is some reason, then, for thinking that, despite the critics' dire warnings, luck egalitarianism is the left's best hope. In the next section this claim will be supported with an examination of a well-known rival theory.

7. Democratic Equality

Earlier in this chapter I have considered, and in the main rejected, Anderson's criticism of luck egalitarianism as harsh to some and insulting to others. I will now focus on the viability of her theory of democratic equality as an egalitarian theory.

Anderson sets out three characteristics of her theory, as contrasted with the luck-egalitarian ideal of equality of fortune, that sketch a 'rough conception of equality'. I will argue that the first and third characteristics do not contrast with luck egalitarianism and that the second is inferior to the luck-egalitarian view. 'First, democratic equality aims to abolish socially created oppression. Equality of fortune aims to correct what it takes to be injustices created by the natural order.' [104] This contrast between the two theories does not exist. Democratic equality seeks to address some natural disadvantages and, as it does so as a matter of justice, it is hard to see how they can be anything but 'injustices created by the natural order'. For example, Anderson advocates allocating more resources to the disabled where this is needed to ensure their mobility.[105] And equality of fortune obviously seeks to address social injustices, advising, for example, that individuals start with an equal share of resources or opportunities rather than with a share defined by their parents' wealth and status. It is true that the two theories address themselves to different types of natural and social injustice, but this is down to their differing conceptions of equality, as we shall shortly see.

I will consider Anderson's second and third contrasts in reverse order. She claims:

> [T]hird, that democratic equality is sensitive to the need to integrate the demands of equal recognition with those of equal distribution . . . People must not be required to grovel or demean themselves before others as a condition of laying claim to their share of goods.[106]

This contrast should, I hope, appear doubtful given the arguments of section 3. Luck egalitarianism makes no demeaning demands of its citizens. Furthermore, on at least one issue, democratic equality falls foul of the charge of insulting citizens that Anderson aims at luck egalitarianism. Democratic equality seems to express pity, as is shown well by the question of the resources which are required in order for a person to appear in public without shame. In developed countries, access to frequent showers and changes of clothes are required, but elsewhere they are not. Consequently some kind of local assessment is necessary to establish what is required for people to have equal standing (in Anderson's sense). Such an assessment requires looking at those who are 'respectable' – which is to say the more advantaged – and giving the unrespectable – the disadvantaged – whatever it is that makes the respectable respectable. But such relative assessments leave democratic equality open to the charge that it insults the disadvantaged by pitying them.[107] Anderson replies that social norms are the object of assessment and 'one need not compare what the worst off have compared to the better off'.[108] But this response fails to bite as it incorrectly assumes that comparisons between the advantaged and disadvantaged must be made directly in order for the latter to be pitied. The social norms Anderson appeals to will themselves have been established by the better off, and will be held as the standard to which the worst off, being so pitiable when left to their own devices, are to be raised. On the question of insulting its citizens, democratic equality fares no better, and perhaps worse, than luck egalitarianism.

So on to Anderson's second, and for us final, contrast: 'democratic equality is what I shall call a relational theory of equality: it views equality as a social relationship. Equality of fortune is a distributive theory of equality: it conceives of equality as a pattern of distribution.' [109] There is something to this contrast, which will now be explained and assessed.

Anderson adopts Amartya Sen's 'capabilities' approach, where '[a] person's capabilities consist of the sets of functionings she can achieve, given the personal, material, and social resources available to her'.[110] Democratic equality is achieved where there is a guarantee of access to 'three aspects of individual functioning: as a human being, as a participant in a system of co-operative production, and as a citizen of a democratic state'.[111] The main contrast between this conception of equality and that of luck egalitarians is the *scope* of equality. Luck egalitarians seek to equalize their chosen good, whatever that is (resources for Dworkin, opportunity for welfare for Arneson, access to advantage for Cohen, and so on); all disadvantages in this good are therefore up for redress. Anderson, however, stops far short of this, stating that the capabilities relevant to her three aspects of functioning 'do not include all functionings or all levels of functioning'.[112]

What does upholding access to the 'three aspects of individual functioning' amount to? The first aspect merely guarantees access to food, shelter, clothing, medical treatment, and freedom of thought and movement. The third aspect guarantees rights of political participation, including the franchise and freedom of speech, and access to public spaces and services. Neither of these requirements would worry the staunchest conservative.

The second aspect guarantees (1) access to education, (2) occupational freedom, (3) 'effective access to the means of production', (4) 'the right to receive fair value for one's labor', and (5) 'recognition by others of one's productive contributions'.[113] The first two of these guarantees would, again, be unobjectionable to conservatives, while the last is purely symbolic, having no distributional effect. The third is more egalitarian, guaranteeing that able-bodied persons who are willing to work are not denied the opportunity to do so. But note that the 'effective access' requirement does nothing to challenge the kind of unequal *ownership* of the means of production experienced in contemporary societies. Consequently its egalitarian effects are limited, especially given Anderson's acknowledgement that '[t]he biggest fortunes are made not by those who work but by those who own the means of production'.[114] This impression is reinforced once the effects of the fourth guarantee are spelled out. All that Anderson tells us about fair value is that '[s]ociety may not define work roles that amount to peonage or servitude, nor, if it can avoid it, pay them [workers] so little that an able-bodied person working full time would still lack basic capabilities'.[115] It is clear that 'basic capabilities' means access to food, shelter, clothing, and the like. So from what Anderson says – and from what she does not say – 'fair value' for the labour of those at the bottom end of full-time employment could amount to less than that set by current minimum-wage laws in Britain and the United States, given that these provide for basic capabilities and some non-basic capabilities. In sum Anderson guarantees citizens at best the status of the lower working class and at worst the status of the underclass.

Now let us consider how well this accommodates egalitarian thinking. Nagel states the egalitarian's position succinctly:

> I do not think that our sense of priority for improvements of those lower down on the scale is exhausted by the case of the absolutely needy. Of course they have first priority. But the distinction between the unskilled and the skilled working class, or between the lower middle class and the upper middle class, or between the middle class and the upper class, presents the same intuitive ranking of relative importance.[116]

Anderson is asking us to cast all thoughts about distributive justice aside once the resources to guarantee *very* bare minimums are in place. But distributions above a minimum level may be greatly significant to justice if they, for example, enable someone to achieve their life's ambition.[117] Moreover, where the minimum is set as low as Anderson sets it, class divisions are permitted at all levels of the social structure, in stark contradiction of egalitarian intuitions.

The affront to equality becomes most apparent when we consider democratic equality's account of *intergenerational justice*. If internal resources were presumed equal, Anderson asks, '[w]ould democratic equality demand that external resources be divided equally from the start, as equality of fortune holds? There is no reason to think so.'[118] From the position Anderson develops there is, indeed, no reason to think so. But we would do well to be sceptical about any theory that is so ambivalent about the choice/circumstance distinction. Anderson's view entails that all inequalities in resources, including those in wealth and ownership of the means of production, may be passed between generations, provided the bare minimum capabilities are upheld.[119] The door for intergenerational definition of life chances is thus propped open. To egalitarians this is anathema. The Dworkinian goal of insensitivity to unchosen circumstance is obviously preferable.

In the light of these considerations, Anderson's claim that substantial compensation for bad luck is disrespectful takes on a sinister tone. As Dworkin remarks, 'the canard that aid to the unlucky insults them has been, for centuries, a shield for the indifference of the rich not the dignity of the poor'.[120] Furthermore, Anderson's ambivalent attitude towards luck and responsibility yields wildly counter-intuitive conclusions in many areas of public policy. If C and D are both given the opportunity to insure, and C does and D doesn't, this is surely at least prima facie relevant for the assignment of scarce resources.[121] Similarly, Anderson's failure to attach a threshold of responsibility to the social minimum invites repeated abuse of the resources it provides.[122] It seems incredible that Anderson, were she to distribute scarce organs, would not give priority to those with faulty organs through bad brute luck over those who have repeatedly needed and received replacement organs due to their willingness to damage their bodies through excessive alcohol intake.[123] Alcohol abuse *may* stem purely from genetic or environmental factors for which the individual is not at all responsible, but some medical conditions are manifestly genetic. Certain brute bad luck presents a stronger case for assistance than merely possible brute bad luck. Here the Dworkinian goal of sensitivity to choice seems to approximate egalitarian intuitions far more effectively.

159

In this section, I have been concerned for the most part with criticism of the theoretical bases of Anderson's theory, and with working out its implications that she leaves unsaid. What she actually says about public policy is less offensive to the egalitarian. A reason for this might be that Anderson's discussion is pitched at a lower level of abstraction than the theories she criticizes and, in some cases, may dovetail with the implementation of those theories.[124] This suggestion is borne out by the proximity of the luck-egalitarian responses to the problems of abandonment of the negligent and the vulnerability of dependent caretakers that I suggested earlier and Anderson's own solutions to these issues.[125] But such proximity detracts nothing from my central case: at the points on which luck egalitarianism and democratic equality diverge, the former offers the preferable account of equality.

8. Concluding Remarks

In this chapter a wide range of arguments against luck egalitarianism has been considered. One recurrent feature of my responses has been the emphasis on distinguishing between different forms of luck egalitarianism. In particular, I have maintained that welfarist luck egalitarianism can see off the majority of the objections raised, including all the insult arguments, without any modification to the theory. This gives us further cause for favouring equal opportunity for welfare. Observe in particular that, while Cohen's equal access to advantage can offer some resistance to objections on account of the welfare component of its conception of advantage, it is not as robust as equal opportunity for welfare. For example, Anderson's stigmatization, Wolff's threat to self-respect, and Shiffrin's endangered autonomy would all be permitted at higher levels under equal access to advantage, because the welfare losses they bring about would be counterbalanced by the improved (more responsibility-sensitive) resource distributions possible only where they occur.

Some of the injury arguments proved to provide some issues that needed addressing. In one area I have suggested that even welfarist luck egalitarianism faces a minor problem – specifically, its failure to secure basic needs. But I have emphasized the fact that the theoretical problem here does not really translate into any practical problem. I also suggested that, in order to deal with the problem of dependent caretakers, luck egalitarianism needs to be extended to account better for the value of procreation and looking after children. This would have more practical impact than the accommodation of basic needs, but requires very little modification of luck egalitarianism.

Finally, my findings regarding the egalitarian credentials of luck egalitarianism have been unequivocal. It seems clear that, to use the terms of the third condition for substantive egalitarianism introduced in the previous chapter, *the theory pursues equality in a dimension that is valuable to egalitarians.* As equal opportunity for welfare also meets the first two conditions, I maintain that this form of luck egalitarianism is substantively egalitarian. Sufficientarian theories, such as Anderson's, fail both the first condition and, on the evidence presented in this chapter, the third condition. There are, of course, more convincingly egalitarian rivals to luck egalitarianism, the most obvious of which is outcome egalitarianism. I have made no attempt to show that this is less egalitarian than luck egalitarianism, my purpose being rather to show how the latter is also plausible as an account of what equality demands. In the final part of this book I will argue that luck egalitarianism is a more attractive theory of justice than outcome egalitarianism, but also that there is more to justice than any theory of equality – including luck egalitarianism – can allow.

Notes

1 Anderson 1999a. Although Fleurbaey 1995 raises many important issues, some of which Anderson's piece takes up, it did not have the initial impact of the later article.
2 Dworkin 1977, 272–3.
3 Fleurbaey 1995, 52.
4 Fleurbaey 1995, 46.
5 See Chapter 1, note 26.
6 Fleurbaey 1995, 47.
7 Kymlicka 1995, 192; see also Kymlicka 1989.
8 Cohen 1999, 94.
9 Cohen 1999, 94.
10 Fleurbaey 1995, 47.
11 Other conditions for identifying compensable belief-related costs are put forward in Jones 1994 and Miller 2002.
12 Sen 1987, 34.
13 For discussion of measures of inequality see Chapter 3, note 37.
14 The most famous advocates of resources and social primary goods are Dworkin (2000) and Rawls (1996; 1999) respectively. While Rawls uses a fairly conventional objective conception of resources which includes basic liberties, income and wealth, and the 'social bases of respect' (but not the psychological phenomenon itself), Dworkin's

conception of resources is strongly influenced by beliefs, ambitions, attitudes, and tastes, and is exposed to the informational difficulties that that kind of subjectivism generally implies.

15 The best-known statement of welfarist luck egalitarianism is Arneson 1989. There Arneson subscribed to an informed preference satisfaction account of welfare; he now endorses an objective account (Arneson 2000c). Cohen (1989) subscribes to a resource-welfare hybrid position.

16 Shiffrin 2000, 245.

17 Note that the penalizing of fraudsters may itself be a negative side effect where such persons are both generally disadvantaged and non-responsible. This might lead luck-egalitarian policy-makers to introduce another level of information gathering to discriminate between different offenders and impose lesser penalties on the less responsible. If this is impossible or inefficient, the overall levels of investigation and punishment might be decreased, or the information gathering may be stopped altogether.

18 It is argued later that, even in cases of urgent health-care needs, the problem with luck egalitarianism is largely illusory in practice and, in any case, easily rectifiable in principle.

19 Arneson 2000b, 115; White 1997, 70–2, 79.

20 Anderson 1999a, 306, original emphasis.

21 Witness, for example, the letter Anderson imagines might accompany cheques from the State Equality Board. It is addressed to 'the disabled', 'the stupid and untalented', and 'the ugly and socially awkward', and drills home the message that '[y]our defective native endowments or current disabilities, alas, make your life less worth living than the lives of normal people' (Anderson 1999a, p. 305). To say that such a letter would not serve the luck egalitarian end of minimizing unfair disadvantage is a considerable understatement.

22 Anderson 1999a, 306.

23 Arneson 2006, 14.

24 Wolff 1998, 108–12.

25 Wolff 1998, 113.

26 Wolff 1998, 114.

27 See Wolff 1998, p. 104 n.16, p. 116. Dworkin's subjective resourcism is, in this regard and others, closer to welfarism than it is to conventional, objective resourcism. Presumably a person subject to shameful revelation will envy a person not subject to shameful revelation who is otherwise similarly positioned. In Dworkin's terms, the former is therefore disadvantaged.

28 For a similar argument in support of the different conclusion that welfarist luck egalitarianism recognizes the injustice of the 'five faces of oppression' identified by Iris Marion Young, see N. Barry 2006, 93–7; see also Young 1990.

29 Wolff 1998, 114.
30 Nicholas Barry (2006, 95, 105 n.62) maintains that 'if luck egalitarianism were applied to the world today, few individuals could seriously
   be considered responsible for their unemployed status, particularly
   if we accept that a job must be suitable for individuals if they are to
   accept it', on account of the shortage of appropriate jobs. If this claim
   was true, the luck egalitarian might have a conclusive reason not to
   make investigations, for the reason indicated in the text. But I think
   the claim is probably an exaggeration. Even if there is a high level of
   cyclical, classical, Marxian, and/or structural unemployment (which
   is the variety Barry mentions, though not by that name), and therefore
   many people will inevitably be unemployed until macroeconomic circumstances change, those people that actually are unemployed may
   be distinguished from the employed by factors for which they are
   responsible. The former group may have chosen riskier careers, not
   searched as thoroughly for jobs, or been unwilling to make the same
   personal sacrifices (for instance, moving to a different city); a small
   minority of this group may also actually not want to be employed.
31 Wolff 1998, 117–18.
32 Anderson 1999a, 306, original emphasis.
33 Kaufman 2004, 828.
34 Sobel 1999.
35 Arneson 2000a, 344.
36 Anderson 1999b.
37 Van Parijs 1995, 73, original emphasis.
38 Dworkin 2003, 192.
39 Anderson 1999a, 307, original emphasis.
40 Dworkin 2002, 117 n.19.
41 Dworkin 1981, 293–5.
42 Arneson 1989, 83–4; 1990, 176; Cohen 1989, 908, 916; Rakowski
   1991, 74–5.
43 Anderson 1999a, 295–6, original emphasis.
44 Anderson 1999a, 296–7.
45 Fleurbaey 1995, 40–1.
46 See also Scheffler 2003a, 33; Mason 2006, 193.
47 The main differences between this choice of the state and the choice
   of the Samaritan in 'The Parable of the Good Samaritan' are that in
   the former case the roadside victim is known to be responsible for his
   condition, and that the relevant moral duties are clearly matters of
   justice, not charity; see Chapter 6, note 6.
48 Dworkin 2002, 114.
49 Dworkin 2002, 114.
50 This kind of reasoning bears an affinity with Anderson's (1999a, 319)
   argument that a prohibition on acquiring the sources of someone's

guaranteed freedoms (these will be described below) may be justified in non-paternalistic fashion where it bases 'inalienable rights on what others are obligated to do rather than on the right bearer's own subjective interests'.

51 Anderson 1999a, 301.
52 Arneson 1997b, 239; see also Arneson 2002, 371; Van Parijs, 1995.
53 Rakowski 1991, 80.
54 Rakowski 1991, 76 n.4.
55 Roemer 1993, 150–2.
56 Anderson 1999a, 328–9.
57 Roemer 1993, 150.
58 In this case the luck egalitarian can return a similar answer to Anderson's, which is to tax cigarettes to pay for lung cancer treatment. The rationale for this would be similar to that for general health taxation – to provide treatment without allowing the negligent (smokers) to free-ride on the prudent (non-smokers).
59 Alexander Kaufman (2004) holds both that luck egalitarianism's 'aggressive' application of responsibility considerations unacceptably denies aid to negligent victims, and that the actual positions developed by Arneson, Cohen and Dworkin permit them to offer aid to such persons. But it should be kept in mind that there are several positions attributable to each of these writers, and some of them are harsher than the ones Kaufman focuses on. Arneson has moved from equal opportunity for welfare to responsibility-catering prioritarianism (see Chapter 6), and has also pointed out an ambiguity in the former principle (see section 5.7). I discuss Dworkin's positions at length in Chapter 1, and Cohen at length in Chapter 2; see also Chapter 1, note 66 on the latter.
60 Whether this is actually so depends on the structure of the taxation system. Another obvious qualification here is that under some arrangements some persons may buy extra health coverage. But that presents no special problem in this context as the inequality will be traceable to differential exercises of responsibility, and Bert will still get his treatment.
61 Anderson 1999a, 297, original emphasis.
62 Anderson 1999a, 299.
63 Anderson 1999a, 300.
64 Anderson 1999a, 297–8.
65 Dworkin 2000, 327.
66 Anderson 1999a, 300.
67 Anderson 1999a, 324; see Rakowski 1991, 153.
68 Dworkin 1981, 294.
69 Cf. Rakowski 1991, 109.
70 Mason 2000, 243; see also Mason 2006, 182–8.

71 Anderson 1999a, 303.
72 Dworkin 2002, 116.
73 Shiffrin 2000, 239.
74 Shiffrin 2000, 239.
75 Shiffrin 2000, 243.
76 An alternative approach justifies responsibility sensitivity itself on grounds of autonomy, self-respect, and other values that are considered valuable, and limits its scope where it comes into conflict with these values; see Brown 2005.
77 Shiffrin 2000, 243. It is arguable that even those with favourable welfare levels for which they are not responsible should be accommodated on utilitarian or other non-egalitarian grounds; see Chapter 6. But I do not see how this might undermine the *egalitarian* credentials of luck egalitarianism, which is what I am concerned with here.
78 Arneson 2000b, 111.
79 Young 2001, 8.
80 See Chapter 5.
81 Fleurbaey 2001, 526.
82 Fleurbaey 2001, 527.
83 Anderson 1999a, 288.
84 Arneson 1997a, 332; 1997b, 238–9; 2006, 17; 1989, 85–6; Cohen 1989, 916–17; N. Barry 2006, 98, 101.
85 One of the 'justice-based arguments for equality' that David Miller identifies (without endorsement) hinges on related doubts about distinguishing what persons are responsible for from such things as the effects of their native endowments; see Miller 1997, 229.
86 See Coram 1998, 130; 1997, 66.
87 N. Barry 2006, 98.
88 N. Barry 2006, 102.
89 Freeman 2006, 129–30.
90 See Chapter 6 below and N. Barry 2006, 99–101.
91 Scheffler 2003a, 14–15.
92 Vallentyne 2006, 434.
93 Each of these characters is discussed in Dworkin 1981 and/or Cohen 1989. The first and sixth originate in Arrow 1973 and Scanlon 1986.
94 Philips 2004, 17.
95 Armstrong 2003, 417.
96 Freeman 2006, 135, 134.
97 See Cohen 2004, 6–7, 13, 17–18. For these and related reasons, Thomas Scanlon (2006) suggests that it is no easy task establishing just how far Cohen's (avowedly luck egalitarian) account differs from Rawls's (evidently non-luck egalitarian) account.
98 Fleurbaey 2001, 501; see also Armstrong 2003, 415; 2006.

99 See Rawls 1999a; 1996.
100 Hayek 1960.
101 Wolff 1998, 112.
102 Indeed, the chapter devoted to luck egalitarianism in Stuart White's introductory book *Equality* includes a section on luck egalitarianism's alleged 'threat to liberty' alongside a section on its alleged promotion of 'social and political inequality'; see White 2006, ch. 4.
103 See B. Barry 2005.
104 Anderson 1999a, 313.
105 Anderson 1999a, 320.
106 Anderson 1999a, 314.
107 Sobel 1999.
108 Anderson 1999b.
109 Anderson 1999a, 313.
110 Anderson 1999a, 316; Sen 1992.
111 Anderson 1999a, 317.
112 Anderson 1999a, 318; see Stark 2002, 38.
113 Anderson 1999a, 318.
114 Anderson 1999a, 325.
115 Anderson 1999a, 325.
116 Nagel 1991, 69–70.
117 Arneson 2002b, 178.
118 Anderson 1999a, 320.
119 It might be thought that Anderson's guarantee to uphold the third aspect of individual functioning limits some such inequalities. John Rawls argues that equal citizenship might be jeopardized where 'inequalities of wealth exceed a certain limit' as money is converted into political power (Rawls 1999a, 246; see also 198–9). Anderson, however, makes no such argument, nor would she be entitled to on her account of the conditions of citizenship, which has much more limited scope than Rawls's. Importantly, she stipulates only that citizens are equal in having the same formal rights and number of votes, not in having equal political power.
120 Dworkin 2002, 116.
121 Christiano 1999.
122 Arneson 2000a, 348–9.
123 Sobel 1999.
124 See Arneson 2000a, 345; Cohen 2003, 244.
125 See Anderson 1999a, 323–5, 330–1 and notes 50 and 58 above.

Part 3

Luck Egalitarianism as an Account of Justice

—

5

Responsibilitarianism

---

1. Introductory Remarks

Luck egalitarianism holds that variations in the levels of advantage held by different persons (that is, inequalities) are justified if, and only if, facts about those persons' choices or opportunities have made them responsible for those variations. One of the most important things to notice about such statements is *the defining role given to both equality and responsibility.* One can truthfully say that luck egalitarianism is just as much a form of 'responsibilitarianism' – that school of theories that seeks to make distributions sensitive to responsibility – as it is a form of egalitarianism – that school of theories that seeks to make distributions equal in some significant sense. This book has so far followed the majority of discussions of luck egalitarianism in focusing on luck egalitarianism's egalitarianism, and has supported most of its claims – and particularly those of equal opportunity for welfare – in this area. This chapter will seek to right the balance by considering issues relating specifically to luck egalitarianism's responsibilitarianism, although equality will continue to play a major role. The issues discussed will be of broader interest if, as will be suggested here, responsibilitarianism implies luck egalitarianism.

Responsibilitarian considerations may bolster luck egalitarianism in a number of ways. If luck egalitarianism truly is a theory that is both egalitarian and responsibilitarian, luck egalitarianism may be able to draw on a wide range of arguments (including some desert-, entitlement-, and autonomy-based arguments) which are near relatives of responsibility-based arguments. Elaborate (neo-)Lockean and (neo-)Kantian arguments might be adopted, *mutatis mutandis*, from both traditions. More straightforwardly, there is great appeal in both the responsibilitarian idea that, when some person is responsible for bringing about some state of affairs, he should incur the costs or the benefits associated with it, and the egalitarian idea that all persons ought, *ceteris paribus*, to hold the same level of advantage.[1] Perhaps these ideas need sometimes to be overridden, but we need good reasons for doing so.[2] Furthermore, the juxtaposition of these ideas hints that luck egalitarianism is more than a theory formed from the combination of two independently weighty principles; the principles are, in fact, not only compatible but complementary, supporting judgements and arguments more attractive than those supported by either responsibilitarianism or egalitarianism independently. Recall, for instance, the attractiveness of the suggestion that it is unfair for some to be worse off than others through no fault of their own.[3] Or, again, the powerful argument for luck egalitarian principles that appeals to the ideals said to underpin existing practices of equality of opportunity, the roots of which some have attributed to Rawls.[4] Why is the impact of inherited social, economic, and natural assets morally arbitrary, as Rawls supposes?[5] One compelling answer is that persons are not responsible for this initial distribution. It therefore provides no justification for inequality.

I will make no attempt to describe the details of any of these potentially elaborate arguments here. I will rather restrict myself to two types of responsibility-based arguments for luck egalitarianism that require relatively little interpretation and exegesis of existing works. The first type, which I present in section 3, holds that luck egalitarianism is not only attractive for responsibilitarians relative to other egalitarianisms, but that the endorsement of it (or of a distributively identical theory) is actually implied by full responsibilitarianism in normal circumstances. Where there are different levels of attributive responsibility, in a sense slightly different from Thomas Scanlon's, responsibilitarians must make distributions reflect those variations and nothing else.

The second and principal type of argument is explored in the second half of the chapter. Much of the recent, largely negative reassessment of luck egalitarianism has, unusually for a matter of political philosophy, been motivated by metaphysical considerations.[6] Particularly damaging, if correct, is the claim that luck egalitarianism is committed to metaphysical libertarianism – the view that incompatibilist free human action is possible – despite reasonable doubts over that doctrine's truth. Why, it may be asked, deny assistance to 'the lazy' or 'the reckless' if they may be, metaphysically speaking, just as non-responsible for their disadvantages as the congenitally disabled and naturally untalented are for theirs?

I will argue that luck egalitarianism may be plausibly construed as sensitive to metaphysics-based concerns such as these. In section 4, I argue that the 'libertarian assumption' allegation itself rests upon the assumption that luck egalitarians are committed to rewarding certain kinds of actions regardless of whether or not those who perform them are actually responsible for performing them. But this assumption is at odds with the reference to responsibility that lies at the heart of luck egalitarianism. It follows that luck egalitarianism would not be undermined were it actually the case that both metaphysical libertarianism (hereafter, libertarianism for short) and compatibilism were false. If the lazy or reckless are not actually responsible for their disadvantages, then luck egalitarianism will not, in principle, penalize them. In this regard luck egalitarianism is better positioned than outcome egalitarianism which must assume, in precisely the sense intended by luck egalitarianism's critics, hard determinism or an equivalent position.

The critics attempt to strengthen their hand by suggesting that luck egalitarianism does not sit well with compatibilism. My response, given in section 5, is firstly, that it has not been shown that there are any relevant differences in the moral implications of compatibilism and libertarianism, and secondly, that even if there were such differences, luck egalitarianism would be able to accommodate them by modifying its prescriptions.

The defence of luck egalitarianism of sections 4 and 5 invites the further objection that luck egalitarianism is, in the inevitable absence of a resolution of the free-will problem, practically impotent. If luck egalitarians cannot know whether those who *appear* to be responsible for their disadvantages are *really* responsible for them, then they cannot know whether to compensate such persons. I meet this criticism in section 6 with the proposal that a luck egalitarian government ought to distribute advantage on the basis of an educated guess about the metaphysics of responsibility. I suggest that a committee of specialists might be well qualified to make such a guess.

The first task, however, is to arrive at a more detailed account of the responsibilitarian position, and in particular, the roles of attributive and substantive responsibility.

2. Attributive and Substantive Responsibility

What does making distributions responsibility sensitive mean? 'Responsibility' is a word that can refer to more than one concept. According to Thomas Scanlon's well-known definition, 'responsibility as attributability' – or, as I will call it, *attributive responsibility* – tells us which things a person can actually be held responsible for bringing about. *Substantive responsibility,* by contrast, tells us the moral significance of the things which someone is attributively responsible for – whether they are good or bad, how good or bad they are, whether they give rise to rights and duties, and what the content of those rights and duties are.[7]

In my view a responsibilitarian theory is sensitive to both forms of responsibility. But attributive responsibility sensitivity is the distinguishing feature of responsibilitarianism. If we want to place a distinct notion of responsibility at the heart of our theory, substantive responsibility will not do. As S. L. Hurley observes, '"[s]ubstantive responsibility" seems closer to desert or institutional accountability or entitlement than to responsibility'.[8] A purely substantive responsibility-sensitive account of distributive justice need not be swayed by which things particular people are actually responsible for bringing about, since it may view the moral (and, hence, distributive) significance of persons' attributive responsibilities as minor relative to other morally weighty matters, such as end-state distributions. A genuinely responsibilitarian theory of distributive justice is one which sets distributive shares largely according to attributive responsibility. This position is at the heart of luck egalitarianism.

I say this with two provisos. First, the sense of attributive responsibility I have in mind differs from Scanlon's sense. On his definition, one might be attributively responsible for some good or bad outcome without there being any corresponding substantive responsibility. Here, attributive responsibility might justify blame, but not sanctions. For example, an individual might be attributively responsible for some act (for example, the taking of drugs) on account of it reflecting their 'judgment-sensitive attitudes'.[9] But if this person had no real alternative choice in the matter (for example, they were addicted to drugs) no substantive responsibility-based rights or duties may arise. As we shall see in section 5, basing distributions on this kind of attributive responsibility would be unjust.

I will be concerned with a stronger sense of attributive responsibility. The theory needs to be sensitive to what Hurley calls 'thoroughgoing, blame-licensing, *accountability-implying* moral responsibility'.[10] Hereafter I will call this attributive responsibility, and leave aside the Scanlonian sense of attributive responsibility. I do not need to deny that Scanlon's non-distributively relevant responsibility exists, but nor do I need concern myself with it. The relevant kind of attributive responsibility, like the non-relevant Scanlonian kind, tells us who is responsible for what without telling us whether that is a good or a bad thing. But, where there are good or bad things, it will imply good or bad distributive consequences.

Second, and as mentioned above, substantive responsibility must play a limited role. As noted, attributive responsibility tells us who is responsible for what but does not identify some of these responsibilities as good and bad. Obviously responsibilitarianism does not reward people to the extent that they are attributively responsible for things, regardless of the nature of those things. Someone who is 100 per cent responsible for their failure to hold down a job will, in principle, be entitled to *less* than someone who is only partially responsible for that failure, although they are *more* attributively responsible for it. Furthermore, we cannot just say that, to the extent that some person is responsible for bringing about some state of affairs, whatever that might mean, the consequences that result from that state of affairs are assigned to that person. We need to know which kinds of consequences to assign.

An individual's action might have the consequences that advantage levels are (1) constant in terms of that individual's resources, (2) a little higher in terms of that individual's welfare, (3) a little lower in terms of total societal resources, (4) much lower in terms of societal welfare, and (5) higher for the worse off and lower for the better off. So we need to decide not only which account of advantage to adopt but also whether we are going to reward maximizing behaviour or behaviour promoting a particular distribution. If maximization is favoured, we need to decide whether the relevant kind of maximization is individual or societal. So we need to apply three things in combination with the particular attributive responsibilities that we identify: an account of advantage; an account of virtue (including, perhaps, an account of fair distribution), *or* an account of prudence, *or* a combined account of the two; and a principle stating that individuals are to be rewarded in proportion to the extent to which they realize the ends set out by the account of morality and/or prudence.

These three elements together I will call substantive responsibility. It is subject to the important limitation that it is solely in the role of identifying the relevant consequences of attributively responsible acts. It is assumed that, whatever the relevant consequences may be, they are of central distributive significance. For example, if utilitarianism is the favoured account of morality, it is restricted to telling us how much each attributively responsible act is worth, on account of its utility promotion, and hence what each person should get on account of their responsible acts. We would not ask the different question of which distribution would promote utility. If I act so as to promote utility, but am myself a poor converter of resources into utility for reasons for which I am not attributively responsible, I would benefit under this scheme. The substantive responsibility functions purely as a means of working out the distributive implications of attributive responsibility.

I think that our intuitive notion of substantive responsibility places some limited restrictions on the reasons available to us in our selection of the relevant consequences. Usage suggests that someone might be acting (substantively) responsibly whether they act self-interestedly or benevolently. But the pursuit of some distributive patterns may not qualify for either category, in which case such a pursuit appears to be irresponsible. This may be the case with outcome equality, because it may prefer to reduce everyone's holdings. While some people hold that a responsible state may act like this, few or none hold that a responsible individual can. Prioritarian actions may count as benevolent, however. For example, a donation to improve the level of care in a hospital in a poor area may count as a perfectly responsible use of money, even if higher overall advantage levels could have been secured by making the same donation to a more efficiently run hospital in a richer area. So if we favour the beneficent or moral account of responsibilitarianism, (5) might count in favour of the agent's entitlement, as might (2). If we favour the self-interested or prudential model of responsibilitarianism, (4) might decrease the agent's claim. I would personally wish to discount (1) and (3), because I hold that welfare is the appropriate measure of advantage, but that position is not required for responsibilitarianism.

I will not take a particular stance on the question of whether to favour a moral or prudential account.[11] Given the intuitive breadth of substantive responsibility, the default position is a combination of the two. But there may be a stronger narrow view. One significant category of narrow views is *desert* views, according to which each person receives that which they deserve. These views are always moral, not prudential – you might be responsible for owning a fortune after befriending an aged wealthy widower purely for inheritance purposes but you could not, unless you planned to use the money to do great good, thereby become deserving of the fortune. Desert views also agree that a desert base – the grounds for deserving praise, blame, reward, or punishment – must be some relevant fact about the individual,[12] but they disagree about what might count as a desert base. While some philosophers state that the base must be something for which the person was at least in part (attributively) responsible, others dispute this.[13] It seems, then, that while many desert views could be described as versions of responsibilitarianism that incorporate moral accounts of substantive responsibility, others could not be so described.

The argument of this section may be summarized thus: responsibilitarianism assumes (i) that the relevant consequences of attributive responsibility set distributive shares, insofar as this is possible, and (ii) that the relevant consequences are identified by substantive responsibility. If this is right, the general failure of political philosophers (including, prior to this chapter, this one) to specify which sense of responsibility they have in mind when discussing responsibility-sensitive theories is understandable. An act which is responsible in the way that justifies responsibilitarian reward is one which is both attributively responsible and substantively responsible in its consequences. A negligent, penalty-justifying act is one which is attributively responsible but substantively irresponsible in its consequences. So the important kind of responsibility is neither purely attributive nor substantive, but rather something combining the two.

3. From Responsibility Sensitivity to Equality

How, then, does the above account of responsibilitarianism relate to equality? The complementariness of responsibilitarianism and equality can be well illustrated by reference to an argument that may be thought to bolster the position of the critic of luck egalitarianism. Hurley has claimed that responsibilitarian objectives such as 'luck-neutralization' can neither specify nor justify egalitarianism.[14] Suppose that it is the case that no egalitarian theory can be specified, nor its specifically egalitarian character justified, by reference to responsibility alone – that is, in Christopher Lake's words, that 'there is nothing discernibly egalitarian in the idea that individuals should benefit or suffer according to what they are responsible for'.[15] It may be thought that it follows that luck egalitarianism is on shaky ground. But no reason has been given for thinking that responsibility sensitivity and equality cannot be combined in the way I have suggested, as long as it is understood that the latter is not rooted in luck neutralization.[16] Equality could be independently posited in the fashion of what Hurley calls the 'equality-default view', which holds that 'equality should be taken as a default position . . . perhaps on some other basis [than responsibility considerations]'.[17] It could be buttressed by a certain interpretation of the weak egalitarian principle discussed in Chapter 3, according to which like cases should be treated alike. Samuel Freeman suggests that the luck egalitarian might say this: 'if human beings are equals in relevant respects, namely with regard to their lack of responsibility or desert for their natural talents (or for differences in natural talents), it should follow they should be treated equally with regard to the effects of their natural talents'.[18] And luck neutralization could still help to justify a particular egalitarian theory *as a whole*. If the idea of rewarding some genuine choices and penalizing others is, all things considered, intuitively appealing, then any egalitarian theory which embodies this idea is, *ceteris paribus*, more attractive than any egalitarian theory which does not. If this idea is more compelling than the idea that all should be equal regardless of considerations of responsibility, then luck egalitarianism is to be preferred to outcome egalitarianism. Thus, if Hurley's observation shows luck egalitarianism to be on shaky ground, it is by virtue of the unsteady foundation of its egalitarianism. Responsibilitarians may be discouraged from endorsing luck egalitarianism once it is apparent that its egalitarianism is not derived from its responsibilitarianism. But egalitarians should have no such worry over it.

If it was accepted that one could be serious about responsibility sensitivity without advocating any form of substantive equality, those of a responsibilitarian bent might nevertheless favour luck egalitarianism, at least over other egalitarian positions. From what I have said, that might be one coherent position among many. But, in fact, I think responsibilitarians have significant egalitarian commitments – specifically, luck egalitarian-type commitments.

Consider the following sequence of events:

(a) Doe starts greatly disadvantaged relative to Roe,
(b) Doe acts more responsibly than Roe,[19]
(c) Doe is rewarded and Roe penalized for this; but
(d) Doe still ends up disadvantaged relative to Roe (albeit less disadvantaged than he had been at the beginning).

This is the kind of inegalitarian situation Hurley and Lake seem to suppose the responsibilitarian can be satisfied with. But can she? At first glance, perhaps she can. Let us say that Doe has indeed benefited, and Roe lost out, in proportion to their (relative) attributive responsibility (events [b] and [d]). But luck – at least, in the interesting *thin* sense where it is just the inverse of attributive responsibility[20] – has clearly not been neutralized, as Doe ends up in a worse situation than Roe, even though Doe acted more responsibly. In other words, there are variations in advantage that are not accounted for by variations in attributive responsibility. We know that that is enough for the luck egalitarian to say that (d) is an unjust outcome. I find it hard to see how anyone who is claiming to reward people *solely* on the basis of those things for which they are responsible could disagree. Clearly, (a) has strongly influenced (d), but neither Doe nor Roe are attributively responsible for their relative standing in (a), and it is therefore an illegitimate influence on the outcome according to a strict responsibilitarian.

Hurley's response here would presumably be that 'people are no more responsible for an equal distribution of goods that are a matter of luck than they are for an unequal distribution'.[21] That is true, but it does not follow that the responsibilitarian should be unconcerned about how *initial distribution affects the final distribution*. The responsibilitarian's problem with (d) was not that Doe was entitled to an equal starting position – he was not – but rather that he had become entitled to be advantaged relative to Roe on account of their actions. Until choice or control (or whatever else makes for responsibility) occurs, the responsibilitarian has no moral compass, and no distribution is unjust. But as soon as anyone becomes responsible for anything, the responsibilitarian's sole objective is to redistribute in a way that responds to that attributive responsibility. Those who start with more can claim no advantage on that score.

Of course, someone might view (d) as more acceptable if they endorsed responsibilitarianism in some more limited sense. Given appropriate background facts, a right libertarian might suggest that he rewards responsible action, within the parameters set by historical entitlement.[22] But a system of entitlements that allows relatively negligent persons to finish with much more than relatively prudent persons is obviously inconsistent with a fully responsibility-sensitive distribution.[23]

What, then, would the responsibilitarian require in cases such as that of Doe and Roe? How do we reward and penalize persons according only to what they are responsible for? An obvious answer is to replace (a) with

(a') Doe and Roe start equally advantaged.

The knock-on effect of this is that (d) is replaced with

(d') Doe ends up advantaged relative to Roe.

An equally good alternative is to make the following addition to the initial sequence of events:

(e) Assets are redistributed such that Doe *finally* ends up advantaged relative to Roe.

In other words, once (a) and (b) have occurred, strict responsibilitarians must seek to bring about sequences of the shape (a), (b), (c), (d), (e). Alternatively, in anticipation of events of type (b), they may aim to bring about the sequence (a'), (b), (c), (d'). (A hybrid, involving less unequal starting points than [a] and less extensive redistribution than [e], is also an option.) Whichever route is taken, the result is that responsible Doe is advantaged and less responsible Roe is disadvantaged. The extent of the advantages and disadvantages will be proportional to responsibility. Where there is responsible action, responsibilitarians advocate a view that is equivalent to full-blown luck egalitarianism. Thin luck neutralization leads us to (one kind of) equality.[24]

4. The Metaphysical Case for Luck Egalitarianism

Some writers will be unmoved by the argument of the preceding section because they object to luck egalitarianism on grounds that are equally applicable to responsibilitarianism. A general worry of critics of luck egalitarianism is that, in bringing choice and responsibility to centre stage in political philosophy, it entered treacherous waters. Specifically, it opened itself up to the *libertarian assumption objection*. Samuel Scheffler writes that 'luck egalitarianism invites the objection that, like the political philosophies of the anti-egalitarian right, it tacitly derives much of its appeal from an implausible understanding of the metaphysical status of choice'.[25] Luck egalitarianism takes the choice/circumstance distinction to be distributively decisive, but this distinction can be deep enough only if free will is possible, and in particular, if libertarianism is correct.[26] As Saul Smilansky notes, from a hard determinist perspective, '[G. A.] Cohen's idea that there can be the sort of non-arbitrary 'genuine choice' which could justify some inequality would be simply seen as mistaken'.[27] These remarks, together with the notorious intractability of the free-will problem, suggest that luck egalitarianism assumes an undoubtedly controversial (and, according to some, implausible) metaphysical theory.

I will not attempt to give any kind of full exploration of the free-will problem here. But exploration of the relationship between metaphysics, justice and luck egalitarianism does, I hope to show, suggest that the latter is well positioned. Consider, then, five preliminary comments on the suggestion of the previous paragraph.

Note first that the critic of luck egalitarianism must, in the case of luck egalitarianism at least, view the findings of philosophy as trumping widely held views about the social and political organization of society. The free-will problem is not, it can safely be assumed, at the forefront of most persons' thoughts about justice. With this the consistency of certain combinations of anti-luck egalitarian arguments is threatened.

Take, for instance, the position that luck egalitarianism is undermined by *both* its suspect metaphysics and its divergence from commonplace moral judgements. The luck egalitarian's insistence that inequalities in the presence of a history of equivalent exercises of responsibility are morally wrong is rejected by Scheffler at least in part on the basis that this view lacks popular support. I maintain that the claim that luck egalitarianism fails to coincide with 'the social and political conception of equality' is both more open to doubt than Scheffler acknowledges and of questionable descriptive and normative importance.[28] But even were it valid and weighty, it undercuts, and is undercut by, the metaphysical argument that Scheffler presents alongside it. If one allows that an account of distributive justice may be disproved on the ground of the weakness of its metaphysics, one surely ought to grant that the wholly metaphysically ignorant 'more common or intuitive view' is likely to be undermined in this way. Conversely, if one believes that the test of a political theory is the popularity of its prescriptions, one ought to view the distinctly ivory tower issue of the metaphysical credentials of such a theory as immaterial.

The second point, which has more importance for the main argument, concerns the precise sense in which luck egalitarianism is said to assume libertarianism. There is surely no conceptual need for a luck egalitarian to premise her theory on this (or any other) metaphysical theory. What difficulty is there in her saying 'I know that you are not really responsible for this outcome, for hard determinism is true; but you certainly look responsible for it, so I'm going to hold you responsible for it'? The difficulty, surely, is a normative one, and so too, I take it, is the assumption – that is, luck egalitarianism looks far more plausible if it rewards and penalizes in a manner that is genuinely (that is, according to the correct metaphysical theory) responsibility sensitive, rather than in an arbitrary manner that is superficially responsibility sensitive. The assumption, then, is largely metaphysical in character but morally motivated.

The final three points can be stated more briefly. The first is that libertarianism is not obviously wrong. Some political philosophers are happy to assert that libertarianism seems implausible to them without so much as an argument to that effect.[29] But this is not an uncontroversial conclusion among metaphysicians; far from it.[30] The next point is that, further objections (such as the unfairness of compatibilism-based inequality objection addressed in the next section) notwithstanding, luck egalitarianism assumes only (in the sense just described) *either* metaphysical libertarianism *or* compatibilism. Some luck egalitarians, indeed, think the second of those options the more promising.[31] The final preliminary is that the libertarian-assumption objection does itself rely upon the credibility of a certain controversial metaphysical theory – hard determinism.[32] Theories of justice that do not give choice a central role are likely to be undercut, and luck egalitarianism appear preferable, if libertarianism or compatibilism is shown to be correct. There will, at least, be no metaphysical grounds for objecting to luck egalitarianism.

With these points the ground has been prepared for the luck egalitarian's central argument, the *metaphysical uncertainty argument*. She begins by observing that the best construal of luck egalitarianism understands luck *thinly* with regard to responsibility, that is, as its inverse.[33] I am unlucky in this sense if I suffer from a disadvantage for which I am not responsible. Thick luck, by contrast, comes in many varieties, each of which has certain substantive content. Conceptions of thick luck will often fail to coincide with thin luck as their content is 'more specific than the negation of our bottom line judgments about responsibility'.[34] For instance, I am unlucky only in the particular thick sense of lack of regressive control of causes if I can or could control all the causes of my disadvantage, and all the causes of those causes.[35] Suppose that I had control over the causes of my disadvantage, but not over their causes. If responsibility requires only non-regressive control, then I am unlucky in this particular thick sense, but I am not unlucky in the thin sense. Those who have been described as luck egalitarians often use luck thickly, most often when referring to brute luck and option luck, which place the focus on the presence or absence of choice.[36] But the use of thin luck is no departure from the core ideas of luck egalitarianism – most luck-egalitarian works explicitly specify that it is the presence or absence of responsibility that is pivotal.[37]

Note that the focus on thin luck means there are as many different luck egalitarianisms as there are ways of defining free will and responsibility (and hence luck). The most obvious divide is between libertarian and compatibilist views, but neither of these groups is homogeneous: on the one hand there are non-causal, event-causal, and agent-causal accounts; on the other there are multiple viewpoints, mesh, reasons-responsive, and Strawsonian accounts. There are, of course, other accounts, and subdivisions within these accounts.[38] But luck egalitarianism itself is not committed to either libertarianism or compatibilism, far less any particular formulation of free will and responsibility. It simply favours that account which is correct, or most correct.

If this is all granted, then even in the metaphysical worst-case scenario that hard determinism is true, luck egalitarianism would be in no worse a state in the relevant regards than other forms of egalitarian justice. If hard determinism is assumed, then equal opportunity for welfare is in all possible circumstances equivalent to the outcome-egalitarian principle of equality of outcome. If no one is responsible for any of their preferences, equal opportunity for welfare's policy of compensating for those and only those disadvantages for which persons are not responsible amounts to equality of welfare's policy of compensating for all disadvantages.[39]

This should be a familiar point.[40] Yet it casts doubt on Scheffler's claim that 'the appeal of luck egalitarianism may seem tacitly to depend on a form of metaphysical libertarianism'.[41] Without libertarianism, and even without compatibilism as well, luck egalitarianism's metaphysics-based appeal is equal to that of its main rival. Furthermore, the metaphysical-uncertainty argument naturally pushes to a stronger conclusion. Given our actual and inevitable uncertainty over which answer to the free-will problem is correct, luck egalitarianism is at a prima facie advantage over outcome egalitarianism, whose categorical insensitivity to responsibility is either equivalent to luck egalitarianism's sensitivity (if hard determinism is true) or prima facie counter-intuitive (if libertarianism or compatibilism is true). Outcome egalitarianism would be subject to the counterpart of the libertarian-assumption objection – the *hard determinist-assumption objection* – with no possibility of recourse to a metaphysical-uncertainty argument, for metaphysical certainty is assumed. Of course, the metaphysics-based moral

counter-intuitiveness may be overcome by some independent normative argument to the effect that responsibility for one's disadvantage
should not preclude compensation for that disadvantage.[42] But clearly
no such argument is available from metaphysics – indeed, as I said,
some arguments of this type may be not be available to the metaphysically disposed. Engagement with the free-will problem leads us to
what is, if anything, an embarrassing conclusion for luck egalitarianism's critics, and an emboldening one for its advocates.

5. Compatibilism

So far I have treated compatibilism and libertarianism as though, so
far as distributive justice is concerned, they were equivalent. Some may
suspect that it is precisely this conflation that has powered my argument, for the critics claim that the two theories are not equally welcome
to luck egalitarians. Scheffler notes that, according to libertarianism,
'genuinely voluntary choices belong to a different metaphysical category than do other causal factors. If the distinction between choices
and unchosen circumstances is viewed as a fundamental metaphysical
distinction, then it may seem capable of bearing the enormous political
and moral weight that luck egalitarianism places on it.'[43] Compatibilism
is less conducive to luck egalitarianism as, '[i]n the absence of such a
conception [of the metaphysical status of genuine choice], it is simply
not clear why choice should matter so much: why such fateful political
and economic consequences should turn on the presence or absence
of genuine choice'.[44] The idea here appears to be that, while it is true
that agents may have Scanlonian attributive responsibility for their
actions if compatibilism is correct, those grounds for moral appraisal
do not justify the particular substantive-responsibility judgements
made by luck egalitarians. In other words, fully responsibility-sensitive
distribution is inappropriate where the responsibility in question is
merely compatibilist-attributive responsibility. This is the *unfairness
of compatibilism-based inequality objection.*

But why exactly does the particular way in which choices are
genuine matter to luck egalitarians or to anyone else interested in distributive justice? Why is one type of attributive responsibility a more
plausible basis for distribution? Without answers to these questions,
the objection is little more than the assertion that compatibilism just
is not enough for the luck egalitarian's purposes.

Scheffler attempts to answer these questions by linking compatibilism with a specific variety of luck-egalitarian unfairness. He starts

by noting that, according to compatibilists, 'the relation of choice to the agent's values, deliberations, and preferences will make the presence or absence of choice an important factor in many contexts. Still, it will be only one factor among others, and its relative importance will vary depending on the context.' [45] Scheffler believes that the status of choice in a compatibilist scheme creates particular problems for the luck egalitarian:

> [A] talent for choosing wisely is just one human skill among others. What we call practical wisdom is affected in complex ways by other traits of character and temperament, and is not itself distributed equally among people . . . Nor can luck egalitarians say that the choices made by those who are less skilful choosers are for that reason alone less genuine choices, for luck egalitarians hold that, if there are genuine choices, then people may reap the rewards of the good ones and must bear the costs of the foolish ones.[46]

The claim, then, is that the luck egalitarian's willingness to punish those who choose badly seems especially harsh when combined with a compatibilist account of responsibility, as those choices do not themselves belong to any special metaphysical category, *and* are affected by each individual's practical reasoning capability which varies from one individual to another. Clearly, a particular account of responsibility is assumed here. But, even if we were to allow that, the argument is misconceived. A poor choice-making capability is a disadvantage just like any other for the luck egalitarian if it may result in a loss in advantage, as is the case here. As such it will give rise to compensation unless the individual is responsible for it.[47] Scheffler does not state whether, in the kind of cases he has in mind, the 'less skilful choosers' are responsible for their lack of skill. But, if they are responsible for it, there is nothing obviously wrong with penalizing them for that, just as it may be appropriate to compensate them where they are not responsible.[48]

Marc Fleurbaey has this to say in support of the unfairness of compatibilism-based inequality objection:

> Even if a compatibilist account may provide grounds for moral attitudes of praise or disparise, it is more questionable whether it could justify differences of welfare or advantage between people. The presence of an identified deterministic factor explaining a person's behavior gives her very good arguments for complaining about any penalty in welfare or advantage imposed by equal opportunity institutions, or symmetrically, seriously undermines any claim to preferential treatment yielding

a higher outcome. In brief, the equal opportunity approach faces a sort of dilemma: its ethical appeal is stronger with an incompatibilist view of free will than with a compatibilist one, but the doubt problem is then also more acute.[49]

Here the focus is on the kinds of judgements of substantive responsibility that are appropriate given compatibilism. While Scheffler's argument might suggest that attributive responsibility in such metaphysical circumstances has no substantive significance, Fleurbaey's accepts that it might, but just not in the way that luck egalitarians imagine.

Were Fleurbaey's person's 'very good arguments for complaining about any penalty in welfare or advantage' actually to materialize independently of the outright rejection of compatibilism – that is, if it was accepted that the negligent were not, on the grounds of responsibility, to be disadvantaged but were nevertheless an appropriate object of non-disadvantaging dispraise – that would suggest that theories of justice should distinguish between compatibilism and libertarianism in a way that I have not up to now considered. But there are two good reasons for thinking that this need not worry the luck egalitarian. First, it does not seem obvious to me that any such arguments will emerge. We usually want to back up a justified expression of praise or dispraise with action of some kind. It seems wholly inadequate to respond to grossly irresponsible or even malicious behaviour with a mere shake of the head. We cannot, for instance, tolerate 'moral hostage taking' by those who know that an egalitarian society will pay for their destructive or extravagant behaviour.[50] Assuming that such persons are, determinism notwithstanding, responsible for their behaviour, it may well strike us as wrong to subsidize their reprehensible choices. Less drastic irresponsibility is typically met with correspondingly less drastic, though still significant, sanctions.

Second, if my hunch is mistaken, and some substantial compatibilism-based inequalities can be shown to be unfair, the relevance of compatibilist-attributive responsibility to distributive justice would have been diminished. But luck egalitarianism would remain a distinctly attractive position as long as libertarianism is viable and/or some compatibilism-based inequalities are fair. Even if these were not possibilities, luck egalitarianism would fare no worse than outcome egalitarianism as its judgements of substantive responsibility would reflect this state of affairs. In other words, the conclusion need only be that luck egalitarianism should not treat any positive result regarding the truth of compatibilism, however limited its moral implications, as though it justified fully responsibility-sensitive distributive measures. This can be accommodated readily enough.

6. Metaphysics meets Public Policy

It appears that luck egalitarianism is a coherent and distinct distributive theory on the assumption of either libertarianism or compatibilism although the latter may place limits on the degree of responsibility sensitivity that is appropriate. If hard determinism is assumed, luck egalitarianism remains coherent although, in that case, it is much harder to distinguish it from outcome egalitarianism. We are left, however, with the question of what a government (or other distributive body) ought to do in the real world where we can make no such assumptions. Outcome egalitarians have an easy answer: distribute advantage equally.[51] 'Non-metaphysical' luck egalitarians might recommend that we reward and penalize wherever certain criteria for responsibility are satisfied, regardless of whether metaphysically genuine responsibility has actually been exercised.[52] Although the notion of attributive responsibility would have to be changed – arguably, beyond recognition – for such a theory to count as responsibilitarian, it would at least be coherent. But this position falls squarely in the sights of the libertarian-assumption objection – it rewards or penalizes where there is the mere veneer of responsibility. Alternatively, if luck egalitarians insist that distribution occurs only where the presence of genuine responsibility is beyond dispute, they will have to wait for the free-will problem to be resolved, in which case the uncertainty that is the source of their metaphysical strength invites fatal criticism at the level of application. As Fleurbaey comments, 'egalitarianism would be seriously endangered of being practically impotent if it was held hostage by metaphysics'.[53]

Can luck egalitarians take metaphysics seriously, as I have urged they should, and still offer concrete distributive proposals? I believe they can, provided they accept the pragmatic solution of legislating on the basis of our best metaphysical guess. I will describe how this might be done in probabilistic terms, but other methods are equally compatible with luck egalitarianism.

Imagine a society consisting of A and B, who each holds fifteen units of advantage, and C, who holds sixty-nine units of advantage. A is, doubts about free will aside, fully responsible for his disadvantage relative to C; it has arisen, say, from decisions that he made but that

C declined. B, however, is not responsible for her disadvantage; her actions are equivalent to those of C. (C is therefore responsible for his advantage over A but not responsible for his advantage over B.) Let us assume that we cannot increase or decrease the number of units in the society; redistribution is the only means of redressing the inequalities we find there. In the first scenario hard determinism is correct, and equal opportunity for welfare recommends, with equality of welfare, that thirty-six units be extracted from C and the product distributed equally between A and B, leaving each person with thirty-three units. In the second scenario libertarianism or (full, distribution-relevant) compatibilism are correct, and equal opportunity for welfare recommends that twenty-seven units be extracted from C and the entire product handed to B, leaving B and C with forty-two units and A with the fifteen units with which he began.

The problem, as I said, is that we do not know whether hard determinism, libertarianism, or compatibilism are true. But what is our best guess? If we had no reasons for or against these theories, we might do best to invoke the principle of insufficient reason, and treat each theory as though it were equally likely to be correct.[54] In that case, if we restrict our attention to the three theories (including compatibilism only in its full sense and excluding any of the recent revisionist theories), the distribution is defined by both the first two scenarios, though the weight of the second is double that of the first (as two of the three theories recommend the second). Equal opportunity for welfare would on that basis recommend that thirty units be extracted from C, with the product divided unevenly between A and B, leaving A with twenty-one units, and B and C with thirty-nine units each.

It is generally supposed, however, that we *do* have reasons, albeit radically inconclusive ones, for and against metaphysical theories. For this reason the principle of insufficient reason is inapplicable. Nevertheless, a probabilistic approach appears to be reasonable. Governments have various ways of arriving at educated guesses; luck egalitarianism has no preference here, other than favouring greater accuracy over lesser accuracy. I will describe one option here: a *responsibility committee* composed of some of the leading authorities on the relevant metaphysical issues. The committee would be representative in terms of the positions (hard determinism, libertarianism, and so on) initially held by each member, though they may change during the course of the committee's deliberations. It would be charged with surveying the research appropriate to its topic and would ultimately provide the distributive arm of the government with their assessments of the likelihoods of each of the two scenarios, and any variations (such as ones involving the minimal, non-distribution-relevant compatibilism suggested by the unfairness of compatibilism-based inequality objection), being correct. It would be a simple task then to establish the appropriate distributive regime. For example, if the specialists decide that the first scenario (or some equivalent involving minimal compatibilism) is twice as likely to be true as the second, equal opportunity for welfare would recommend that thirty-three units be extracted from C, with the product divided unevenly between A and B, leaving A with twenty-seven units, and B and C with thirty-six units each.

I am confident that there is no consensus among the leading metaphysicians in developed anglophone countries that either hard determinism or outright libertarianism/compatibilism is correct. I am also confident that there is no reason to believe that such a consensus would arise from the committee's deliberations. On these grounds I speculate that the committees of these countries would settle on compromises that give some weight to both hard determinism and libertarianism/compatibilism.[55] The distributions mentioned in the two preceding paragraphs are embodiments of such compromises.[56] In practice, luck egalitarians will give some weight to equalizing opportunities and outcomes. Thus, the typical luck-egalitarian compensation pattern mentioned in the introduction – compensation for disadvantages arising from congenital disability, poor native endowment of talent, and birth into unfavourable social or economic circumstance, but no compensation for disadvantages arising from choices to make more or less effort, or to pursue some goals rather than others – receives a qualified endorsement, the main divergence being that there will be some (though less than full) compensation for disadvantages apparently arising from choices. Other ways of arriving at a decision (including Roemer's method mentioned below) are, for parallel reasons of demography, likely to have a similar outcome.

Imperfect as the committee of specialists approach may be, I think it is a reasonable enough method. Our best guess is that metaphysicians comprise the group best qualified to make the required decision.[57] We could, at any rate, do worse. Consider John Roemer's contrasting view. He puts forward an 'algorithm by which any society, with its particular views concerning the extent to which persons can overcome their circumstances by acts of will, can implement an egalitarianism of opportunity consonant with those views. In this sense, my proposal is political and not metaphysical.'[58] Such an approach treats society as a whole as the appropriate decision-making body. But this group is severely underqualified. The vast majority of the population will begin with no or virtually no philosophical expertise. Public debate may be all but worthless, for proponents of rival views may find that logical argumentation is a less effective way of persuading others than rhetoric and emotional appeal.[59] We want members of the decision-making body to make judgements about the truth rather than merely express their preferences. We are less likely to get this as the body gets larger and less familiar with the topic. Many members of the public may be motivated by unreflective attitudes, stereotypes, and self-interest. As Fleurbaey observes, Roemer's proposal is a 'dangerous tool for wanton applications of biased ideologies . . . It would be just too easy if hard metaphysical issues could always properly be decided by politicians and voters.'[60] We have no reason for thinking that the metaphysicians would actually fare worse than the general public's complete stab in the dark, and some reason for hoping that they would do better.[61] In some spheres, democracy may further luck-egalitarian ends; in this one, however, it does not.

Perhaps it would be said that the committee would itself be ideologically biased, or even deterministically driven. The second problem obviously runs very deep. But we have good reasons for wanting to arrive at an informed decision, and unfortunately there is no way of getting to one without running this epicycling risk. I also cannot say that the first problem would not arise, but I think it less serious in the case of the committee than that of most alternatives, given the knowledge and ability of the members, and the time set aside for consideration and discussion of the relevant problems. They ought also to be less prone to being moved by self-interest.[62] Short of randomly assigning probabilities to the two scenarios, we can never be sure to have eradicated the threat of ideological bias. Certainly, any political philosopher who simply assumes her favoured metaphysical theory is being anything but ideologically neutral. If there is a fully neutral method, then luck egalitarianism is open to it; if there is not, then the committee will suffice.

7. Concluding Remarks

In section 3 it was urged that, in normal circumstances (ones involving responsible action), those committed to responsibilitarianism must subscribe to luck egalitarianism, or to an identical position. If

they endorse the equality-default view as well, they will straightforwardly be luck egalitarians; if they do not, they can maintain a principled difference with luck egalitarianism (because they disagree on
how to distribute in the absence of responsibility) that has no impact
wherever responsibility has been exercised. Although this is a significant finding, and one which runs contrary to the views of several
writers, its most obvious effect is a defensive one. Opponents of luck
egalitarianism suppose that one can have full responsibilitarianism
without agreeing with the luck egalitarian that initial distributions
should have no impact on post-responsible act outcomes, but to the
best of my knowledge no one has ever subscribed to a theory that
they believe is both fully responsibilitarian and non-egalitarian; or
if they have, they have done so only because they have not distinguished between responsibility and related concepts such as actual
choice, historical entitlement, and merit. It is, nevertheless, possible
that the argument connecting responsibilitarianism and luck egalitarianism may increase the intuitive attractiveness of the latter to
some persons (principally political libertarians) when taken in combination with the arguments found in the rest of the chapter which,
inter alia, present a case for focusing on responsibility rather than,
say, choice.

The principal argument of sections 4 to 6 was that egalitarians
have very good responsibility-based reasons for being luck egalitarians. Reference to metaphysics shows that luck egalitarianism is at an
advantage relative to outcome egalitarianism (and related positions),
being superior in its use of responsibility and equal in the practical
applicability of that account. This is not necessarily to say that luck
egalitarianism ought to be favoured over other accounts of equality
(including outcome egalitarianism). Such accounts may be buttressed
by moral objections to luck egalitarianism that do not appeal to
metaphysics. But the argument does indicate that luck egalitarianism
is, in the relevant respects, far better placed than is often supposed.
Furthermore, given the arguments of Chapters 3 and 4, it is not at all
clear that any of the many more practical moral objections to luck
egalitarianism can do much to undermine that theory. Overall, luck
egalitarianism appears to be in a position of great strength, at least
as regards its egalitarianism and responsibilitarianism.

These considerations create the appropriate context for understanding the nature of an ambiguity in the notion of equal opportunity for welfare. Richard Arneson has noted that, according to his
classic 1989 article 'Equality and Equal Opportunity for Welfare',

[e]quality of opportunity for welfare obtains between Smith and Jones if their expected welfare given reasonably prudent conduct is the same. Facing these equal prospects, Smith and Jones may make exactly the demanded reasonably prudent choices, yet one enjoys better luck, and Smith ends up leading a miserable existence, while Jones lives well.[63]

The brute luck of lightning striking Smith but missing Jones who is standing right next to her can still affect the distribution of welfare. This might motivate us to bring about 'equal opportunity for welfare in the strict sense', which guarantees equally prudent persons the same level of welfare. But this may be unacceptably insensitive to option luck. Suppose two persons take part in high-stakes gambling, with differing results. Arneson observes that,

> [e]ven though strict equal opportunity is violated here, one might argue that in the morally relevant sense, these two individuals did have equal opportunities for welfare, because the eventual differences in their welfare prospects came about only through a process that both mutually agreed to undergo under conditions of full information against a background of equal initial prospects.[64]

Thin-luck egalitarianism refuses to take a binding decision on this or similar issues. It just favours whichever conception of equal opportunity for welfare is consonant with the best account of where attributive responsibility lies. Arneson's discussion highlights certain aspects of the cases that appear to be relevant to responsibility, such as the presence and circumstances of choice, but there are undoubtedly other, even more intractable matters that make Arneson's refusal to take sides here quite sensible. Intuition suggests that neither of the two conceptions of equal opportunity for welfare that Arneson describes is fully satisfactory. It may be that the truly responsibility-sensitive conception comports better with our intuitions about distributive fairness. But those particular intuitions are no way of deciding what makes for responsibility, and they may ultimately be frustrated.[65]

A precursor to the main argument of this chapter is Cohen's famous acknowledgment of the anxiety 'that to make choice central to distributive justice lands political philosophy in the morass of the free will problem'. He 'unreassuringly' replied that 'we may indeed be up to our necks in the free will problem, but that is just tough luck. It is not a reason for not following the argument where it goes.' [66] On one reading, the implication of this appears to be that, before responsibilitarianism came along, political philosophers did not have to worry about metaphysics.[67] Such a view grants too much ground to the critic. If hard determinism is indisputably correct, outcome egalitarianism appears to be the obvious option for metaphysically minded egalitarians. (I have noted that this scenario does not, in point of fact, undermine luck egalitarianism, but that would hardly be worth arguing for were there never to be any dispute over practical recommendations.) But for political philosophy to assume that this is the case is for the field to have its head in the sand. If libertarianism or compatibilism are true, the attractions of outcome egalitarianism are far less obvious. Given our actual metaphysical uncertainty, it is quite reasonable to ask how responsibility might be accommodated by a theory of equality, if only to test how equality of advantage fares against such a theory. If luck egalitarianism did not exist, it would have to be invented. For the reasons suggested above, those political theorists who take responsibility and metaphysics seriously should be amazed that we ever did without it.

Notes

1 See Steiner 2002; Scanlon 2002, 45–6.
2 See Chapter 6 of this work.
3 Temkin 1993, 13, 17, 200. For similar formulations see Arneson 1989, 85; Cohen 1989, 920; Nagel 1991, 71. Though consistent with equal opportunity for welfare, the 'no fault' suggestion defines far less, its egalitarianism and responsibilitarianism being highly conditional; on its consistency with non-egalitarian results see Arneson 1999b, 227–31.
4 Will Kymlicka's (1990, 58) statement of this argument credits the 'basic premiss' but not the 'conclusion' to Rawls (1999). Other writers see less of a connection between Rawls and luck egalitarianism; see Scheffler 2003a; Freeman 2006, ch. 4; Matravers 2007, ch. 3. The argument is, of course, just as forceful whether Rawls has anything to do with it or not.
5 Rawls 1999a, 62–5.
6 Fleurbaey 1995; 2001; Scheffler 2003a; 2005; Smilansky 1997; Risse 2002; Matravers 2002a; 2002b; Hurley 2003. Note that such considerations are moral as well as metaphysical. Philosophical accounts of responsibility seek to draw moral conclusions from metaphysical and also moral arguments. For instance, compatibilist moral argument may show how a deterministic metaphysics is compatible with responsibility. For presentational convenience I describe such considerations as metaphysical throughout this chapter because their metaphysical character distinguishes them from the other moral arguments explored in this book.
7 Scanlon 1998, 248.
8 Hurley 2006, 453.

9 Scanlon 1998, 290.
10 Hurley 2003, 92, emphasis added.
11 Note that, on the moral account, we might have had a more direct argument for compensating dependent caretakers than that given in 4.5.
12 Feinberg 1970.
13 Cf. Miller 1989, 167–70; Feldman 1996.
14 Hurley 2003, ch. 6.
15 Lake 2001, 98.
16 Arneson 2001.
17 Hurley 2003, 153–4, 172. This view does seem to have appeal of its own; see Berlin 1961, 131; Miller 1997, 226; Parfit 1995, 15.
18 Freeman 2006, 121; see also Matravers 2007, 67.
19 That is, the consequences of the things for which Doe is attributively responsible are more advantageous than the consequences of the things for which Roe is attributively responsible. (I will make no more clarifications of this kind. I think my intended meaning is generally conveyed well enough without them.)
20 See Hurley 2003, 107–8.
21 Hurley 2003, 151.
22 Cf. Nozick 1974.
23 Another difference between right libertarianism and responsibilitarianism is the former's focus on actual choice rather than responsibility; see Nozick 1974, 160. The limited responsibilitarianism of right libertarianism mentioned in the text would be further eroded where persons cannot be held fully responsible for the choices they make.
24 For the different argument that the neutralization of either *bad* thin luck, or thick luck (which is tied to one or another particular substantive view of responsibility), can offer some justification for egalitarianism, see Lippert-Rasmussen 2005.
25 Scheffler 2003a, 18; see also Matravers 2002, 560.
26 In one place Scheffler (2003a, 17–18) says that '[s]ome luck-egalitarian writings seem implicitly to suggest that whatever is assigned to the category of unchosen circumstance is a contingent feature of the causal order, which is not under the individual's control and does not implicate his or her personhood, whereas voluntary choices are fully under the control of individuals and constitute pure expressions of agency'. He clearly does not take himself merely to be drawing attention to the misleading signals of particular luck egalitarians. Earlier in the same paragraph he asserts that 'the degree of weight that the luck egalitarian places on the distinction between choices and circumstances seems, on its face, to be both philosophically dubious and morally implausible'. Given this and the thrust of his other remarks, it is reasonable to assume that Scheffler believes that luck egalitarianism is morally reliant upon libertarianism.

27 Smilansky 1997, 156.

28 See 3.6.

29 Scheffler 2003a, 17–18; 2005, 13.

30 See note 56 below.

31 Rakowski 1991, 76–7, 113–15; Roemer 2003, 262. Mathias Risse maintains that the argument of Roemer's book *Equality of Opportunity* assumes the impossibility that *both* libertarianism and compatibilism are correct; see Roemer 1998. Whatever the validity of this criticism, however, Risse (2002, 743 n.40) states that it is inapplicable to the theories of Cohen, Dworkin, and Arneson.

32 If the unfairness of compatibilism-based inequality objection could be upheld, the libertarian assumption objection would rely upon either hard determinism or compatibilism being correct.

33 Hurley (2002, 79–80) states that '[w]hat is a matter of thin luck for [an] agent is just what he is not responsible for, and what he is responsible for is not a matter of thin luck for him'. A terminologically different but, in effect, identical strategy would be to replace the term 'luck egalitarianism' with 'responsibility-sensitive egalitarianism'. A similar strategy is taken in some of Arneson's more recent papers, although the theory he now espouses ('responsibility-catering prioritarianism') is, strictly speaking, non-egalitarian. See 6.7. I generally take the thin luck strategy, however, as the phrase 'luck egalitarianism' appears to be entrenched.

34 Hurley 2002, 80.

35 See Hurley 2002, 81–4.

36 Dworkin 1981, 293–5; Arneson 1989, 83–4; 1990, 176; Cohen 1989, 908, 916; Rakowski, 74–5.

37 Other criteria, such as control or (genuine) choice, are also often mentioned. See the works cited in the preceding note. In such cases it is often assumed that control and choice coincide with responsibility. I think it evident that, were responsibility and such other factors to come into conflict, it would be the latter with which Arneson and Cohen would dispense. Larry Temkin (1993, 18 n.33) also holds that egalitarian distributive justice is in part dependent upon 'the mare's nest of free will'. Roemer and Dworkin seem to disagree, however (see note 52 below). For discussion of control- and reason responsiveness-based versions of luck egalitarianism see Mason 2006, ch. 7; for discussion by political philosophers of these and other accounts of responsibility see Hurley 2003, part I; Matravers 2007, ch. 2.

38 For good overviews of contemporary libertarianism and compatibilism see Clarke 2004; McKenna 2004.

39 This is not, of course, to say that, on this assumption, equal opportunity for welfare does itself reduce to equality of welfare. Even though the two principles' recommendations would be identical in even the

most unusual circumstances, the justification for these recommendations would be different (see note 48 below).

40 See Arneson 1989, 86; Cohen 1993, 28; cf. Arneson 2006, 9.

41 Scheffler 2003a, 19.

42 For arguments of this type and my responses see Chapter 4 of this work.

43 Scheffler 2005, 12.

44 Scheffler 2005, 13.

45 Scheffler 2005, 13.

46 Scheffler 2005, 13.

47 Scheffler suggests that the importance that Arneson attaches to choice
is particularly questionable given his acknowledgement that some
are better at making choices than others; see Scheffler 2005, 26 n.18;
Arneson 2002a, 371; 1999a, 496. But as we saw in 2.1, Arneson and
other luck egalitarians explicitly state that interpersonal variations
in ability to use options effectively should be taken into account.
For example, those who act irresponsibly owing to their upbringing
would not be penalized for their irresponsibility; see the works cited in
Chapter 4, note 84.

48 A possible response to the argument of this paragraph is foreshad-
owed by Dworkin, who argues that no tastes are genuinely chosen as
those that might appear to be are ultimately traceable to uncultivated
second-order tastes; see Dworkin 2000, ch. 7; 2004, 346–7, 391 n.22.
Likewise, it might be claimed that no individual can really choose to
develop or neglect their choice-making capability in the required way,
as any such choices will be influenced by their initial capability. These
arguments raise questions that cannot be answered without going
too far afield. Fortunately they do not need to be answered for our
purposes, as luck egalitarianism could, in any event, accommodate
the arguments. Cohen's response to Dworkin's argument is, *mutatis
mutandis*, equally applicable here: '[i]t is a matter of principle for
equal opportunity for welfare that tastes are compensated for only if
and when and because they are (to put it crudely) not chosen, however
often (including never) they are *in fact* chosen, and equality of welfare
denies that principle. That deep difference of principle would survive
even if it should turn out that all tastes are unchosen . . .' (2004, 19,
original emphasis. If luck egalitarianism refused to reward or penalize
any choices then it obviously could not be subject to the charge that it
disadvantaged less skilful choosers.

49 Fleurbaey 1995, 40.

50 See Keller 2002; Dworkin 1981, 228–40. Notice that Fleurbaey's argument is concerned with any loss in advantage. I do not think it would
be much more compelling if restricted to the case of basic needs. While
I am not especially attracted to Keller's (2002, 538–9) proposal, *pace*
Sen and Anderson, that a wheelchair should be denied to someone who

has taken the deliberate decision to cut off their legs, it does strike me as more morally plausible than the suggestion that such a person should suffer no welfare deficit whatsoever on account of their actions (assuming that there is responsibility for those actions). If a wheelchair was provided but deliberately destroyed or given away by its new owner, I think society would probably be justified in then taking Keller's harder line; see the final paragraph of 6.8.

51 A related position ensures outcome equality of some types of advantage or goods but not others. Typically, basic liberties fall into the former category whereas happiness falls into the latter; other goods, such as wealth, fall on different sides of the line according to different versions of the general position; cf. Rawls 1999a; Fleurbaey 1995; Anderson 1999a; Scheffler 2003a. Insofar as a variant of this position ensures outcome equality, it is susceptible to the hard determinist assumption objection. Insofar as it fails to equalize advantage, its egalitarian credentials are undermined although this is not for reasons that are relevant to the present argument; for criticism of Anderson's position, see section 4.7.

52 This is, I believe, Roemer's stance; see the discussion following in the text. It also shares significant similarities with Dworkin's position. He insists, for instance, that resource distribution be option luck- and choice-sensitive but brute luck- and circumstance-insensitive, with no requirement that the choices that give rise to option luck are metaphysically genuine; indeed, the relevance of the choice/circumstance distinction is based on the claim that it 'tracks ordinary people's ethical experience' (Dworkin 2000, 289–90; see also 6). Brian Barry has also proposed a choice-based egalitarianism, which he calls 'semi-choicism', that is free from metaphysics; see B. Barry 1991; Matravers 2007, 80–4. Finally, Andrew Williams has mentioned in correspondence with Scheffler the possibility of a luck egalitarianism grounded in Scanlon's 'Value of Choice' view, which holds that a person can have no complaint about actual outcomes where the opportunities assigned to them generally prevent harm, rather than the more conventionally luck egalitarian 'Forfeiture View' which bases valid complaints on the presence or absence of voluntariness; see Scheffler 2005, n.20; Scanlon 1998, 258–9.

53 Marc Fleurbaey 2001, 502; cf. Williams 1997, 52.

54 The best-known discussion of the principle of insufficient reason in political philosophy is in Rawls 1999a, sec. 28. Rawls refuses to apply it, though on notoriously dubious grounds. See Harsanyi 1975.

55 By 'settle' I do not mean to imply that unanimous agreement is the necessary outcome of the committee's debates. We might assign each member of the committee equal power in setting its recommendation in the absence of unanimity. This is possible because the committee

provides probability scores rather than policy documents. The committee could decide, say, that the first scenario is twice as likely to be true as the second either by unanimous agreement, or on the grounds that there are twice as many convinced hard determinists as there are libertarians and compatibilists combined, or on the grounds that this is the balance of power struck between those who hold a compromise position and those who take a hard line.

56 Derk Pereboom (1995, 21) reports that 'the demographic profile of the free will debate reveals a majority of soft determinists' and 'a minority' of libertarians; '[s]eldom has hard determinism . . . been defended'. This suggests that there will be a compromise, but one strongly biased towards the libertarian/compatibilist viewpoint.

57 See Arneson 2006, 10.

58 Roemer 1993, 149.

59 See Hampton 1989, 807.

60 Fleurbaey 2001, 503. See also Fleurbaey 1995, 39.

61 Fleurbaey (2001, 503) makes a different claim: 'The problem with [Roemer's] political approach is that it is interesting only if society is indeed likely to decide correctly where responsibility lies.' In my view neither the committee nor society is actually likely to make the (metaphysically) *correct* decision. I maintain only that the former is likely to make a *better* (i.e. less wrong) decision than the latter.

62 The danger of self-interest could be limited by exempting the members from the effects of their findings and placing them under the rule of certain predefined norms (such as those resulting from the previous committee's deliberations).

63 Arneson 1997b, 239.

64 Arneson 1997b, 239–40.

65 There is, then, the paradoxical possibility that the distributive intuitions of outcome egalitarians are right even though, given metaphysical uncertainty, it is unreasonable for them to subscribe to their theory, and that the distributive intuitions of the typical luck egalitarian – that distributions should be at least partially sensitive to commonplace conceptions of responsibility – are wrong, even though it is reasonable for them to subscribe to their theory. The most likely way for all this to be the case would be if hard determinism is true.

66 Cohen 1989, 934.

67 Though plausible, I do not believe that this is the correct reading. Scheffler (2003a, 18) seems to disagree, maintaining that Cohen is speaking as a luck egalitarian rather than as a political philosopher when he says 'we may indeed be up to our necks', and interpreting Cohen's 'tough luck' comment as ironic.

6

The Components of Justice

1. Introductory Remarks

We have found that the problems that critics most identify with luck egalitarianism are more illusory than real. Both its egalitarian and responsibilitarian credentials appear to be quite solid. Furthermore, reasons have been given for doubting some writers' confidence that their favoured theories are unproblematically egalitarian (for example, Anderson's 'democratic equality') or responsibility sensitive (for example, right libertarianism). It has been maintained that, in normal circumstances, luck egalitarianism (or a view with identical implications in those circumstances) is the only truly responsibilitarian show in town. The field of egalitarian rivals has also been thinned; and although there is no reason for doubting that various outcome-egalitarian theories (for example, equality of welfare) are substantively egalitarian, such theories suffer once responsibility considerations are brought into the picture. In short, luck egalitarianism appears to be the best way of accommodating both equality and responsibility sensitivity in a theory of distributive justice.

Although this finding is significant, it cannot be the final word on the theory. There may be more to distributive justice than equality and responsibility sensitivity. In this final chapter I will take into account further demands of justice – principally, those concerning absolute (non-comparative) levels of advantage – which show luck egalitarianism to be deficient in certain significant and less significant respects.

The most prominent deficiency of the latter variety was mentioned in 4.4. It was shown that luck egalitarianism is in principle open to leaving the negligent to their fates, even where this treatment may strike us as somehow disproportionate to the 'offence'. As noted there, and in 4.6, this 'Bad Samaritanism' is not much of a problem in practice; but Chapter 4 left the theoretical problem unaddressed, as the focus was on the largely practical issue of whether luck egalitarianism satisfied the third condition for substantive egalitarianism.

The argument of this chapter begins in earnest in section 2, where it is maintained that a minimally pluralistic luck egalitarianism can rule out Bad Samaritanism.

The rejection of Bad Samaritanism requires very little modification of luck egalitarianism even at the level of principle. Several related, but rather more serious, complications are then introduced, starting in section 3 with an application of the familiar problem of 'levelling down' to luck egalitarianism. In section 4 the specifically luck-egalitarian problems of 'diverging down' and 'responsibility levelling' are set out alongside a demonstration of luck egalitarianism's tendency to make 'expensive resource transfers'. In section 5, the various effects of these problems are explored, while section 6 examines the susceptibility to these problems of pluralistic versions of luck egalitarianism. The most developed response to said problems, Richard Arneson's 'responsibility-catering prioritarianism', is set out, (re)interpreted, and extended in section 7. It is maintained in section 8 that, even with its reference to prioritarianism, responsibility-catering prioritarianism still has an insufficient regard for absolute levels of well-being, on account of its responsibilitarianism. But this problem may be rectified by a particular precise formulation of the position.

2. The Pluralist Response

Two responses are open to the luck egalitarian who wishes to preclude Bad Samaritanism. The first of these is the *equality-first response*. Kasper Lippert-Rasmussen describes egalitarianism's preference-ordering over distributions thus:

> *Best* – Equality reflecting equivalent exercises of responsibility (A).
> *Second best* – Inequality reflecting differential exercises of responsibility (B).
> *Third best* – Inequality (or, for that matter, equality) failing to reflect differential exercises of responsibility (C).[1]

The difference between conventional luck egalitarianism and the equality-first response is at the top end of the ordering: while the former treats A and B as equivalent, the latter differentiates between them, treating A as preferable to B.[2] It is not immediately evident that the equality-first response copes with negligent victim cases at all. For the inequality between the negligently uninsured and injured Bert, and some injured but insured person, is a matter of differential responsibility, and is as such a case of B. Were Bert treated we would then be looking at a case of C. Thus, treating Bert does not appear to be recommended by the equality-first response. This response, however, provides the normative grounding for a system of public health insurance that we found to be lacking in equality of opportunity for advantage. This is because such a system could be structured so as to give rise to A rather than B or C, for it would put all persons, including Bert, into the position of being insured against injury.

The equality-first response may be strong enough to see off negligent-victim cases. Unfortunately, it looks to be so strong that it renders luck egalitarianism utterly repulsive. Note that the key problem for egalitarian planners in bringing about A would be ensuring that individuals exercise their responsibility equivalently, for they can sort out equal distributions after the event. The obvious way of maximizing the occurrence of responsibility equivalency would be by limiting the choice and control available to individuals, such that their exercises of responsibility tend to be equivalent. This leads to a particularly pernicious variation on egalitarianism's levelling-down theme.[3] Were the state to put every citizen in pitch-black solitary confinement for twenty-four hours a day, then their exercises of responsibility would be far more equivalent than were they to lead more normal lives. But it is hard to imagine a more perfect dystopia. In fairness it should be said that Lippert-Rasmussen claims only to be describing egalitarianism. But even if equality does not reject this scenario, justice clearly does,[4] and with it the equality-first response.

Our reasons for rejecting the equality-first response lead us to a more successful luck-egalitarian response, which I will call the *pluralist response*. This grants that outright luck egalitarians may be Bad Samaritan, but that this shows only what we know already – that justice (or morality generally) should be in part guided by considerations that are not egalitarian in any usual sense.[5] Candidate non-egalitarian considerations include charity, priority to the worst off, utility, sufficiency, solidarity, and direct reference to basic needs. Here I will consider the last of these.[6] For present purposes, basic needs are defined as those things which are so important for an individual that they must be satisfied regardless of normal responsibility considerations; in this case the basic need appears to be life. (If, as Fleurbaey seems to suggest, a very large welfare loss is something that justice must take into account, then whatever prevents that may be a basic need. But that is not necessarily the only reason we might have for calling survival a basic need.)

On the *luck egalitarianism plus basic needs* view, justice simply slips out of her luck-egalitarian clothes when she encounters cases such as Bert and plays the Good Samaritan. But it should be clear that she generally remains distinctly luck egalitarian. In the first place, cases of basic-need deprivation are likely to be rare in a luck-egalitarian world because, unlike present societies, all persons will (on reasonable empirical assumptions) initially have adequate means.[7] In the vast majority of cases luck egalitarianism is the only basis for distribution. There is no need to 'forgive' *all* those whose negligence has left them significantly disadvantaged by compensating them at the expense of the prudent.[8] Compensation is reserved for cases of exceptional disadvantage.

Furthermore, while all instances of basic-need deprivation are cause for concern, responsibility considerations may play a role in helping us decide how to respond to that concern. There is, for instance, nothing to stop the government from sending medical bills to those negligent who have immediate needs and have (or will have) the assets to pay. We may choose to make Bert's treatment a lower priority than that of prudent persons otherwise identically positioned, place him in a less luxurious hospital, and so on. We can, then, ensure that negligent victims receive treatment without falling back into some form of outcome egalitarianism, and without altering our judgements in the great majority of cases. This version at least of the pluralist argument retains a luck-egalitarian flavour.

An obvious reply to this move is that it just is not good enough to offer Bert treatment on purely non-egalitarian grounds. Fleurbaey asserts that '[i]t is obviously a matter of *egalitarian* distributive justice that the satisfaction of basic needs should be given priority in the distribution of resources'.[9] But I simply do not believe that this is obviously true. It is quite crucial that the strictest egalitarian sees no injustice where everyone's basic needs are unsatisfied. All are equally destitute.[10] Whether an individual's basic needs are to be satisfied as a matter of justice is, according to outcome egalitarianism, contingent on the circumstances of other persons, just as it is contingent on various practical and metaphysical factors under luck egalitarianism.

It seems, then, that assertions such as Fleurbaey's are false unless egalitarian justice is construed more broadly. But that broader construal must include some kind of non-comparative (that is, strictly non-egalitarian) requirement such as basic-needs satisfaction, in which case the difference between the proponent of the pluralist argument and the critic is largely verbal: the former says justice equals their conception of equality plus basic-needs satisfaction; the latter says justice equals their conception of equality and that alone but defines equality in such a broad way that it includes basic needs. Some space remains but it is not, as the critic requires, to do with equality's sensitivity to basic needs. Furthermore, it is, on the face of it, as plausible for the luck egalitarian to describe her reference to basic needs as part of her (primarily luck-egalitarian) conception of equality as it is for the critic to describe her similar reference as part of her (primarily non-luck-egalitarian) conception of equality.

At this point a more specific, and apparently egalitarian, objection might be raised. The critic might urge that equality must have something to say about a situation where some persons' basic needs are unsatisfied while others have sufficient resources to meet those unsatisfied needs without leaving their own needs unsatisfied. Equality does indeed tell us something about that situation but it is just the same thing it tells us about the situation where all have their basic needs satisfied but some are far more advantaged than others – that is, that there is a major inequality. Equality does not tell us to treat correcting the former inequality as a higher priority.

This objection simply attempts to smuggle basic-needs satisfaction in under a controversially broad conception of equality. The reference to basic needs is at least bordering on the gratuitous for, as already shown, basic needs strictly speaking have no particular importance for egalitarians. Without it the objection is simply that egalitarians disapprove of a situation where some have (much) more than others. This is obviously true of outcome egalitarianism. But the very point of dispute is whether we can sensibly conceive of equality in other ways. If inequalities reflect differential exercises of responsibility, there is nothing obviously wrong about saying that everyone is being treated equally and that the distribution is equal in the appropriate sense or one of the appropriate senses. This applies as much for a serious outcome inequality, such as one where basic needs are an issue, as it does for a minor one, for the differential exercises of responsibility are, by hypothesis, correspondingly serious. The objection cannot be rendered compelling without implicitly appealing to the special value of basic-need satisfaction, but that value has little to do with egalitarianism and can be accommodated equally well by luck egalitarianism.

The basic-needs version of the pluralist response may take into account paternalistic considerations similar to those attributed in section 4.4 to Eric Rakowski and, in particular, Ronald Dworkin. As it is now a matter of justice to ensure that basic needs are met, it is not enough to hope or to expect that the basic needs of negligent victims will be met by private individuals. This broader luck egalitarianism now offers a reason to introduce a public health-care system.

Elizabeth Anderson holds that the paternalism of moves such as this introduces a new kind of insult:

> In adopting mandatory social insurance schemes for the reasons they offer, luck egalitarians are effectively telling citizens that they are too stupid to run their lives, so Big Brother will have to tell them what to do. It is hard to see how citizens could be expected to accept such reasoning and still retain their self-respect.[11]

All systems of social insurance are paternalistic in some way. Anderson does not want to rule out social insurance *tout court*, but says that the reasoning offered by luck egalitarians is particularly insulting. I am not so sure. A luck-egalitarian government that wished to bring about a public health service might say something like this to its citizens:

> Everybody knows that if there is no social insurance scheme some people will be negligent and not insure themselves against injury. Everybody also knows that when such persons get injured, our society, being humane, will view providing them with treatment as a moral obligation. Institutional arrangements that leave some persons morally obligated to pay for the negligence of others are unfair. Therefore we must tax everyone to pay for universal health care.

There is no affront to prudent citizens' self-respect in this reasoning. Perhaps we might like to say that the would-be negligent are insulted. If their negligence had an impact only upon themselves, this insult might be unacceptable. But this is not the case, and the cost of the insult to them cannot be thought to outweigh the alternative, which is unfairly to ask the prudent to pay for other people's negligence. The form of pluralistic luck egalitarianism just described gives us reasons for opposing both basic needs going unmet and basic needs being met at the expense of altruistic individuals. The former reason is obvious. The latter reason is that individuals should not be disadvantaged for acting on moral principles that are endorsed as such by the state.

3. Levelling Down

The addition of a principle securing the basic needs of negligent victims is only a very limited constraint on luck egalitarianism, especially where it is made conditional in the way just outlined. But this principle fails to address another serious problem, which was hinted at in the preceding section. The problem is one of *inefficiency* – the use of resources in ways which benefit no one, or produce much smaller overall benefits for society than alternative uses – and it comes in four forms.

Outcome egalitarianism strikes some persons as unacceptable on account of its openness to *levelling down*. In many circumstances, the easiest and most effective way of securing a more equal distribution is to destroy some or all of the holdings of the better-off party or parties. In an extreme case, it might be expedient physically to harm the better-off person(s). In both cases, the action may be justified even if there is no benefit to the worse-off party. If, as committed economic egalitarians, we are concerned about the gap between rich and poor in a particular society, we would reduce the income and wealth of the rich, even if this does not improve the circumstances of the poor. If we are committed welfare egalitarians, we might find that the best way of narrowing or closing the gap between the position of the eternal optimists and clinically depressed is to cause the former pain and injury, whether or not this eases the depressives' depression.

Luck egalitarianism is also likely sometimes to favour levelling down, although only in cases where the patterns of responsibility and advantage lead it to recommend distributions identical with, or much like, those of outcome egalitarianism. The most straightforward pattern occurs where persons have acted equally responsibly but some of these persons hold more than others. As long as equality can be realized (or best approximated) by reducing the holdings or other benefits of the better off without benefiting the worse off, this is what luck egalitarianism will recommend. A similar approach might be taken where both levels of advantages and responsibilities are unequal, but the size of the difference in advantage is greater than is justified by the differences in responsible action.

What, then, is the nature of the objection to this levelling down? Two main varieties of the objection may be identified. The differences between the two are brought out by a simple example. Suppose that we can choose between two states of affairs for a society divided into two equally sized classes. There are no variations in the levels of advantage held by members of the same class. The first state of affairs, X, has one class holding ten units of advantage, and the other class holding four units of advantage (10, 4). The second state of affairs, Y, has each class holding three units of advantage (3, 3). This represents the most extreme kind of case of levelling down, since the worst-off group is actually disadvantaged by the egalitarian's favoured distribution. I will call the recommendation that each individual be disadvantaged a recommendation of *gross inefficiency*.

The *strong* form of the levelling-down objection is as follows:

(i)   egalitarianism implies that Y is better than X *in at least one respect*;

(ii) Y is not better than X *in any respect*;
      therefore,

(iii) egalitarianism is false.[12]

It is clear that, in a certain uninteresting and descriptive way, Y is better than X in certain respects. It is, for example, better in respect of *persons having one unit of welfare*; and as regards *reducing welfare*. What we are interested in is whether Y is or is not *morally* better than X in any respect; or more precisely, whether Y is or is not better than X in any respect that is *a matter of justice*. Giving people one unit of welfare and reducing welfare do not by themselves make things better in any way as regards justice.

It is, of course, clear that, in the descriptive sense, Y makes things better in respect of equality of outcome. It also makes things better as regards equal opportunity for welfare if individuals have acted equally (or fairly equally) responsibly or the worse off group in X have acted more responsibly. Things are also better as regards responsibility-sensitive envy-test equality if individuals have acted equally (or fairly equally) responsibly or the worse-off group in X has acted more responsibly, *and* Y is closer to envy freeness than A, as might be expected.[13] But are any of these respects matters of justice?

Equal opportunity for welfare may appear to reflect one dimension of justice. Dworkin has argued that

> a community that accepts the demand of equal concern must have some answer to the question why its laws and policies allow some people to secure lives of greater excitement, interest, and achievement than others can, even when no one is starving or even badly off measured historically. Equal concern is essentially a comparative concept.[14]

It seems that it is a basic requirement of justice that the advantages some people have over others are either set on a principled basis (as luck egalitarianism proposes to do) or negated altogether (as outcome egalitarianism demands). For the reasons given in earlier chapters, luck egalitarianism (and especially equal opportunity for welfare) might be thought to justify some inequalities. We might describe inequalities that are justified on the grounds of responsibility as *equitable* ones: 'If one individual receives less than another owing to their own choice, then the disparity is not considered inequitable; if it arises for reasons beyond her control, then it is inequitable.' [15] Likewise, equalities are equitable if they reflect equally responsible action, but inequitable if they do not.

Let us allow, for the moment, that Y may be morally better than X, provided that the inequalities in X are not justified on responsibility grounds. We could then still accept the strong levelling-down objection where the inequalities in X were justified on responsibility grounds, because we can see nothing better about Y: everyone is worse off than they were in A, and there is not even the saving grace that unfair inequalities have been removed. But we cannot accept the strong levelling-down objection where the inequalities in X were *not* justified on responsibility grounds, since Y has just that saving grace.[16]

The strong levelling-down objection may not, then, be effective as a criticism of the most viable form of luck egalitarianism (equal opportunity for welfare). The same cannot be said of the *weak* form, which holds the following:

(i*)   egalitarianism implies that Y is better than X, *all things considered*;
(ii*) Y is not better than X, *all things considered*;
        therefore,
(iii*) egalitarianism is false.[17]

While some persons, perhaps for the reasons mentioned earlier, may be comfortable with the notion that Y may be better than X in one regard, virtually no one would be prepared to agree with (i*) that Y was, on the whole, a better state of affairs. It makes things worse for every individual, and the one benefit – the removal of inequitable variations in advantage – does not even come close to compensating fully for that.[18] Cases of levelling down are similar to Bad Samaritan cases, in that they demonstrate strict luck egalitarianism's complete indifference to absolute – that is, non-comparative – levels of advantage. Here, luck egalitarianism overlooks Pareto improvements – those which would benefit at least one person without placing any extra burden on any other – and more generally 'undervalues the moral significance of having more resources in people's hands'.[19] Yet absolute societal levels of advantage comprise a key factor to consider when assessing whether a distribution is just. This is the one thing that all forms of utilitarianism definitely get right.

4. Diverging Down, Responsibility Levelling and Expensive-Resource Transfer

Luck egalitarianism's vulnerability before the weak levelling-down objection is not its only display of inefficiency. Three other phenomena are worthy of note. First, there are some scenarios in which the luck egalitarian will harm certain parties' interests, for nobody's benefit, in a way which is perhaps best described as *diverging down*. Suppose one person has acted more responsibly than another but that their advantages are identical; or, alternatively, that the more responsible person has lower levels of advantage than the less responsible person. A luck-egalitarian distributive body may, under some quite plausible conditions, find that the best way of introducing the required disparity (or something approaching that) is to penalize the less responsible person although this does not benefit the responsible person. In an extreme case, gross inefficiency may occur, as the most effective way of bringing about the appropriate inequality may involve worsening every individual's position. For example, suppose that, perhaps following the intervention of outcome egalitarians, Y (3, 3) now holds in the two-class society described earlier, but that one class is much more responsible than the other. A luck egalitarian would favour a move to Z, where the responsible class holds two units of advantage and the irresponsible class holds one unit of advantage (2, 1).

The (un)attractiveness of diverging down depends very much on context. Something very much like it is often viewed as unobjectionable in criminal law. It may be just to punish someone for committing a murder or a rape even if doing so will not benefit other persons (there are no deterrent effects, the victim's families and public do not take any comfort from the sentence, and so on). But luck egalitarianism proposes to diverge down in cases where the irresponsible person has not acted maliciously; they need only have acted somewhere below the societal average. Take, for instance, the example of punishing someone for failing to make the same effort at work as others, where that punishment is not linked to advantages for the more responsible, and where the effort made is only small relative to that of the highly motivated majority. It also appears that the grossly inefficient variety of diverging down may be unacceptable, even where (unusually) the harm to the responsible is a necessary side effect of punishing serious wrongdoing.

Luck egalitarianism also suffers from *responsibility levelling*. This is another serious source of inefficiency, even though it is not as obvious in this case as it is in the case of Lippert-Rasmussen's equality-first view described earlier. Since luck egalitarianism is equally satisfied with a situation in which all persons act equally responsibly and receive the same levels of advantage (welfare, resources, or whatever), and a situation in which individual levels of advantage vary with their levels of responsibility, it has no direct reason for depriving everyone of opportunities to vary their levels of responsibility. It is a virtual certainty, however, that, given the limitations of both information gathering and schemes of rewards and penalties, as well as metaphysical doubts, it will be impossible to make individual levels of advantage and responsibility correspond with one another in the appropriate ways where the levels of responsibility vary considerably, as they would under normal circumstances. The luck egalitarian may, then, have reasons for imposing draconian limits on the kinds of activities open to persons. Such measures would very likely result in a large welfare loss across society, and may conceivably be grossly inefficient. For instance, the moves from X (10, 4) to Y (3, 3) or Z (2, 1) might be recommended if these latter distributions better reflected individual responsibility levels.

The final variety of luck-egalitarian inefficiency is the *expensive resource transfer*. The previous varieties involved decreasing some persons' levels of advantage without thereby advantaging other persons'. Here, by contrast, some persons are disadvantaged in a way that benefits others. Typically this will involve a redistribution of impersonal resources.[20] The problem is the lack of concern with the cost of extracting the benefit, relative to that benefit.

Suppose, as we did back in section 1.2, that B is seriously and permanently disabled. As a result, she strongly disidentifies with her disability, and favours the bundle of resources of the non-disabled but otherwise identical A. Let us recall that B was not responsible for her disability. According to responsibility-sensitive envy-test equality, B qualifies for compensation up to the level at which she no longer envies A's resources. According to equal opportunity for welfare, she qualifies for compensation up to the level at which she matches A's level of welfare.

My earlier discussion of this case concluded that envy-test equality's way of setting compensation for disabilities appears acceptable to disabled persons such as B. The same should be true of the approaches of the responsibility-sensitive version of that theory and equal opportunity for welfare, provided that such persons are not responsible for their disabilities. But all of this may seem unacceptable to A; indeed, it may appear unfair to him. As B considers her disability to be a severe disadvantage, she would require significantly larger quantities of impersonal resources than non-disabled people in order for her bundle of resources or level of welfare to be equal to theirs. These may go far beyond what is required for the basic capability of mobility. Indeed, it is possible that a large proportion of a society's wealth could be distributed to her. Such extensive redistribution will occur if it is both the case that B's conception of her disability is sufficiently negative that she cannot be satisfied by anything less, and that each increase in wealth improves her assessment of her overall bundle of goods (even if only infinitesimally). This latter condition may well be the case if the extra money makes expensive care services or medical treatment available to her, or even if it enables her to buy that tropical island she has her eye on.

I do not think that this outcome is avoided where policy-makers have taken on board the insights of the social approach to disability.[21] To be sure, it may be reasonably cost-effective to increase a disabled person's assessment of her bundle of goods by removing *basic* social restrictions,

> whether those restrictions occur as a consequence of inaccessible built environments, questionable notions of intelligence and social competence, the inability of the general population to use sign language, the lack of reading material in Braille or hostile public attitudes to people with non-visible disabilities.[22]

But costs spiral out of control when we attempt actually to *equalize* her bundle of goods. In the first place, *fully* removing those social restrictions may be very costly. For example, providing a Braille copy of every book in every library in a state would cost many billions of pounds, yet it is hard to see any other way of arriving at equal access to written materials for the sighted and blind.

More importantly, even were such social restrictions removed, a vast range of experiences enjoyed by the majority would remain closed to many disabled people. On the envy test, someone's inability to watch the sun rise or run a marathon is just as much a source of deprivation as a lack of Braille books or wheelchair access, provided they attach as much value to those experiences. Of course, this is more likely to be the case for those who go blind or deaf than for the congenitally disabled, as the former's preferences and tastes have been arrived at with the knowledge of such experiences. But even if it was only this group that attached value to such experiences, we are left with a group of people who cannot be compensated by any amount of Braille or ramps, and who may only be satisfied when they are compensated financially. If they value a whole range of lost experiences very highly, there may be virtually no upper limit to the compensation, for that compensation should be at least equal to the cost to that individual of their disability.

Luck egalitarianism's refusal to recognize that there is a balance to be struck between the levels of advantage of the (equally responsible) better off and worse off leaves it in conflict with our considered moral judgements. It views the former group's resources or welfare as being of disvalue, since they expand inequality, and holds that such goods should be given to the worse off, no matter how small the benefit they may be able to get from them. But intuitively, both the size of the cost imposed on the better off in the course of bringing about a benefit for the worse off, and the size of that benefit, matter. As the cost a possible measure promises for the better off gets increasingly out of proportion to the benefit it promises for the worse off, that measure becomes decreasingly attractive.[23] Such transfers are most unappealing where the advantage to the worse off is negligible, and the disadvantage to the relatively better off is great.[24] The moral disvalue will be especially weighty, even to those who would identify themselves as egalitarians, where the resources are being moved from persons who do not enjoy particularly high standards of living by, say, historical or international standards, but who are nevertheless better off. The lack of any trade-off here leaves luck egalitarianism defenceless before the classic criticism that egalitarian policies might leave many, and possibly a majority, in a state of deprivation.[25] This impression is only reinforced by the likely presence of the earlier three types of inefficiency; if they are present in their less common, grossly inefficient forms, matters are dire indeed.

5. The Effects of Inefficiency

Luck egalitarianism's fatal flaw is none of the usual suspects. It is neither excessive responsibility sensitivity, nor an inability to be sufficiently responsibility sensitive, nor even a failure to be truly egalitarian. Luck egalitarianism's weakness is equality's weakness: a failure to recognize the value of increases in absolute, non-comparative levels of well-being. Whether the absolute levels of well-being in question are those of the negligent needy, as in Samaritan cases, or of the non-proportionately more responsible better off, as in the standard cases of levelling down, diverging down, responsibility levelling, and expensive resource transfer, or of the non-negligent worse off, as in the first three varieties of inefficiency (and especially in their grossly inefficient manifestations), they are utterly disregarded, with potentially serious practical consequences. Here I will offer a few speculations about these consequences.

As a preliminary, it might reasonably be asked how the findings of the previous section can possibly sit comfortably with my generally positive findings regarding luck egalitarianism, especially as found in Chapter 4. It should, then, be recalled that that earlier discussion was limited to luck egalitarianism's egalitarian credibility. Consideration of the treatment of the better off was, for this reason, generally avoided.[26] Moreover, my argument here does, with one important proviso, tend to support my earlier findings regarding luck egalitarianism's treatment of the worse off. The irresponsible worse off (if there are any) will, as I said in earlier chapters, often benefit from empirical and metaphysical doubts about their levels of responsibility; even where there are no such doubts, and they are penalized, this appears unsatisfactory only in the extreme cases which section 2 above aimed to combat. In most empirical circumstances, luck egalitarianism's focus on the comparative well-being of responsible but worse-off persons would result in these persons receiving a decent level of advantage. The best way of making individual levels of advantage correspond to individual levels of responsibility is not, generally, to destroy social assets on a grand scale. Because responsibilities vary so much, levelling down is not usually an appropriate strategy. It is most often more effective to move resources to the more responsible from the less responsible using redistributive mechanisms modelled on those that are already in place. And it is particularly hard to see grossly inefficient levelling down, or for that matter grossly inefficient diverging down, getting much use. Disadvantaging the equally or less responsible better off (levelling down) or disadvantaging the less responsible equally well off (diverging down) will rarely require disadvantaging more responsible individuals.[27] That final class of disadvantaging is itself a barrier to the efficacy of the overall policy, since it offsets the decreasing (levelling down) or increasing (diverging down) of inequality.

Here, though, is the proviso: responsibility levelling *might* make luck egalitarianism very bad for everyone, including the non-irresponsible worst off. The choiceless and lifeless dystopia mentioned in section 2 would be a luck egalitarian Utopia. More standard manifestations of Utopia, or (less idealistically) of a well-ordered or good society, would also be luck-egalitarian Utopias, *if only* individual levels of responsibility could be recorded with unerring accuracy (which they presumably never could be), and *if only* we had definitively solved the free-will problem (which we presumably never will).[28] Since these are such big 'if onlys', the luck egalitarian Utopia would probably take something like the original, distinctly non-vote-winning form. Of course, there may very well be practical reasons for a (it is to be hoped by now purely hypothetical) strict luck egalitarian to abandon that ideal. It is hard to imagine many rallying to the cause (but perhaps a few people of great power might be enough), and there may be difficulty in running the new arrangements if somehow they were put in place (but even if it was necessary to have many administrators, all living in more normal, choice-making circumstances, things would overall be very responsibility sensitive). Whether these issues could be overcome or not is, I think, an open question. It is clear that full-blown luck egalitarianism is open to the most appalling injustice in principle, and perhaps also in practice. It is possible that the worse off would be made (even) worse off along with everybody else.

The variety of inefficiency which would be most likely to have a public policy impact is, I think, expensive resource transfer. Although the effects here will not worsen the situation of the worse off – quite the contrary – they may be terrible none the less. Some persons suffer from circumstances which are conspicuously both deeply disadvantaging and beyond their control. Those with any of a wide range of severe congenital disabilities may fall into this category. In addition, some of those disadvantaged persons who had an unfavourable social and economic 'start in life' may also fall into this category. In both cases, it may be that even very large expensive transfers in resources are insufficient to equalize appropriately. In the former case, reasons for this have already been provided. In the latter case, unfavourable early socialization may make it impossible for these persons to hold down jobs (or even to have the motivation to work). Given the clear depressive effect of unemployment, the compensation called for may go far beyond that required to equalize economic circumstances with workers. Where even only a small subset of profoundly unhappy people cannot be satisfied with the most extensive resources, the

majority in a luck-egalitarian society may find itself subject to pau-
perization by the bottomless pit of compensable disadvantage.

It should be emphasized that the underlying causes of these potential problems are not those identified by the outspoken opponents of
luck egalitarianism. Nor, indeed, do they correctly identify the most
likely ill effects. The worse off may, in certain special circumstances,
be disadvantaged but a broader disadvantaging is much more foreseeable. The writers who have been most sensitive to this real danger are
luck egalitarians such as Arneson, Cohen, Rakowski, Temkin, and
(if he is to count as a luck egalitarian) Dworkin, who have made it
plain that justice must take account of absolute levels of well-being.[29]
So perhaps luck egalitarianism can be modified to meet the problems
identified thus far.

6. The Pluralist Response Reprised

In this section I will explore a few ways in which the worst effects
of luck egalitarianism's inefficiency can be negated by reprising the
pluralist response described earlier in this chapter. The aim is to
see whether there is any combination of luck egalitarianism and (a)
familiar independent principle(s) which consistently yields distinctly
egalitarian and responsibilitarian conclusions, but without conflict-
ing with our other notions of justice. I will maintain that no such
combination appears to be available.

The natural place to start is with the pluralistic luck egalitarianism already described, which ensures that basic needs are met. Under
any of several plausible construals of basic needs, this could rule
out the most pernicious possible effects of luck egalitarianism, such
as the severe responsibility levelling just described. But many less
acute problems would remain. This approach would not prevent the
occurrence of any of the varieties of inefficiency outlined above nor
would it even prevent gross inefficiency. It sees no wrong in making
many people's situations much worse off if that both maintains very
minimal standards of living and reduces responsibility-corrected
inequality, even if this does not benefit the worse off. Except in cases
of extreme irresponsibility, if we can make people's lives go better, we
should make them go better. This applies to everyone, and most of all
to the worse off. Justice is not satisfied merely because luck egalitarianism is satisfied, nor merely because basic needs are satisfied,[30] nor
even if both are satisfied.

These comments suggest that a *luck egalitarianism plus maximin* combination might fare better. Here, we first of all ensure that the worst-off group are as well off as is possible, and then go about securing the luck-egalitarian objective (insofar as this is consistent with the maximining). If we wish still to take responsibilitarianism seriously, we might choose only to maximize the levels of advantage of the worst-off persons who are not responsible for their circumstances. Whichever construal we adopt, the extreme problems corrected by luck egalitarianism plus basic-needs satisfaction remain corrected, and some of the remaining problems are combated. Gross inefficiency is removed, because some persons (the worst off or the worst off non-irresponsible) will undoubtedly benefit. The garden varieties of levelling down, diverging down and responsibility levelling will also appear to be less pronounced, since the (non-irresponsible) worst off will at least benefit in absolute terms from the overall redistributive strategy.

This combination does, nevertheless, face serious difficulties. Firstly, the less severe character of the first three varieties of inefficiency does not mean that these problems have gone away. They are inevitably bound up with egalitarianism, and so long as a combination of principles includes an egalitarian element (such as luck egalitarianism), that combination is, to some extent, recommending counter-intuitive distributions. Maximin obscures rather than resolves the difficulty here.

Secondly, even if this combination is presented in the form that takes responsibility sensitivity quite seriously, it fails to be genuinely luck egalitarian. Since the maximin component has lexical (that is, unconditional) priority over the luck-egalitarian component, there is little more than a nod to egalitarianism. Certainly, it would fail to satisfy the criteria for substantive egalitarianism described in Chapter 3, for essentially the same reasons that straightforward maximinism failed to satisfy them. Conversely, if greater priority is granted to the luck-egalitarian component, the benefits the maximinism affords start to evaporate.

Thirdly, some definition of the worst-off group is necessary, but any such definition will appear to be quite arbitrary. The most famous advocate of maximin, John Rawls, admits that '[a]ny procedure [for identifying the worst-off group] is bound to be somewhat ad hoc', but maintains that 'we are entitled at some point to plead practical considerations, for sooner or later the capacity of philosophical or other arguments to make finer discriminations must run out'.[31] Quite what Rawls means by 'practical considerations' is obscure. At any rate, because there are other theories and principles which can claim, with some plausibility, to get further on the strength of the arguments, luck egalitarianism plus maximin must rate weaker on this score.

Finally, and most gravely, this combination fails to address the problem of expensive resource transfer. Maximin provides an alternative rationale for costly removals of resources from the better off. The aim is to benefit those who are worst off (not worse off)[32] in absolute terms (not comparative terms). But this rationale leads us in much the same direction as the luck egalitarian's rationale. Within a given society, the worse or worst off in absolute terms comprise the same group as the worse or worst off in comparative terms. The worse/worst-off distinction may have substantial effects on distributions, but the difference in the levels of exposure to the expensive resource transfer problem experienced by (luck) egalitarianism and maximin is impossible to specify in advance, and will depend on both the circumstances and the size of the stipulated worst-off group. In short, luck egalitarianism plus maximin limit the scope of luck egalitarianism but in such a way that, as regards expensive resource transfers, much the same effects follow.

A *luck egalitarianism plus utilitarianism* combination may appear to be the natural way of insulating our theory against the danger of excessively expensive resource transfers. While this is not the only advantage of the combination, there are also difficulties. Chief among these is the positive correlation between the extent to which the various efficiency problems are tackled, and the extent to which the egalitarianism and responsibilitarianism of the theory are compromised. This also held for luck egalitarianism plus maximin, but a separate explanation is necessary, since there are differences in which efficiency problems may be addressed. In both cases, there appears to be no satisfactory weighting of the two components.

Suppose we give lexical priority to the utilitarian component. Here, there can be no expensive resource transfers, nor any levelling down, diverging down or responsibility levelling. Since every distribution will optimize the levels of advantage (that is, utility) in society, there will be no inefficiency. There will be no responsibility sensitivity, however, except in the unusual situation that there are two or more ways of maximizing advantage, and some of these reward the responsible and penalize the irresponsible better than others. Even where there is not lexical priority for utilitarianism, but it has a heavy weighting in the overall distributive theory, we will find that distributions are responsibility sensitive in only a limited way. The egalitarianism of the overall theory is similarly undermined where the utilitarianism is prominent.[33] Moreover, and as the first criticism of luck egalitarianism plus maximin urges, the weakness of luck egalitarianism is not removed by giving another principle a major role.

To go to the other extreme of the spectrum, we could give lexical priority to the luck-egalitarian component. Here, the responsibilitarian and egalitarian credentials of the theory are in no doubt, since the utilitarianism can kick in only where luck egalitarianism is equally happy with more than one alternative. But this approach gives virtually no protection against any of the four forms of inefficiency. Even if we drop the lexical priority, so long as luck egalitarianism has a significant role in setting distributions, it will drag them in inefficient directions.

It should also be mentioned that luck egalitarianism plus utilitarianism would offer limited protection against Bad Samaritanism. It is often the case that satisfaction of the basic needs of the negligent needy is a good way of promoting utility. For example, the benefits, in terms of overall levels of advantage, brought about by state provision of food or simple medical treatment are generally disproportionate to their costs. The Samaritanism is limited, however, as some medical treatments or other ways of meeting basic needs may be so expensive that the utilitarian has better ways of using her resources. This may apply in the example of Bert. Since luck egalitarianism does not recommend assisting the needy negligent no matter how inexpensive that assistance may be, the bar of acceptable expense is raised where utilitarianism has anything less than lexical priority.

The best combination of the principles canvassed here strikes me as being a three-way meeting of *luck egalitarianism plus utilitarianism plus basic-needs satisfaction*. I would not give basic-needs satisfaction the lexical priority that has, until now, been implicitly assumed, because that approach faces a further criticism which, while of little practical significance, has some relevance theoretically. The criticism draws attention to a certain variety of expensive resource transfer. In this kind of case, the basic needs of some person(s) are unsatisfied in a way that is very expensive to correct. This kind of case lacks practical significance relative to the general phenomenon of expensive resource transfer for two reasons. First, because basic needs are (presumably) to be defined in largely objective fashion, they do not provide the redistributive blank cheque that subjective measures of disadvantage, such as present-mood welfare deficits or envy, do when they are combined with a principle eliminating disadvantage. An extremely unhappy person is potentially a source of limitless claims for compensation under a subjective account, whereas a person lacking basic needs can be entitled only to the resources necessary to satisfy those needs – for instance, the money needed to pay for food or medicine. Second, since the reason for the redistribution is the satisfaction of basic needs, rather than the mere removal of disadvantage, however small that disadvantage may be, inefficient redistribution appears acceptable at higher levels. This point, in tandem with the first, suggest that basic-needs-mandated inefficiency must be extreme for it to be unacceptable, and that extreme cases of basic-needs-satisfaction-mandated inefficiency are unusual. Even so, it is conceivable that, say, the only way of satisfying someone's right to life is to provide them with a regular supply of a drug that is so expensive that its provision will seriously undermine the standard of living of many thousands of people, though not in a way that can be said to undermine their basic needs. In this way, then, basic-needs satisfaction may appear to be too open ended in principle, even if adopted in the semi-responsibility-sensitive form mentioned in section 2 (I revisit this issue at the close of the chapter).

Within this best combination, the satisfaction of basic needs might be given a heavy weighting that falls short of lexical priority. Luck egalitarianism and utilitarianism might be given roughly similar weightings to one another. In some cases basic needs might go unsatisfied, particularly where the pulls of responsibility sensitivity and utility are united in their opposition to such satisfaction. The utilitarian component would provide resistance to luck egalitarianism's inefficiency, while the luck-egalitarian component would give the overall proto-theory access to some of the considerations of justice that fall outside of the utilitarian's narrow view.

7. Responsibility-Catering Prioritarianism

I think the distributive recommendations of a more precise formulation of the luck egalitarianism plus utilitarianism plus basic needs combination would be quite intuitively sound. The bad news for luck egalitarianism's prospects is that this is still not the best account of justice. The good news is that there is a better account which is significantly responsibilitarian and maybe also be egalitarian.

The better account I have in mind is a variant of Arneson's *responsibility-catering prioritarianism*. This, in effect, combines responsibilitarianism with utilitarianism and prioritarianism; that is, it is a responsibility-sensitive version of the limited priority for the worse off view described in Chapter 3. This form of prioritarianism holds that '[t]he moral value of a gain is (1) greater, the greater the welfare or utility it affords the person, and (2) greater, the lower the person's lifetime utility or welfare prior to receipt of this gain'. Responsibility-catering prioritarianism adds a further dimension of moral value:

> (3) if [the person] is worse off in welfare than others, the moral value of the gain we might achieve for her is greater, the lower the individual's responsibility for her present condition, and if she is better off than others, the moral disvalue of the loss we might impose on her is greater, the greater the individual's level of responsibility for her present condition.[34]

(1) is, of course, the utilitarian component of responsibility-catering prioritarianism. It is natural to read it as a statement of the core idea of classical (total) utilitarianism, since there is no reference to the effects of the act on the size of the population (and hence, on average utility). I will set this matter aside, since the difference between classical and average utilitarianism is relevant only to population policy.

(2), the prioritarian component, is essentially a statement of leximinism,[35] though the usual radical impact of that principle is, of course, limited by (1) and (3). The focus on welfare levels across an entire life should be noted. I argued in Chapter 2 that, if someone happens to be happy but has been living an unhappy life overall, they are nevertheless advantaged right now. But this approach to defining present welfare levels is quite consistent with Arneson's view that, as far as prioritarian (or, indeed, egalitarian) justice is concerned, the relevant factor in deciding the importance of an individual's claim for assistance relative to the claims of others is how much higher or lower the lifetime welfare of that individual is relative to that of those others.[36] Indeed, I hold that giving priority to the worse off may mean making the presently happy and (hence) advantaged even happier and more advantaged, if their moods (or whatever else makes for welfare) have been disadvantageous historically.

The responsibilitarian component, (3), is that which is of most interest to the present study. The concern of the remainder of this section and the next will be this final component, and variations on it. Significant responsibility sensitivity appears to be present since (a) advantaging of those who are less responsible for their disadvantaged position (*the less negligent disadvantaged*) is to have priority over advantaging of those who are more responsible for their disadvantaged position (*the more negligent disadvantaged*), and (b) disadvantaging of those who are less responsible for their advantaged position (*the less responsible advantaged*) is to have priority over disadvantaging of those who are more responsible for their advantaged position (*the more responsible advantaged*).[37] We should, I think, interpret the priorities here as lexical, so that a gain of even one unit of welfare for the less negligent disadvantaged should be secured even if this prevents a gain of a hundred units of welfare for the more negligent disadvantaged. This will not lead to the extreme, responsibility-insensitive distribution – with the slightly more responsible receiving a never-ending supply of resources from the state – that it may appear to. The less negligent or more responsible will become the more negligent or less responsible when their welfare levels reach a certain level relative to the initially more negligent or less responsible, as they will have become responsible for a smaller proportion of their welfare level. Where the priority is anything less than unconditional the distribution is not as responsibility sensitive as it might be.

Still, without further stipulations, full responsibility sensitivity is not achieved even within the confines of (3), since there may still be variations in advantage that are not accounted for by variations in responsibility. In the first place, we might point out that there is no reason of responsibility for limiting the priorities described in (a) and (b) to advantaging and disadvantaging respectively. We might, then, favour

(a*) the welfare of the less negligent disadvantaged is to have priority over that of the more negligent disadvantaged;

(b*) the welfare of the more responsible advantaged is to have priority over that of the less responsible advantaged.

These are not equivalent to (a) and (b), since a distributive body may be in a position to decide which disadvantaged group to disadvantage further or which advantaged group to advantage further. It is clear what responsibilitarianism has to say about such questions.

(a*) and (b*) do not go far enough, as there are some priorities between more and less responsible groups which they do not address. This is because there is space for two groups which Arneson does not name. (a), (b), (a*), and (b*) all identify the relevant issue as 'the individual's level of responsibility for her present condition', and treat higher levels of such responsibility as a justification for lower welfare for the worse off and higher welfare for the better off. But some advantaged persons may have behaved so responsibly that, from the responsibilitarian's perspective, they should hold even more than they do. Such persons may have performed tasks that were advertised by the state or some other reliable body as giving rise to major benefits which they are yet to receive. Saying merely that they are fully responsible for their welfare level does not do them justice. Contrariwise, some disadvantaged persons may have behaved very irresponsibly, and therefore be entitled to even less than they actually hold, were we to concern ourselves with responsibility sensitivity. They may have acted in ways which are generally known to further their existing disadvantages, without yet having been penalized. They have been less responsible than any similarly disadvantaged persons who are fully responsible for their disadvantaged circumstances, but who have not performed these additional negligent acts.

Let us call these two new groups the *super-responsible* and the *grossly negligent*. Since the first of these groups is the most favoured by responsibilitarianism, these further rules of treatment might be stipulated:

(c) the welfare of the super-responsible advantaged is to have priority over that of the grossly negligent disadvantaged and the less responsible advantaged.
(d) the welfare of the more negligent disadvantaged and the less negligent disadvantaged is to have priority over that of the grossly negligent disadvantaged.
(e) advantaging the super-responsible advantaged is to have priority over disadvantaging (or maintaining the position of) the super-responsible advantaged.

The justification for (c) is that we know that the super-responsible advantaged are more responsible than the other three named groups. The grossly negligent disadvantaged and the less responsible advantaged are responsible for less than they hold, while the more responsible advantaged are responsible for either less than they hold, or for exactly what they hold. Since the super-responsible advantaged are responsible for more than they hold, they have an entitlement to any 'non-responsible surplus' – that is, that part of persons' advantage for which they are not responsible – held by other groups. Since the more responsible advantaged may be fully responsible for what they hold, they may sometimes have no surplus. But the grossly negligent disadvantaged and the less responsible advantaged do always have a surplus – in the first case for obvious definitional reasons, and in the second case because they are less responsible than a group (the more responsible advantaged) which is itself at most fully responsible for their welfare level (i.e. non-super responsible). No priority for the super-responsible advantaged over the less negligent disadvantaged and the more negligent disadvantaged can be established in advance, as these groups may actually be responsible for as much or more than they hold. They are only more or less negligent relative to other disadvantaged persons.

The justification for (d) is familiar. The more negligent disadvantaged are *at worst* responsible for their disadvantage, the less negligent disadvantaged are not even as irresponsible as the former group, but the grossly negligent disadvantaged are *worse than responsible for their disadvantage*. But priority over the grossly negligent disadvantaged for the two of the three advantaged groups that were not given it under (c) cannot be given anywhere, because these two groups are not necessarily better than the grossly negligent disadvantaged in respect of responsibility for their holdings.

(e) is justified simply on the grounds that the super-responsible are responsible for more than they hold. It may seem to go without saying, since it might be supposed that we would also prefer advantaging to disadvantaging. But for the committed responsibilitarian, this is not so, as we shall now see.

8. Inefficient Rules of Responsibility Sensitivity

I believe that responsibility sensitivity recommends these two further stipulations:

(f) disadvantaging the less responsible advantaged is to have priority over advantaging (or maintaining the position of) the less responsible advantaged.

(g) disadvantaging the grossly negligent disadvantaged is to have priority over advantaging (or maintaining the position of) the grossly negligent disadvantaged.

If we wish to advance the cause of responsibility sensitivity in its fullest form, we can not reject (f) or (g), or any principles with the same effects. The less responsible advantaged and the grossly negligent disadvantaged are responsible for (even) less than they hold, so they are entitled to (even) less than they hold.[38] (f) and (g) capture part of the notion I described in section 3 as equity. If a grossly negligent disadvantaged person and a less (or, in the special sense given here, more) negligent disadvantaged person both hold identical welfare levels, and it is only possible to alter this by decreasing the grossly negligent person's welfare level (that is, it is impossible to redistribute in the way [d] sanctions), this decrease is surely mandated by responsibility sensitivity. Without it, there is an inequitable equality; that is, a variation in advantage unjustified on responsibility grounds. (f)'s virtue could be illustrated in a parallel way.

I believe that responsibility sensitivity requires (a*), (b*), (c), (d), (e), (f), and (g). But even this is not enough. They describe only the priorities that should hold for the six groups defined here *by the very definition of those groups*. That definition indicates that some groups are more responsible (and hence entitled to more advantage) than others but, between some groups, there is no such ordering. Further specific rules would need to be given – for example, the rule that, where the more responsible advantaged are fully responsible for their welfare level, they have priority over the grossly negligent disadvantaged. Further divisions within the groups may also be useful. For instance, the grossly negligent disadvantaged and the super-responsible advantaged might each usefully be split into two, more and less negligent/responsible, groups, in order to direct more favourable treatment towards those whose holdings are least favourable relative to their levels of responsibility.

This all roughly follows the general responsibilitarian position that distributions should be proportionate to responsibility. Why, then, the need to set out more specific rules? Firstly, because this is necessary to show that, while some rules of this type, such as (a) and (b), undoubtedly have responsibilitarian motivation and effect, they are not sufficient for responsibilitarianism. If rules this particular are going to be articulated, we need a lot more of them to secure full responsibility sensitivity. Secondly, because a list of rules setting out distributive priorities in the way described above does not have the effect of promoting responsibility-levelling that the general responsibilitarian position might. These rules are limited to specifying how the state should respond to particular histories of individual action, rather than suggesting that the state should get involved in setting the boundaries of that action. (Of course, we may have non-responsibilitarian reasons for altering the choice context.) Finally, because some of these rules, and the parts of responsibilitarianism that they reflect, may seem more attractive than others. I will conclude this section by saying more on this point.

Of the responsibilitarian rules set out above, (f) and (g) are undoubtedly the most controversial. They sanction the phenomena

I described earlier as levelling down and diverging down. Which phenomenon actually occurs depends on the position of the named groups relative to other groups (whether they are better or worse off). If the transfer decreases inequality, on the grounds that the previous inequalities were larger than the deviation in responsibility, we have levelling down; if the transfer brings about responsibility-justified inequality we have diverging down. Either way, we have 'hyperinefficiency': the disadvantaging of one person or more for the benefit of nobody.[39]

In normal distributive circumstances, I find it hard to accept any of the transfers recommended by (f) and (g). The reasons for this have in essence been stated earlier in this chapter. In short, where there is a conflict between giving an individual more, and giving him what he is responsible for, and nothing else enters the equation, we should give him more.[40] This would not be accommodated by a version of responsibility-catering prioritarianism that endorsed (f) and/or (g). Suppose we have the opportunities to increase or decrease the holdings of a less responsible advantaged person and, independently, those of a grossly negligent irresponsible person. In these cases, (1) and (2) offer some pull in favour of advantaging but, on account of (f) and (g), (3) pulls in favour of disadvantaging. Whether these persons are advantaged or disadvantaged will be a matter of the weightings placed on (1), (2), and (3). But, even if (1) and (2)'s weighting is sufficient for advantaging to take place, the extent of that advantaging will be less than optimal, since (3) will still offer resistance. In my view the drag on advantage levels that (f) and (g) introduce to the overall account of justice is unacceptable. A similar drag would also be present in luck egalitarianism plus utilitarianism plus basic needs, since the luck-egalitarian component of that view endorses (f)- and (g)-type rules.

My rejection of (f) and (g) does presume that the strong levelling-down objection mentioned in section 3 above is, after all, sound. It is, I accept, much less obviously correct than the weak levelling-down objection. Endorsing (f) and (g) alongside principles that promote absolute well-being is perhaps plausible in a way that endorsing them without such principles is not. Still, I do not ultimately believe that there can ever be anything better about Y (3,3) than X (10,4), as regards distributive justice, even where Y better reflects responsibility. This stance needs a little explaining.

Y may be better than X in respect of some variety of non-distributive justice. I have criminal justice in mind here. There may be something good about a situation where those who have committed crimes are punished with lower levels of advantage, even in the absence of this punishment producing any benefits for society. The difference here is, presumably, between those acts which are permissible, however irresponsible they may be, and those which are morally wrong. The responsibilitarian does not say that the negligent person is a bad person; they just say that they are not entitled to as much as a non-negligent person. Here, right or wrong comes in only at the level of distribution – some state responses to certain acts are more just than others. But criminal justice may identify some acts and some persons as wrong and bad themselves. That may make the full range of responsibilitarian sanctions more acceptable.[41]

Y may also be better than X in respect of desert. We do not usually think of desert as sensitive to efficiency considerations. A desert base has to be a relevant fact about a person, but the way our unfavourable treatment of an individual affects others is not ordinarily thought of as a relevant fact about that individual. What I deserve cannot be ascertained by looking at the external effects of different deserts. In the previous chapter I said that many desert views can be construed as versions of responsibilitarianism, but it must be unrestricted responsibilitarianism. A principle that rejects (f) and (g) also rejects desert, because it is a core feature of a distributive desert view that undeserving people should be disadvantaged, regardless of whether that benefits anyone. My view is that desert and justice are incompatible on account of the former's disregard for efficiency.

Y may, finally, be better than X as regards equality. But equality does not itself seem to be a component of distributive justice. Certain elements of equality – and more specifically, certain elements of luck egalitarianism – do form part of justice. Although the luck-egalitarian notion of equity is not fully accommodated, since (f) and (g) are rejected, it is reflected in cases (a*), (b*), (c), (d), and (e), which ensure that disadvantages exist only where responsibility justifies them. Overall, this is not strongly egalitarian, since shorn of (f) and (g), the responsibilitarian component of responsibility-catering prioritarianism cannot be said to be substantively egalitarian. It fails to place a relevantly identically positioned person in the same circumstances as another relevantly identically position person for the bare reason that they are in those circumstances, as the first condition for substantive egalitarianism requires.[42] There is no mechanism here for bringing the welfare of the less responsible advantaged and the grossly negligent disadvantaged to the same levels as those of other, identically (ir)responsible people.

My favoured revision of the responsibilitarian component of responsibility-catering prioritarianism might be called (3*) or *restricted responsibilitarianism*. It lacks (f) and (g), but has a full array of rules of lexical priority for more responsible persons over less responsible ones. The basic idea of restricted responsibilitarianism is that persons should receive what they are responsible for, *except where giving them something they are not responsible for disadvantages nobody.* The italicized limitation on responsibilitarianism is required since, without it, responsibility-catering prioritarianism has a pro tanto reason for reducing welfare in a way that benefits no one.

(1), (2), and (3*) together form a very attractive account of distributive justice. (1), the utilitarian component, tackles all four forms of inefficiency described earlier, while (2), the leximin component, provides a pull away from Bad Samaritanism and moves resources towards the worse off, even when they are not the worst off, in a more efficient fashion than egalitarianism. (3*) gives us a strong, but importantly restricted, responsibilitarian thrust. Of course, (1) may also give some limited pull towards Bad Samaritanism, while (2) may provide support for the final variety of inefficiency (expensive resource transfer). I think our considered judgements drag us in two directions here, and the best we can do is settle on that compromise between the calls of efficiency and priority for the worse/worst off which strikes us as most appropriate. Responsibility-catering prioritarianism is ahead of the game, in that, unlike the pluralistic luck egalitarianisms discussed at the end of section 6 above (including the attractive luck egalitarianism plus utilitarianism plus basic needs combination), none of its components (including restricted responsibilitarianism) offers any backing whatsoever for the first three varieties of inefficiency. The remaining compromises in responsibility-catering prioritarianism appear to be the only ones which are unavoidable.

Bert is a case in point. Here responsibility-catering prioritarianism takes into account a whole range of factors which appear to be relevant – the benefit aid might give to the victim; the extent of their irresponsibility for their situation; the cost of that aid to non-victims; and the extent of the non-victims' responsibility for their holdings. In certain circumstances responsibility-catering prioritarianism may justify a denial of assistance. This may be the case if Bert consistently refuses to insure having been repeatedly involved in accidents, particularly if we think he deliberately caused those accidents.[43] There may come a point where someone is so persistent or wilful in their negligence or maliciousness that they can be considered to have waived all their rights to aid. Similarly, where Bert can be assisted only at crippling cost to a host of responsible persons, or where the benefit to Bert is negligible (his basic needs were very nearly met without aid) but the cost fairly high, that expense does not appear to be justified. Where there is a confluence of such assistance-dampening circumstances, responsibility-catering prioritarianism is at a great advantage relative to luck egalitarianism plus basic needs, or any other theory which proposes to ensure that the very badly off are aided no matter what.[44] The restricted form of responsibility-catering prioritarianism has the advantage over the unrestricted form as none of its components object to the surely objectionable action of assisting Bert where this can be done at no cost to anyone else.

9. Concluding Remarks

In this chapter it has been argued that luck egalitarianism fails as an account of distributive justice on account of its failure to acknowledge the value of absolute levels of well-being. This is reflected not only in the Bad Samaritanism that critics have incorrectly identified as a symptom of non-egalitarianism, but also in levelling down, diverging down, responsibility levelling, and expensive resource transfer. The solution is not to replace luck egalitarianism's responsibility sensitivity with a less responsibility-sensitive form of egalitarian justice, since that will inevitably permit Bad Samaritanism, levelling down, and expensive resource transfer. Rather, we should combine responsibility sensitivity with prioritarianism's direct reference to absolute levels of well-being.

Arneson's responsibility-catering prioritarianism is, then, a big step in the right direction. Even so, as he has stated it, it is unsatisfactory, since the responsibilitarian component, (3), gives only a very curtailed description of responsibility-sensitive distribution. Once a fuller description is given, responsibility sensitivity loses some of its attraction on account of its prescription that those who hold more than their responsible share should be disadvantaged, even though this benefits nobody. It appears, however, that we can restrict the component in just such a way that this hyperinefficiency is removed, but responsibility sensitivity is retained in cases where it is non-hyperinefficient. The combination of the restricted version of the responsibilitarian component (3*) with utilitarian and leximin components seems to produce a sound account of justice.

Notes

1 Lippert-Rasmussen 2001, 576.
2 It occurs to me that the reasons that motivate this differentiation probably have counterparts that would motivate a similar differentiation at the bottom of the ordering. If, as egalitarians, we think that equality reflecting equivalent responsibility is better than inequality also reflecting responsibility, then we are likely to think that equality not reflecting responsibility is better than inequality not reflecting responsibility. This point does not affect the argument in the text.
3 See sections 4 and 5 below for an examination of this problem (responsibility levelling as I call it there) as found under conventional luck egalitarianism.
4 Temkin 1993, 282.
5 Apart, that is, from reflecting equality in the weak sense mentioned in 3.1.
6 Cohen (1989, 940) mentions charity, but this simply grants, improbably, that Bad Samaritanism may be just (Fleurbaey 1995, 40). Arneson's responsibility-catering prioritarianism reflects responsibilitarian, prioritarian, and utilitarian concerns; see sections 7 and 8 below. An equality of opportunity for advantage-sufficiency combination would have identical effects in Bad Samaritan cases as the equality of opportunity for advantage-basic needs combination explored in the text. I refer to the latter formulation as sufficiency is unnecessarily wide reaching. Harry Frankfurt's (1988, 152) version, for example, requires that each person 'is content, or . . . it is reasonable for him to be content'. A basic needs approach, by contrast, allows conditions in which people are discontented on reasonable grounds. Anyone who is moved by a pseudo-Samaritan case, in which pseudo-Bert is not under threat of death but is just discontented (with, say, the uncomfortable conditions of the hospital in which he is being treated at society's expense), may favour sufficiency over basic needs; I personally do not find this new case compelling. Similarly, I find considerations of social solidarity, as Shlomi Segall (2007) favours, less pressing than basic needs considerations, and too wide ranging in their implications.
7 See 4.6.
8 Fleurbaey (1995; 2002; 2005) makes this compensation conditional on there being a change of mind or regret on the part of the negligent disadvantaged person. But I do not see how this kind of cognitive or emotional change is relevant to justice. As Dworkin (2002, 113 n.8) notes, Fleurbaey's proposal 'seems an almost literal case of allowing people to eat cake and have it too'.
9 Fleurbaey 1995, 41, emphasis added; see also Scheffler, 2003a, 24.
10 See Lippert-Rasmussen 2001, 561.

11 Anderson 1999a, 301.

12 Adapted from Brown 2003, 114. Brown presents this as the levelling-down objection, without distinguishing between stronger and weaker versions.

13 But observe that peculiar psychological patterns would have to hold in the society for the 'official' version of equality of resources to endorse Y.

14 Dworkin 2004, 356.

15 Le Grand 1991, 87.

16 For more general arguments against the strong levelling-down objection, see Temkin 1993, ch. 9; 2003; Brown 2003.

17 The weak form is suggested by one interpretation of 'The Slogan' identified by Temkin, but he thinks that a strong interpretation of The Slogan that corresponds to what I have called the strong levelling-down objection is the only interesting interpretation; see Temkin 1993, 248, 256–8. This is understandable given Temkin's pluralism – he thinks that any 'reasonable egalitarian' will care about things other than equality (Temkin 2003, 63, 68; 1993, 13, 282) – but the weaker interpretation is very interesting when considering the main, non-pluralistic versions of outcome egalitarianism and luck egalitarianism.

18 See Rakowski 1991, 48–9.

19 Arneson 2004a, 89. Arneson actually makes the comment in the course of discussing Dworkin's equality of resources. Note that Dworkin's insurance markets would actually reflect this 'moral significance', because persons could be expected to go some way to maximizing resources when selecting the appropriate levels of insurance. See 1.6 and 1.7 above; cf. Dworkin 2002, 122–5; 2004, 355–6.

20 There are other, more dramatic ways that this might be achieved. For example, a distributive body might disable one of the better-off people, to make an otherwise envious and unfairly worse-off person feel better about their circumstances. I disregard this kind of approach in the text, because it raises issues concerning bodily integrity that would distract from the relevant points. A pluralistic luck egalitarianism would, in any case, have little difficulty in accommodating a principle that would prevent deliberately disabling policies.

21 See 1.2.

22 Oliver 1990, xiv.

23 See Arneson 2004a, 89; 1999a, 495; 2004b, 187.

24 Rakowski 1991, 49.

25 Otsuka 2002, 46.

26 My discussion of the last of Elizabeth Anderson's insult arguments mentioned in 4.3 is the obvious exception to this. The discussion was necessary as Anderson seems to hold that this particular form of harming the better off is inegalitarian.

27 At least, if we restrict our focus to impersonal resources; see note 20 above.
28 The necessity of the second condition is on account of the need to know the extent to which prima facie responsible or irresponsible actions should be rewarded or penalized. The dystopian administrators do not need to satisfy this condition, because there is no question of reward or penalization as no individual will act more or less responsible.
29 For Arneson's proposal in this direction, see sections 7 and 8 below. Cohen and Rakowski make weaker, but still significant, concessions; see Cohen 1989, 908–10, 935 n.66; Rakowski 1991, 53 n.36. Regarding Temkin's position here, see note 17 above; regarding Dworkin's position, see Chapter 1 as well as note 19 above and Dworkin 1981, 329–30.
30 Cf. 4.7.
31 Rawls 1999a, 84.
32 Inequality can, of course, be reduced without improving the position of the worst off (or, for that, worsening the position of the best off). Differences between the intermediate groups (the worse off and better off) are also objects of egalitarian concern; see Chapter 3, note 37. Maximin, by contrast, focuses exclusively on the worst off.
33 See Knight 2009b, and 3.5 above.
34 Arneson 1999a, 497. For a similar formulation, see Arneson 2004b, 192; cf. Arneson 2000a; 2000b.
35 See 3.5.
36 Cf. Rawls 1999a, 56; Nagel 1991, 69.
37 By 'worse off in welfare' and 'better off', Arneson probably means to refer to lifetime welfare levels, given what he says about (2). At any rate, I would intend the advantaged and disadvantaged positions to be established in this historical fashion.
38 Cf. Kagan 1999, 300.
39 The term for the phenomenon (but not its present application) is from Vallentyne 2000, 9. A grossly inefficient transfer is necessarily a hyper-inefficient one, but the reverse is not true. Rules (f) and (g) are not grossly inefficient, because they say nothing about the circumstances of those whose holdings are equal to or less than their responsible share.
40 Arneson 2006, 15.
41 Cf. Arneson 2006, 6.
42 See 3.2.
43 J. G. Ballard's (1973) car-crash-obsessed character, Vaughan, springs to mind, although his insanity may diminish or eliminate his responsibility for his actions.
44 Anderson's democratic equality is another obvious example; see 4.7.

Conclusion

A More Efficient Luck Egalitarianism

Luck egalitarianism is now something of a default position among philosophical egalitarians, with a whole industry of articles and, increasingly,[1] books focusing on its core idea of making equality respond to individuals' responsible action. But is this elevated place in the academy deserved? Is this core idea outright mistaken?

It might well be wondered where the apparent success of responsibility-catering prioritarianism leaves luck egalitarianism. I argued that restricted responsibilitarianism – the principle that persons should receive what they are responsible for, except where giving them something they are not responsible for disadvantages nobody – is clearly responsibility sensitive, though not fully so. Given my position that responsibilitarianism and luck egalitarianism are, in all the interesting cases, one and the same thing, it might well be supposed that restricted responsibilitarianism is also significantly luck egalitarian. This is, strictly speaking, quite right. But it should be recalled that the regards in which restricted responsibilitarianism departs from responsibilitarianism include those regards in which responsibilitarian is most obviously egalitarian, in particular cases of levelling down. While it may be quite legitimate to say that restricted responsibilitarianism is luck egalitarian to a large extent, and also that luck egalitarianism is substantively egalitarian, it does not follow that restricted responsibilitarianism is substantively egalitarian.

Responsibility-catering prioritarianism as a whole is obviously less luck egalitarian than restricted responsibilitarianism, since the two other components of it are neither substantively egalitarian nor concerned with responsibility. Even so, responsibility-catering prioritarianism is not only egalitarian in the weak sense described in section 3.1, but also in the sense I described as 'contemporary egalitarian'. That is, it would in most circumstances recommend the 'liberal' (US sense) policies described at the outset of section 3.5; and even where it does not recommend them, contemporary egalitarians might be persuaded that there are good reasons (particularly concerning responsibility or priority to the worst off) for this. I would, then, be willing to accept that responsibility-catering prioritarianism is egalitarian, provided it is understood that we mean one of these senses of egalitarianism. I would also be willing to accept Arneson's suggestion that responsibility-catering prioritarianism is a variety of luck egalitarianism,[2] so long as it was understood that it has, if anything, a stronger claim to being a variety of utilitarianism and prioritarianism, since they are reflected in responsibility-catering prioritarianism by unrestricted components, while luck egalitarianism is reflected only in restricted responsibilitarianism, which is constrained by efficiency considerations.

I will finish with some comments which both highlight a particular significant focus of the book and review the terrain that it has covered. In treating luck egalitarianism as being, at core, the view that inequalities are justified only insofar as they reflect differential exercises of responsibility, and equalities only insofar as they reflect equivalent such exercises, I have used a very tight description. Yet luck egalitarians are not always explicit about the implications their formulations suggest. Certainly, cases where responsibility sensitivity is bad for someone and good for no one are rarely, if ever, discussed in their writings. One might explain this by saying that luck egalitarianism somehow implicitly precludes this most dubious category of responsibility sensitivity. The most promising idea here is to endorse full responsibility sensitivity only where there is no Pareto optimal alternative allocation – that is, only where there is no relaxation of responsibility sensitivity that would advantage at least one person without disadvantaging any other. Luck egalitarianism so construed would reject a non-Pareto optimal responsibility-sensitive distribution where a Pareto optimal responsibility-sensitive distribution is available. This softer version of luck egalitarianism might still be thought of as egalitarian, just as Rawls's difference principle is usually considered egalitarian. In both cases, the egalitarian component (strong luck egalitarianism/outcome equality) is constrained by Pareto optimality, which is considered an unobjectionable non-egalitarian component. This 'Paretian luck egalitarianism' is essentially the same as restricted responsibilitarianism, with the exception that, on the question of how to respond to an absence of responsible acts, it prescribes equality while restricted responsibilitarianism is silent. The position could be revised further such that Pareto optimality applies in the absence of responsible acts.

I believe my focus on the starker, non-Paretian luck egalitarianism is justified on two grounds. First, the best-known 'position statements' by luck egalitarians concentrate on eliminating responsibility-insensitive inequalities, and do not even mention Pareto optimality or anything similar. Caveats to the effect that luck egalitarianism itself should be counterbalanced by other principles are sometimes present, and Dworkin actually introduces mechanisms, such as the hypothetical insurance markets, which insulate equality of resources against the charge of inefficiency that blights more strictly luck-egalitarian positions. But there is no discussion, to my knowledge, of any 'Paretian proviso', far less the suggestion that this is somehow part of luck egalitarianism itself. It is conceivable that, if pushed, this is the position that many luck egalitarians would favour, but it would be several steps too far to conclude that we should disregard what they actually say as this is what most of them always had in mind. Second, the starker position has considerable independent interest. In particular, it is more plausible as an account of egalitarianism, and as an account of responsibility sensitivity.

The first ground was illustrated in the first part of the book, which considered the two best-known theories that have been identified as luck egalitarian – equality of resources, and equal opportunity for welfare. I argued that, on any of the available interpretations, equality of resources would allow levels of advantage to vary where responsibility was constant, in spite of Dworkin's stated intent to design choice-sensitive, circumstance-insensitive distributive mechanisms. Equal opportunity for welfare is more consistently luck egalitarian, especially where a particular affective state account of welfare is adopted.

The second point was supported in the second part of the book, which asked whether luck egalitarianism is satisfactory as an account of distributive equality. Since all major theories of justice are egalitarian in some regard, it was necessary to identify more discriminating conditions for a theory to be genuinely or substantively egalitarian. Three plausible conditions were set out, and various theories (including libertarianism, utilitarianism, prioritarianism, and Dworkinian equality of resources) were shown to fail to satisfy them. Rawls's difference principle is not, on the stated criteria, substantively egalitarian, and Paretian luck egalitarianism is not either. While these views might satisfy the second and third conditions, they would fail the first. They treat likes (in the case of Paretian luck egalitarianism, that means those with equal potential under present

231

conditions for furthering responsibility-weighted welfare, consistent with Pareto optimality) alike, but they do not treat likes alike *because* they are alike. But equal opportunity for welfare clearly meets the first two conditions, and it was argued that it meets the third as well, while being applicable in practice. This is possible only because of its focus on eliminating all varieties of inequity – that is, all instances of inequality that do not correspond to variations in responsible action.

The final part of the book assessed luck egalitarianism's credibility as a theory of distributive justice. It was maintained that luck egalitarianism is plausible as a theory of responsibility sensitivity, and even that full responsibilitarians must usually be luck egalitarians. It is ultimately unsatisfactory as a theory of justice, however, on account of its failure to take account of absolute levels of advantage. It would permit various forms of inefficiency, as well as the abandonment of the negligent needy.

These criticisms are not fully applicable to Paretian luck egalitarianism. Even so, I believe that the arguments of this chapter allow for some fine-tuning of this position, and suggest what its appropriate role in a theory of distributive justice might be. The former issue is, I think, less interesting. No amount of fine-tuning of luck egalitarianism can achieve the same thing as the introduction of utilitarian and prioritarianism principles. And if we want to see how far we can take egalitarianism and/or responsibilitarianism, we cannot refuse to negate advantages for which the holder is not responsible. The latter issue is of greater concern, given that it seems that this kind of luck egalitarianism incorporates the kind of restriction on responsibility sensitivity that is required for responsibility considerations to figure in a theory of justice.

Full-blown, non-responsible-surplus-destroying luck egalitarianism is, I hold, a strong account of both equality and responsibility sensitivity. But egalitarianism and responsibilitarianism do not tell us all we need to know about justice. As a stand-alone theory, luck egalitarianism cannot deliver, since it comes up against the brick wall of absolute levels of well-being. But an appropriately qualified version of it – Paretian luck egalitarianism – can still play a role as a key component of a pluralistic account of justice.

Notes

1   Recent volumes that have luck egalitarianism as a central concern include Hurley 2003; Armstrong 2006; Mason 2006; White 2006; Matravers 2007; Fleurbaey 2008; Knight and Stemplowska (eds) 2009.

2   Arneson 2000a; Arneson 2006, 2.

Bibliography

Anderson, Elizabeth S. 1999a. 'What is the Point of Equality?' *Ethics*, 109, 287–337.

Anderson, Elizabeth S. 1999b. 'Anderson Replies to Arneson, Christiano and Soble'. *Brown Electronic Article Review Service* (1999), ed. J. Dreier and D. Estlund, *World Wide Web*, (*http://www.brown.edu/ Departments/Philosophy/bears/homepage/html*).

Aristotle. 1954. *The Nicomachean Ethics*. Tr. David Ross. London: Oxford University Press.

Aristotle. 1995. *The Politics*. Tr. Ernest Barker. Oxford: Oxford University Press.

Armstrong, Chris. 2003. 'Opportunity, Responsibility, and the Market: Interrogating Liberal Equality'. *Economy and Society*, 32, 410–27.

Armstrong, Chris. 2006. *Rethinking Equality: The Challenge of Equal Citizenship*. Manchester: Manchester University Press.

Arneson, Richard J. 1989. 'Equality and Equal Opportunity for Welfare'. *Philosophical Studies*, 56, 77–93.

Arneson, Richard J. 1990. 'Liberalism, Distributive Subjectivism, and Equal Opportunity for Welfare'. *Philosophy and Public Affairs*, 19, 159–94.

Arneson, Richard J. 1992. 'Property Rights in Persons'. *Social Philosophy and Policy*, 9, 201–30.

Arneson, Richard J. 1997a. 'Egalitarianism and the Undeserving Poor'. *Journal of Political Philosophy*, 5, 327–50.

Arneson, Richard J. 1997b. 'Postscript (1995)'. In Louis J. Pojman and Robert Westmoreland (eds), *Equality: Selected Readings*. Oxford: Oxford University Press.

Arneson, Richard J. 1999a. 'Equality of Opportunity for Welfare Defended and Recanted'. *Journal of Political Philosophy*, 7, 488–97.

Arneson, Richard J. 1999b. 'Egalitarianism and Responsibility'. *Journal of Ethics*, 3, 225–47.

Arneson, Richard J. 2000a. 'Luck Egalitarianism and Prioritarianism'. *Ethics*, 110, 339–49.

Arneson, Richard J. 2000b. 'Egalitarian Justice versus the Right to Privacy'. *Social Philosophy and Policy*, 17, 91–119.

Arneson, Richard J. 2000c. 'Welfare Should Be the Currency of Justice'. *Canadian Journal of Philosophy*, 30, 497–524.

Arneson, Richard J. 2001. 'Luck and Equality'. *Proceedings of the Aristotelian Society*, supplement, 75, 73–90.

Arneson, Richard J. 2002a. 'Review of *Sovereign Virtue*'. *Ethics*, 112, 367–71.

Arneson, Richard J. 2002b. 'Justice Requires Transfers to Offset Income and Wealth Inequalities'. *Social Philosophy and Policy*, 19, 172–200.

Arneson, Richard J. 2004a. 'Cracked Foundations of Liberal Equality'. In Justine Burley (ed.), *Dworkin and His Critics*. Oxford: Blackwell.

Arneson, Richard J. 2004b. 'Opportunity for Welfare, Priority, and Public Policy'. In Steven Cullenberg and Prasanta K. Pattanaik (eds), *Globalization, Culture, and the Limits of the Market: Essays in Economics and Philosophy*. New Delhi: Oxford University Press.

Arneson, Richard J. 2006. 'Luck Egalitarianism Interpreted and Defended'. *Philosophical Topics*, 32, 1–20.

Arrow, Kenneth J. 1973. 'Some Ordinalist–Utilitarian Notes on Rawls' Theory of Justice'. *The Journal of Philosophy*, 70, 245–63.

Ballard, J. G. 1973. *Crash*. London: Cape.

Barrow, Robin. 1991. *Utilitarianism: A Contemporary Statement*. Aldershot: Edward Elgar.

Barry, Brian. 1973. *The Liberal Theory of Justice*. Oxford: Oxford University Press.

Barry, Brian. 1989. *Theories of Justice*. London: Harvester-Wheatsheaf.

Barry, Brian. 1991. 'Chance, Choice, and Justice'. In *Liberty and Justice: Essays in Political Theory*, vol. 2. Oxford: Oxford University Press.

Barry, Brian. 2005. *Why Social Justice Matters*. Cambridge: Polity.

Barry, Nicholas. 2006. 'Defending Luck Egalitarianism'. *Journal of Applied Philosophy*, 23, 89–107.

Benditt, T. M. 1974. 'Happiness'. *Philosophical Studies*, 25, 1–20.

Bentham, Jeremy. 1970. *An Introduction to the Principles of Morals and Legislation*. Ed. J. H. Burns and H. L. A. Hart. London: Athlone Press.

Berlin, Isaiah. 1961. 'Equality'. In Frederick A. Olafson (ed.), *Justice and Social Policy*. Englewood Cliffs, NJ: Prentice-Hall.

Bower, Bruce. 1998. 'Review of *Welfare, Happiness, and Ethics* by L. W. Sumner'. *Philosophical Review*, 107, 309–12

Brandt, R. B. 1979. *A Theory of the Good and the Right*. Oxford: Oxford University Press.

Brandt, R. B. 1982. 'Two Concepts of Utility'. In Harlan B. Miller and William H. Williams (eds), *Limits of Utilitarianism*. Minneapolis: University of Minnesota Press.

Brown, Alexander. 2005. 'If We Value Individual Responsibility, Which Policies Should We Favour?' *Journal of Applied Philosophy*, 22, 23–44.

Brown, Campbell. 2003. 'Giving Up Levelling Down'. *Economics and Philosophy*, 19, 111–34.

Bykvist, Krister. 2002. 'Sumner on Desires and Well-Being'. *Canadian Journal of Philosophy*, 32, 475–90.

Carter, Alan. 2001. 'Simplifying "Inequality"'. *Philosophy and Public Affairs*, 30, 1, 88–100.

Cassell, Eric. 1982. 'The Nature of Suffering and the Goals of Medicine'. *New England Journal of Medicine*, 306, 639–45.

Cassell, Eric. 1991. *The Nature of Suffering and the Goals of Medicine*. Oxford: Oxford University Press.

Christiano, Thomas. 1999. 'Christiano Reviews Anderson'. *Brown Electronic Article Review Service*, ed. J. Dreier and D. Estlund, World Wide Web, (http://www.brown.edu/Departments/Philosophy/bears/homepage/html).

Clarke, Randolph. 2004. 'Incompatibilist (Nondeterministic) Theories of Free Will'. *The Stanford Encyclopedia of Philosophy* (Fall 2004 Edition), ed. Edward N. Zalta, URL=<http://plato.stanford.edu/archives/fall2004/entries/incompatibilism-theories/>

Clayton, Matthew. 2000. 'The Resources of Liberal Equality'. *Imprints*, 5, 163–84.

Cohen, G. A. 1989. 'On the Currency of Egalitarian Justice'. *Ethics*, 99, 906–44.

Cohen, G. A. 1993. 'Equality of What? On Welfare, Goods and Capabilities'. In Martha Nussbaum and Amartya Sen (eds), *The Quality of Life*. Oxford: Oxford University Press.

Cohen, G. A. 1995. 'The Pareto Argument for Inequality'. *Social Philosophy and Policy*, 12, 160–85.

Cohen, G. A. 1999. 'Expensive Tastes and Multiculturalism'. In Rajeev Bhargava, Amiya Kumar Bagchi, and R. Sudarshan (eds), *Multiculturalism, Liberalism and Democracy*. New Delhi: Oxford University Press, 1999.

Cohen, G. A. 2003. 'Facts and Principles'. *Philosophy and Public Affairs*, 31, 211–45.

Cohen, G. A. 2004. 'Expensive Taste Rides Again'. In Justine Burley (ed.), *Dworkin and His Critics*. Oxford: Blackwell.

Cohen, G. A. 'Luck and Equality: A Reply to Hurley'. *Philosophy and Phenomenological Research*, 72, 439–46.

Cohen Christofidis, Miriam. 2004. 'Talent, Slavery and Envy in Dworkin's Equality of Resources'. *Utilitas*, 16, 267–87.

Coram, Alexander T. 1997. 'Social Class and Luck: Some Lessons from Gambler's Ruin and Branching Processes'. *Political Studies*, 45, 66–77.

Coram, Alexander T. 1998. 'Why Social Scientists Should Be Interested in Luck: A Note on Some Fallacies'. *Social Science Quarterly*, 79, 129–39.

Crisp, Roger. 2003. 'Equality, Priority, and Compassion'. *Ethics*, 113, 745–63.

Daniels, Norman. 1996. *Justice and Justification: Reflective Equilibrium in Theory and Practice*. Cambridge: Cambridge University Press.

Darwall, Stephen. 2002. *Welfare and Rational Care.* Princeton, NJ: Princeton University Press.

Dworkin, Ronald. 1977. *Taking Rights Seriously.* London: Duckworth.

Dworkin, Ronald. 1978. 'Liberalism'. In Stuart Hampshire (ed.), *Public and Private Morality.* Cambridge: Cambridge University Press.

Dworkin, Ronald. 1981. 'What is Equality? Part One: Equality of Welfare. Part Two: Equality of Resources'. *Philosophy and Public Affairs*, 10, 185–246, 283–345.

Dworkin, Ronald. 1983. 'Comment on Narveson: In Defense of Equality'. *Social Philosophy and Policy*, 1, 24–40.

Dworkin, Ronald. 2000. *Sovereign Virtue: The Theory and Practice of Equality.* Cambridge, MA: Harvard University Press.

Dworkin, Ronald. 2002. '*Sovereign Virtue* Revisited'. *Ethics*, 113, 106–43.

Dworkin, Ronald. 2003. 'Equality, Luck and Hierarchy'. *Philosophy and Public Affairs*, 31, 190–8.

Dworkin, Ronald. 2004. 'Replies'. In Justine Burley (ed.), *Dworkin and His Critics.* Oxford: Blackwell.

Elster, Jon. 1982. 'Sour Grapes: Utilitarianism and the Genesis of Wants'. In Amartya K. Sen and Bernard Williams (eds), *Utilitarianism and Beyond.* Cambridge: Cambridge University Press.

Feinberg, Joel. 1970. 'Justice and Personal Desert'. In *Doing and Deserving: Essays in the Theory of Responsibility.* Princeton: Princeton University Press.

Feldman, Fred. 1996. 'Desert: Reconsideration of Some Received Wisdom'. *Mind*, 104, 63–77.

Finnis, John. 1980. *Natural Law and Natural Rights.* Oxford: Oxford University Press.

Fleurbaey, Marc. 1995. 'Equal Opportunity or Equal Social Outcome?' *Economics and Philosophy*, 11, 25–55.

Fleurbaey, Marc. 2001. 'Egalitarian Opportunities'. *Law and Philosophy*, 20, 499–530.

Fleurbaey, Marc. 2005. 'Freedom With Forgiveness'. *Politics, Philosophy and Economics*, 4, 29–67.

Fleurbaey, Marc. 2008. *Fairness, Responsibility, and Welfare.* Oxford: Oxford University Press.

Flew, Antony. 1981. *The Politics of Procrustes.* London: Temple Smith.

Frankfurt, Harry G. 1988. 'Equality as a Moral Ideal'. In *The Importance of What We Care About.* Cambridge: Cambridge University Press.

Freeman, Samuel. 2006. *Justice and the Social Contract: Essays on Rawlsian Political Philosophy.* Oxford: Oxford University Press.

Fried, Barbara H. 2004. 'Left-Libertarianism: A Review Essay'. *Philosophy and Public Affairs*, 32, 66–92.

Fried, Barbara H. 2005. 'Left-Libertarianism Once More: A Rejoinder to Vallentyne, Steiner, and Otsuka'. *Philosophy and Public Affairs*, 33, 216–22.

Gert, Bernard. 1998. *Morality: Its Nature and Justification*. Oxford: Oxford University Press.

Goldstein, Irwin. 1980. 'Why People Prefer Pleasure to Pain'. *Philosophy*, 55, 349–62.

Goldstein, Irwin. 1989. 'Pleasure and Pain: Unconditional, Intrinsic Values'. *Philosophy and Phenomenological Research*, 50, 255–76.

Goldsworthy, Jeffrey. 1992. 'Well-Being and Value'. *Utilitas*, 4, 1–26.

Greenawalt. Kent. 1997. '"Prescriptive Equality": Two Steps Forward'. *Harvard Law Review*, 110, 1265–90.

Griffin, James. 1986. *Well-Being: Its Meaning, Measurement and Moral Importance*. Oxford: Oxford University Press.

Griffin, James. 2000. 'Replies'. In Roger Crisp and Brad Hooker (eds), *Well-Being and Morality: Essays in Honour of James Griffin*. Oxford: Oxford University Press.

Hall, Richard J. 1989. 'Are Pains Necessarily Unpleasant?' *Philosophy and Phenomenological Research*, 49, 643–59.

Hampton, Jean. 1989. 'Should Political Philosophy Be Done Without Metaphysics?' *Ethics*, 99, 791–814.

Handley, Peter. 2003. 'Theorising Disability: Beyond "Common Sense"'. *Politics*, 23, 109–18.

Hare, R. M. 1973. 'Rawls' Theory of Justice, II'. *Philosophical Quarterly*, 23, 241–52.

Hare, R. M. 1981. *Moral Thinking: Its Levels, Method, and Point*. Oxford: Oxford University Press.

Hare, R. M. 1997. 'Justice and Equality'. In Louis P. Pojman and Robert Westmoreland (eds), *Equality: Selected Readings*. Oxford: Oxford University Press.

Harsanyi, John C. 1975. 'Can the Maximin Principle Serve as a Basis for Morality? A Critique of John Rawls's Theory'. *American Political Science Review*, 64, 594–606.

Harsanyi, John C. 1982. 'Morality and the Theory of Rational Behaviour'. In Amartya Sen and Bernard Williams (eds), *Utilitarianism and Beyond*. Cambridge: Cambridge University Press.

Haslett, D. W. 1990. 'What is Utility?' *Economics and Philosophy*, 6, 65–94.

Haybron, Daniel M. 2000. 'Two Philosophical Problems in the Study of Happiness'. *Journal of Happiness Studies*, 1, 207–25.

Haybron, Daniel M. 2001. 'Happiness and Pleasure'. *Philosophy and Phenomenological Research*, 62, 501–28.

Hayek, Friedrich A. 1960. *The Constitution of Liberty*. London: Routledge & Kegan Paul.

Hinton, Timothy. 2001. 'Must Egalitarians Choose Between Fairness and Respect?' *Philosophy and Public Affairs*, 30, 72–87.

Hinton, Timothy. 2002. 'Choice and Luck in Recent Egalitarian Thought'. *Philosophical Papers*, 31, 145–67.

Hobbes, Thomas. 1996. *Leviathan*. Ed. Richard Tuck. Cambridge: Cambridge University Press.

Hurka, Thomas. 1993. *Perfectionism*. Oxford: Oxford University Press.

Hurley, S. L. 2002. 'Luck, Responsibility, and the Natural Lottery'. *Journal of Political Philosophy*, 10, 79–94.

Hurley, S. L. 2003. *Justice, Luck, and Knowledge*. Cambridge, MA: Harvard University Press.

Hurley, S. L. 2006. 'Replies'. *Philosophy and Phenomenological Research*, 72, 447–65.

James, William. 1956. *The Will To Believe, Human Immortality and Other Essays on Popular Philosophy*. New York: Dover.

Johnston, David. 1994. *The Idea of a Liberal Theory: A Critique and Reconstruction*. Princeton, NJ: Princeton University Press.

Jones, Peter. 1994. 'Bearing the Consequences of Belief'. *Journal of Political Philosophy*, 2, 24–43.

Kagan, Shelly. 1999. 'Equality and Desert'. In Louis J. Pojman and Owen McLeod, *What Do We Deserve?* New York: Oxford University Press.

Kaufman, Alexander. 2004. 'Choice, Responsibility, and Equality'. *Political Studies*, 52, 819–36.

Keller, Simon. 2002. 'Expensive Tastes and Distributive Justice'. *Social Theory and Practice*, 28, 529–52.

Knight, Carl. 2004. 'Liberal Multiculturalism Reconsidered'. *Politics*, 24, 189–97.

Knight, Carl. 2005. 'In Defence of Luck Egalitarianism'. *Res Publica*, 11, 55–73.

Knight, Carl. 2006a. 'The Metaphysical Case for Luck Egalitarianism'. *Social Theory and Practice*, 32, 173–89.

Knight, Carl. 2006b. 'The Method of Reflective Equilibrium: Wide, Radical, Fallible, Plausible'. *Philosophical Papers*, 35, 205–29.

Knight, Carl. 2008. 'A Pluralistic Approach to Global Poverty'. *Review of International Studies*, 34, 713–33.

Knight, Carl. 2009a. 'Egalitarian Justice and Valuational Judgment'. *Journal of Moral Philosophy*, forthcoming.

Knight, Carl. 2009b. 'Describing Equality'. *Law and Philosophy*, forthcoming.

Knight, Carl and Zofia Stemplowska (eds), 2009. *Distributive Justice and Responsibility*. Oxford: Oxford University Press, forthcoming.

Kymlicka, Will. 1990. *Contemporary Political Philosophy: An Introduction*. Oxford: Oxford University Press.

Lake, Christopher R. 2001. *Equality and Responsibility*. Oxford: Oxford University Press.

Le Grand, Julian. 1991. *Equity and Choice*. London: Routledge.

Lippert-Rasmussen, Kasper. 2001. 'Egalitarianism, Option-Luck, and Responsibility'. *Ethics*, 111, 548–79.

Lippert-Rasmussen, Kasper. 2005. 'Hurley on Egalitarianism and the Luck-Neutralizing Aim'. *Politics, Philosophy and Economics*, 4, 249–65.

Lloyd Thomas, D. A. 1968. 'Happiness'. *Philosophical Quarterly*, 18, 97–113.

McKenna, Michael. 2004. 'Compatibilism'. *The Stanford Encyclopedia of Philosophy* (Summer 2004 Edition), ed. Edward N. Zalta, URL=<http://plato.stanford.edu/archives/sum2004/entries/compatibilism/>.

McKerlie, Dennis. 1984. 'Egalitarianism'. *Dialogue*, 23, 223–38.

McKerlie, Dennis. 1996. 'Equality'. *Ethics*, 106, 274–96.

McKerlie, Dennis. 2001. 'Dimensions of Equality'. *Utilitas*, 13, 263–78.

McLeod, Colin M. 1998. *Liberalism, Justice, and Markets: A Critique of Liberal Equality*. Oxford: Oxford University Press.

Marshall, Gordon, Adam Swift, David Routh, and Carol Burgoyne. 1999. 'What Is and What Ought to Be: Popular Beliefs about Distributive Justice in Thirteen Countries'. *European Sociological Review*, 15, 349–67.

Mason, Andrew. 2000. 'Equality, Personal Responsibility, and Gender Socialisation'. *Proceedings of the Aristotelian Society*, 100, 227–46.

Mason, Andrew. 2006. *Levelling the Playing Field: The Idea of Equal Opportunity and Its Place in Egalitarian Thought*. Oxford: Oxford University Press.

Matravers, Matt. 2002a. 'Responsibility, Luck, and the "Equality of What?" Debate'. *Political Studies*, 50, 558–72.

Matravers, Matt. 2002b. 'Responsibility and Choice'. *Critical Review of International Social and Political Philosophy*, 5, 77–92.

Matravers, Matt. 2007. *Responsibility and Justice*. Cambridge: Polity.

Mill, John Stuart. 1969. *Utilitarianism*. Ed. J. M. Robson. Toronto: University of Toronto Press.

Miller, David. 1989. *Market, State, and Community: Theoretical Foundations of Market Socialism*. Oxford: Oxford University Press.

Miller, David. 1997. 'Equality and Justice'. *Ratio*, 10, 222–37.

Miller, David. 1999. *Principles of Social Justice*. Cambridge, MA: Harvard University Press.

Miller, David. 2002. 'Liberalism, Equal Opportunities and Cultural Commitments'. In Paul Kelly (ed.), *Multiculturalism Reconsidered*. Cambridge: Polity.

Montague, Richard. 1967. 'Happiness'. *Proceedings of the Aristotelian Society*, 67, 87–102.

Nagel, Thomas. 1979. *Mortal Questions*. Cambridge: Cambridge University Press.

Nagel, Thomas. 1991. *Equality and Partiality*. Oxford: Oxford University Press.

Narveson, Jan. 1983. 'On Dworkinian Equality'. *Social Philosophy and Policy*, 1, 1–23.

Nozick, Robert. 1974. *Anarchy, State and Utopia*. Oxford: Blackwell.

Nozick, Robert. 1989. *The Examined Life: Philosophical Meditations*. New York: Simon & Schuster.

Nussbaum, Martha. 1988. 'Nature, Function, and Capability: Aristotle on Political Distribution'. *Oxford Studies in Ancient Philosophy*, supp. 1, 145–84.

Nussbaum, Martha. 1990. 'Aristotelian Social Democracy'. In R. Bruce Douglas, Gerald M. Mara, and Henry S. Richardson (eds), *Liberalism and the Good*. New York: Routledge.

Oliver, Michael. 1990. *The Politics of Disablement*. Basingstoke: Macmillan.

Oppenheim, Felix E. 1970. 'Egalitarianism as a Descriptive Concept'. *American Philosophical Quarterly*, 7, 143–52.

Otsuka, Michael. 2002. 'Luck, Insurance, and Equality'. *Ethics*, 113, 40–54.

Otsuka, Michael. 2003. *Libertarianism without Inequality*. Oxford: Oxford University Press.

Otsuka, Michael. 2004. 'Equality, Ambition, and Insurance'. *Proceedings of the Aristotelian Society* (Supplement), 7, 151–66.

Parfit, Derek. 1984. *Reasons and Persons*. Oxford: Oxford University Press.

Parfit, Derek. 1995. *Equality or Priority?* Lindley Lecture, University of Kansas.

Parfit, Derek. 1996. 'Equality and Priority'. In Andrew Mason (ed.), *Ideals of Equality*. Oxford: Blackwell.

Pereboom, Derk. 1995. 'Determinism *al Dente*'. *Nous*, 29, 21–45.

Philips, Anne. 2004. 'Defending Equality of Outcome'. *Journal of Political Philosophy*, 12, 1–19.

Peters, Christopher J. 1996. 'Foolish Consistency: On Equality, Integrity, and Justice in Stare Decisis'. *Yale Law Journal*, 105, 2031–115.

Peters, Christopher J. 1997. 'Equality Revisited'. *Harvard Law Review*, 110, 1210–64.

Popper, Karl. 1966. *The Open Society and its Enemies*, II, 5th rev. edn, London: Routledge & Kegan Paul.

Price, Terry. 1999. 'Egalitarian Justice, Luck, and the Costs of Chosen Ends'. *American Philosophical Quarterly*, 36, 267–78.

Rae, Douglas. 1981. *Equalities*. Cambridge, MA: Harvard University Press.

Rakowski, Eric. 1991. *Equal Justice*. Oxford: Oxford University Press.

Rawls, John. 1982. 'Social Unity and Primary Goods'. In Amartya K. Sen and Bernard Williams (eds), *Utilitarianism and Beyond*. Cambridge: Cambridge University Press.

Rawls, John. 1996. *Political Liberalism*, paperback edn. New York: Columbia University Press.

Rawls, John. 1999a. *A Theory of Justice*, rev. ed. Oxford: Oxford University Press.

Rawls, John. 1999b. *The Law of Peoples*. Cambridge, MA: Harvard University Press.

Raz, Joseph. 1986. *The Morality of Freedom*. Oxford: Oxford University Press.

Ripstein, Arthur. 1999. *Equality, Responsibility, and the Law*. Cambridge: Cambridge University Press.

Risse, Mathias. 2002. 'What Equality of Opportunity Could Not Be'. *Ethics*, 112, 720–47.

Roemer, John. 1993. 'A Pragmatic Theory of Responsibility for the Egalitarian Planner'. *Philosophy and Public Affairs*, 22, 146–66.

Roemer, John. 1996. *Theories of Distributive Justice*. Cambridge, MA: Harvard University Press.

Roemer, John E. 1998. *Equality of Opportunity*. Cambridge, MA: Harvard University Press.

Roemer, John E. 2003. 'Defending Equality of Opportunity'. *The Monist*, 86, 261–82.

Ryle, Gilbert. 1949. *The Concept of Mind*. London: Hutchinson.

Scanlon, Thomas. 1975a. 'Preference and Urgency'. *The Journal of Philosophy*, 72, 655–69.

Scanlon, Thomas. 1975b. 'Rawls' Theory of Justice'. In *Reading Rawls*, ed. Norman Daniels. New York: Basic Books.

Scanlon, Thomas. 1986. 'Equality of Resources and Equality of Welfare: A Forced Marriage?' *Ethics*, 97, 111–18.

Scanlon, Thomas. 1998. *What We Owe to Each Other*. Cambridge, MA: Harvard University Press.

Scanlon, Thomas. 2002. 'The Diversity of Objections to Inequality'. In Matthew Clayton and Andrew Williams (eds), *The Ideal of Equality*. Basingstoke: Palgrave Macmillan.

Scanlon, Thomas. 2003. 'Rawls on Justification'. In Samuel Freeman (ed.), *The Cambridge Companion to Rawls*. Cambridge: Cambridge University Press.

Scanlon, Thomas. 2006. 'Justice, Responsibility, and the Demands of Equality'. In Christine Synowich (ed.), *The Egalitarian Conscience: Essays in Honour of G. A. Cohen*. Oxford: Oxford University Press.

Scarre, Geoffrey. 1996. *Utilitarianism*. London: Routledge.

Scheffler, Samuel. 2003a. 'What is Egalitarianism?' *Philosophy and Public Affairs*, 31, 5–39.

Scheffler, Samuel. 2003b. 'Equality as the Virtue of Sovereigns: A Reply to Ronald Dworkin'. *Philosophy and Public Affairs*, 31, 199–206.

Scheffler, Samuel. 2005. 'Choice, Circumstance and the Value of Equality'. *Politics, Philosophy and Economics*, 4, 5–28.

Scully, Gerald W. 1974. 'Discrimination: The Case of Baseball'. In Roger Noll (ed.), *Government and the Sports Business*. Washington, DC: Brookings Institution.

Schwartz, Thomas. 1982. 'Human Welfare: What It Is Not'. In Harlan B. Miller and William H. Williams (eds), *Limits of Utilitarianism*. Minneapolis: University of Minnesota Press.

Segall, Shlomi. 2007. 'In Solidarity with the Imprudent: A Defense of Luck Egalitarianism'. *Social Theory and Practice*, 33, 177–98.

Sen, Amartya K. 1980. 'Equality of What?' In S. M. McMurrin (ed.), *The Tanner Lectures on Human Values*, I. Salt Lake City: University of Utah Press.

Sen, Amartya K. 1987. *On Ethics and Economics*. Oxford: Blackwell.

Sen, Amartya K. 1992. *Inequality Reexamined*. Cambridge, MA: Harvard University Press.

Shaw, Patrick. 1999. 'The Pareto Argument and Equality'. *The Philosophical Quarterly*, 49, 353–68.

Shiffrin, Seana Valentine. 2000. 'Paternalism, Unconscionability, and Accomodation'. *Philosophy and Public Affairs*, 29, 3, 206–50.

Sidgwick, Henry. 1962. *The Methods of Ethics*. 7th edn. London: Macmillan.

Smart, J. J. C. 1978. 'Hedonistic and Ideal Utilitarianism'. In Peter A. French, Theodore E. Uehling, Jr., and Howard K. Wettstein (eds), *Midwest Studies in Philosophy*, III. Minneapolis: University of Minnesota Press.

Smilansky, Saul. 1997. 'Egalitarian Justice and the Importance of the Free Will Problem'. *Philosophia*, 25, 153–61.

Sobel, David. 1997. 'On the Subjectivity of Welfare'. *Ethics*, 107, 501–8.

Sobel, David. 1999. 'Sobel Reviews Anderson'. *Brown Electronic Article Review Service*, ed. J. Dreier and D. Estlund, World Wide Web, (*http:// www.brown.edu/Departments/Philosophy/bears*/homepage/html).

Stark, Andrew. 2002. 'Beyond Choice: Rethinking the Post-Rawlsian Debate over Egalitarian Justice'. *Political Theory*, 30, 36–67.

Steiner, Hillel. 1994. *An Essay on Rights*. Oxford: Blackwell.

Steiner, Hillel. 1997. 'Choice and Circumstance'. *Ratio*, 10, 296–312.

Steiner, Hillel. 2002. 'How Equality Matters'. *Social Philosophy and Policy*, 19, 342–56.

Sumner, L. W. 1996. *Welfare, Happiness, and Ethics*. Oxford: Oxford University Press.

Sumner, L. W. 2000. 'Something in Between'. In Roger Crisp and Brad Hooker (eds), *Well-Being and Morality: Essays in Honour of James Griffin*. Oxford: Oxford University Press.

Swift, Adam. 1999. 'Popular Opinion and Political Philosophy: The Relation between Social-Scientific and Philosophical Analyses of Distributive Justice'. *Ethical Theory and Moral Practice*, 2, 337–63.

Tännsjö, Torbjörn. 1998. *Hedonistic Utilitarianism*. Edinburgh: Edinburgh University Press.

Tatarkiewicz, Wladislaw. 1976. *Analysis of Happiness*. Trans. Edward Rothert and Danuta Zielinskn. The Hague: Martinus Nijhoff.

Telfer, Elizabeth. 1980. *Happiness*. London: Macmillian.

Temkin, Larry S. 1993. *Inequality*. Oxford: Oxford University Press.

Temkin, Larry S. 2003. 'Equality, Priority or What?' *Economics and Philosophy*, 19, 61–87.

Tungodden, Bertil. 2003. 'The Value of Equality'. *Economics and Philosophy*, 19, 1–44.

Vallentyne, Peter. 2000. 'Equality, Efficiency, and Priority to the Worse Off'. *Economics and Philosophy*, 16, 1–19.

Vallentyne, Peter. 2006. 'Hurley on Justice and Responsibility'. *Philosophy and Phenomenological Research*, 72, 433–8.

Vallentyne, Peter, Hillel Steiner, and Michael Otsuka. 2005. 'Why Left-Libertarianism is Not Incoherent, Indeterminate, or Irrelevant: A Reply to Fried'. *Philosophy and Public Affairs*, 33, 201–15.

Van Parijs, Philippe. 1995. *Real Freedom for All*. Oxford: Oxford University Press.

Vlastos, Gregory. 1962. 'Justice and Equality'. In Richard B. Brandt (ed.), *Social Justice*. Englewood Cliffs, NJ: Prentice-Hall.

Waldron, Jeremy. 1991. 'The Substance of Equality'. *Michigan Law Review*, 89, 1350–70.

Warner, Richard. 1987. *Freedom, Enjoyment, and Happiness: An Essay on Moral Psychology*. Ithaca, NY: Cornell University Press.

Weirich, Paul 1983. 'Utility Tempered With Equality'. *Nous*, 17, 423–39.

Westen, Peter. 1982. 'The Empty Idea of Equality'. *Harvard Law Review*, 95, 537–96.

Westen, Peter. 1990. *Speaking of Equality: An Analysis of the Rhetorical Force of 'Equality' in Moral and Legal Discourse*. Princeton, NJ: Princeton University Press.

Williams, Andrew. 2002. 'Equality for the Ambitious'. *Philosophical Quarterly*, 52, 377–89.

Williams, Bernard. 1962. 'The Idea of Equality'. In Peter Laslett and W. G. Runciman (eds), *Philosophy, Politics and Society, Second Series*. Oxford: Blackwell.

Williams, Bernard. 1997. 'Forward to Basics'. In Jane Franklin (ed.), *Equality*. London: IPPR.

White, Stuart. 1997. 'What do Egalitarians Want?' In Jane Frankin (ed.), *Equality*. London: IPPR.

White, Stuart. 2006. *Equality*. Cambridge: Polity.

Wolff, Jonathan. 1998. 'Fairness, Respect, and the Egalitarian Ethos'. *Philosophy and Public Affairs*, 27, 97–122.

Young, Iris Marion. 1990. *Justice and the Politics of Difference*. Princeton, NJ: Princeton University Press.

Young, Iris Marion. 2001. 'Equality of Whom? Social Groups and Judgments of Justice'. *Journal of Political Philosophy*, 9, 1–18.

Index